Butterworths Technical and
Scientific Checkbooks

Construction Site Production 4 Checkbook

W H Davies

Butterworth Scientific

London Boston Sydney Wellington Durban Toronto

All rights reserved. No part of this publication may be reproduced or transmitted in any form or by any means, including photocopying and recording without the written permission of the copyright holder, application for which should be addressed to the publishers. Such written permission must also be obtained before any part of this publication is stored in a retrieval system of any nature.

This book is sold subject to the Standard Conditions of Sale of Net Books and may not be resold in the UK below the net price given by the Publishers in their current price list.

First published 1982

© Butterworth & Co (Publishers) Ltd 1982

British Library Cataloguing in Publication Data

Davies, W H
   Construction site production 4 checkbook
   1. Building sites — Management
   I. Title
   624´.068   TH438

ISBN 0-408-00675-7
ISBN 0-408-00656-0 Pbk

Typeset by Tunbridge Wells Typesetting Services Ltd
Printed in Scotland by Thomson Litho Ltd., East Kilbride

Contents

Preface   vii

1 Communications   1
   1.1 Production activity   1
   1.2 Application   1
   1.3 Communication principles   3
   1.4 Methods of communication   3
   1.5 Barriers to communication   5
   1.6 Conclusions   6
   1.7 Questions on communications   6

2 Site layout   8
   2.1 General requirements   8
   2.2 Contract requirements   9
   2.3 Statutory requirements   9
   2.4 Sub-contractor requirements   11
   2.5 Site investigation   11
   2.6 Site boundaries   13
   2.7 Temporary works and services   14
   2.8 Safety aspects   14
   2.9 Offices and administrative provision   17
   2.10 Material storage   18
   2.11 Location of plant   18
   2.12 Planning the layout   19
   2.13 Communicating the layout   19
   2.14 Questions on site layout   23

3 Site administration   25
   3.1 Reports   25
   3.2 External administration   26
   3.3 Internal administration   27
   3.4 Labour administration   31
   3.5 Materials administration   31
   3.6 Drawings administration   37
   3.7 Architects' Instructions   37
   3.8 Delay records   43
   3.9 Dayworks   45
   3.10 Questions on site administration   47

4 Meetings   49
   4.1 Types of site meeting   49
   4.2 Purpose of meeting   51
   4.3 Planning a meeting   53
   4.4 Preparing the agenda   54
   4.5 Arranging meetings   56
   4.6 Chairing the meeting   57
   4.7 Minutes of meetings   57
   4.8 Questions on meetings   60

5 Site resources 62
5.1 Information needs 62
5.2 Material control 64
5.3 Materials waste 69
5.4 Plant task definition 71
5.5 Plant selection and procurement 72
5.6 Plant operation 74
5.7 Plant control 75
5.8 Labour 79
5.9 Questions on site resources 81

6 Sub-contractors 83
6.1 Definitions 83
6.2 Selection 84
6.3 Attendance 87
6.4 Meetings 90
6.5 Coordination 92
6.6 Questions on sub-contractors 95

7 Work study 97
7.1 Introduction 97
7.2 Method study 100
7.3 Time study 106
7.4 Activity sampling 111
7.5 Operations research 115
7.6 Incentives 117
7.7 Questions on work study 123

8 Planning and programming 125
8.1 Introduction 125
8.2 Planning 126
8.3 Programming 128
8.4 Programming techniques 136
8.5 Resource optimisation 141
8.6 Progress reporting 143
8.7 Questions on planning and programming 151

9 Quality control 153
9.1 Quality definition 153
9.2 Responsibilities of the parties 155
9.3 Quality standards 158
9.4 Testing 161
9.5 Sampling 162
9.6 Questions on quality control 167

10 Site cost control 169
10.1 Elements of cost 169
10.2 Cost systems 170
10.3 Graphs and charts in costing 172
10.4 The recording of costs 178
10.5 Site cost control 180
10.6 Questions on site cost control 183

Index 185

Note to Reader

As textbooks become more expensive, authors are often asked to reduce the number of worked and unworked problems, examples and case studies. This may reduce costs, but it can be at the expense of practical work which gives point to the theory.

Checkbooks if anything lean the other way. They let problem-solving establish and exemplify the theory contained in technician syllabuses. The Checkbook reader can gain *real* understanding through seeing problems solved and through solving problems himself.

Checkbooks do not supplant fuller textbooks, but rather supplement them with an alternative emphasis and an ample provision of worked and unworked problems. The brief outline of essential data—definitions, formulae, laws, regulations, codes of practice, standards, conventions, procedures, etc—will be a useful introduction to a course and a valuable aid to revision. Short-answer and multi-choice problems are a valuable feature of many Checkbooks, together with conventional problems and answers.

Checkbook authors are carefully selected. Most are experienced and successful technical writers; all are experts in their own subjects; but a more important qualification still is their ability to demonstrate and teach the solution of problems in their particular branch of technology, mathematics or science.

Authors, General Editors and Publishers are partners in this major low-priced series whose essence is captured by the Checkbook symbol of a question or problem 'checked' by a tick for correct solution.

Preface

This book specifically covers the TEC level 4 syllabus, which is an important part of programmes for higher technicians in construction, surveying, quantity surveying, architecture and civil engineering.

The text is divided into ten chapters which are arranged sequentially so that early information supports later chapters. The sections of chapters are identified using decimal numbering.

A wide selection of questions is included to check and reinforce the reader's understanding of the material. The multi-choice questions are based on the text of the book and the exact meaning of the phrases used can be ascertained by reading the appropriate section.

The completion of this book has been due to the assistance I have received from my colleagues at Preston Polytechnic and to the tolerance shown by my wife. I take this opportunity of expressing my thanks to all those who have contributed to the final product.

W H Davies
Preston Polytechnic

Butterworths Technical and Scientific Checkbooks

General Editor for Building, Civil Engineering, Surveying and Architectural titles:
Colin R. Bassett, lately of Guildford County College of Technology.

General Editors for Science, Engineering and Mathematics titles:
J.O. Bird and A.J.C. May, Highbury College of Technology, Portsmouth.

A comprehensive range of Checkbooks will be available to cover the major syllabus areas of the TEC, SCOTEC and similar examining authorities. A comprehensive list is given below and classified according to levels.

Level 1 (Red covers)
Mathematics
Physical Science
Physics
Construction Drawing
Construction Technology
Microelectronic Systems
Engineering Drawing
Workshop Processes & Materials

Level 2 (Blue covers)
Mathematics
Chemistry
Physics
Building Science and Materials
Construction Technology
Electrical & Electronic Applications
Electrical & Electronic Principles
Electronics
Microelectronic Systems
Engineering Drawing
Engineering Science
Manufacturing Technology
Digital Techniques
Motor Vehicle Science

Level 3 (Yellow covers)
Mathematics
Chemistry
Building Measurement
Construction Technology
Environmental Science
Electrical Principles
Electronics
Microelectronic Systems
Electrical Science
Mechanical Science
Engineering Mathematics & Science
Engineering Science
Engineering Design
Manufacturing Technology
Motor Vehicle Science
Light Current Applications

Level 4 (Green covers)
Mathematics
Building Law
Building Services & Equipment
Construction Technology
Construction Site Studies
Concrete Technology
Economics for the Construction Industry
Geotechnics
Engineering Instrumentation & Control

Level 5
Building Services & Equipment
Construction Technology
Manufacturing Technology

To my parents

1 Communications

1.1 PRODUCTION ACTIVITY

The production of work on site is a result of combining resources in such a way as to manufacture or assemble a marketable item in the most efficient manner.

The first of these resources is land which requires a design and layout to maximise its utilisation.

The second of these resources is capital which it employed to provide materials and mechanical aids to convert the design into reality.

The third resource is labour which is also obtained by capital but has attributes which capital cannot always provide. Money will certainly provide labour but it cannot create the skill needed to carry out the work efficiently. These skills whether belonging to craftsmen or management are the resource required to turn designs and information into a building.

1.2 APPLICATION

The construction industry is in a special category with regard to production. It is one of the few industries which separate the design and production systems. No item of production is the same, even individual units on a housing estate differ in levels, sub-structure work, aspect, and the amount of external works required. Production is also carried out under the most variable of conditions. These factors generate constantly changing circumstances which require a **continuous information flow** to enable site management to function effectively.

That flow of information is the only tool available to the management. The site manager does not move materials, operate plant or carry out a physical production function. The site manager organises, informs, coordinates, orders, instructs and motivates other people to carry out the work. Whatever level or speciality of site management occupied, the effectiveness of performance will depend on the ability to listen, read, speak, write or more importantly to understand and be understood.

The amount of information which is exchanged to complete a complex product is almost unquantifiable. This information increases as more sophisticated buildings are designed and placed on less suitable land in the crowded urban environment.

The information to be communicated in the course of a construction contract is illustrated in simplified form in *Fig 1.1*.

When information has to pass through so many communicators some decay in its accuracy may occur and every attempt should be made to ensure the decay is kept to a minimum.

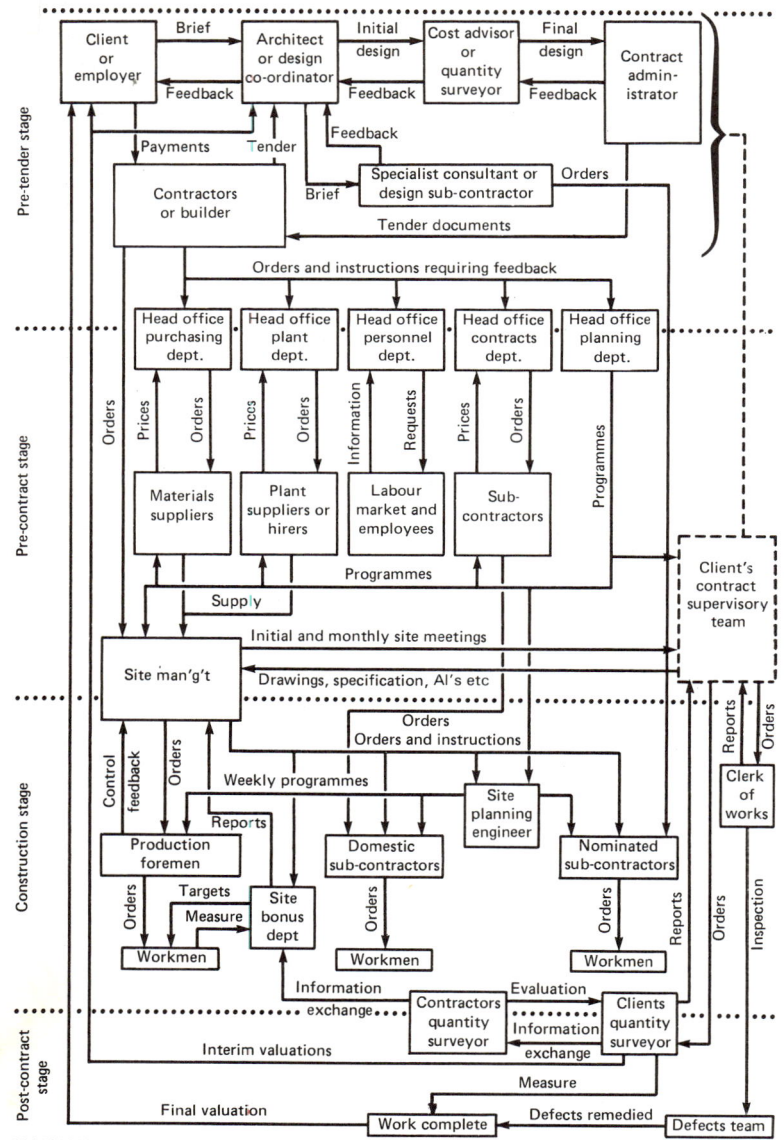

Fig 1.1 Simplified construction contract information flow

Communications from the point of view of a site manager can be viewed from three aspects:

Firstly, as a means of gathering information to ascertain the needs of the employer and architect.

Secondly, as a necessary tool of management to integrate the functions of departments and specialist sections within an organisation.

Thirdly, as a vital link between manager and subordinate to get the job done using person to person communication.

1.3 COMMUNICATION PRINCIPLES

Communication can be defined as the act of **passing information.** Consideration of this definition indicates that when a request is made for information, a transfer of information is conducted indicating that you lack that piece of information requested. The act of passing information can be used to transfer ideas, relay instructions, give orders, tender advice and explain facts.

The first requirement of effective communication is that, what is intended is understood. Secondly, that the understanding should induce the action which was the objective of the communication. Thirdly, the lines of communication should be as short as possible.

The process of communication is shown in *Fig 1.2*. Effective communication should be two-way and therefore **feedback** should be present. Not all circumstances are a two-way process, for example there is no feedback from reading a book. A receiver may be a group of people gathered together or they may be dispersed. Timing between receipt of information and feedback is an important influence on accuracy and understanding. Therefore, person-to-person communications should be most effective.

The stages to be followed in preparing effective communications should initially require a purpose or objective for the transferring of information. The information to be transferred should be properly prepared and in the most suitable form to suit the receiver. Ensure the method to be used will prove the most effective for transmitting the information and for receiving it. Finally, provision should be made for feedback and the need for action on that feedback appreciated.

The points which should be present in all communication should be:

Clarity — easily understood
Presentation — creating a favourable impression;
New information — to attract interest;
Drive — demanding the necessary action;
Tone — affecting attitudes particularly;
Feedback — ensuring that transfer of information is achieved.

1.4 METHODS OF COMMUNICATION

The method of communication chosen should not be the most convenient to the transmitter. The form of communication is not as important as the content. A suitable method of communication should be the most acceptable and effective having regard to its impact on attitudes and stimulation to action. There are three

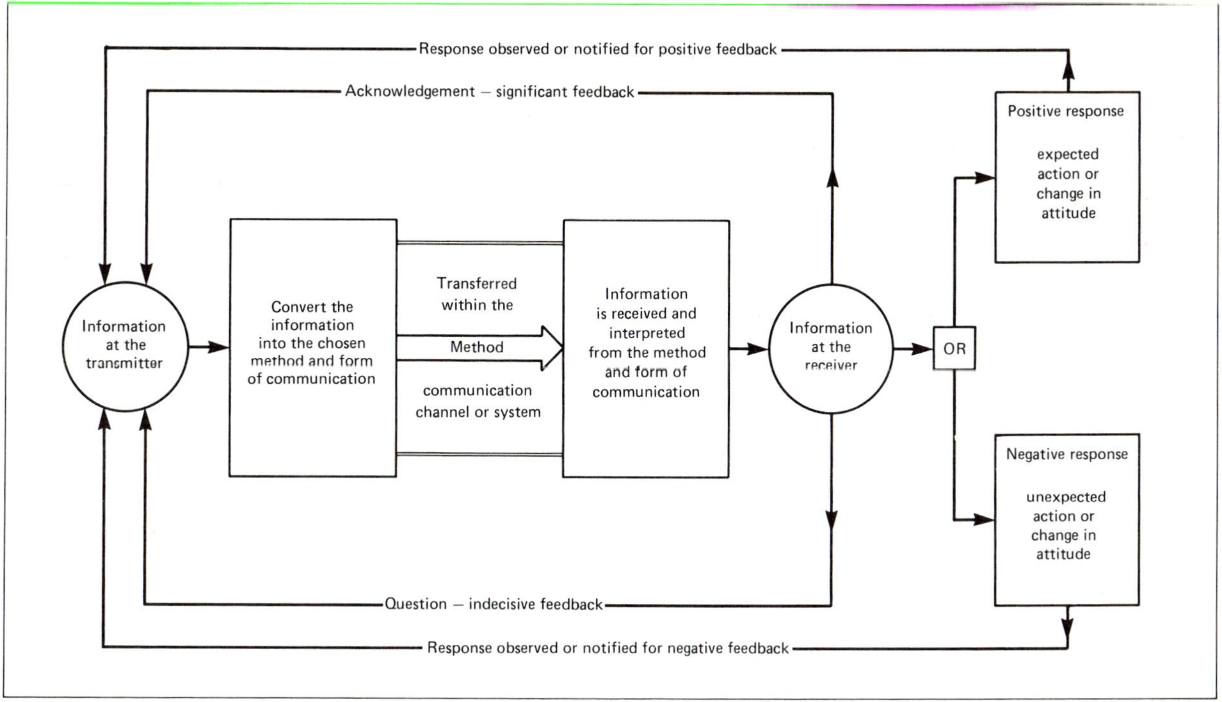

Fig 1.2 The process of communication

basic methods of communication: **written, visual and oral (by mouth),** this last method should not be confused with verbal (by words).

Written communication takes the form of letters, reports, notices, memoranda, books, specifications, bills of quantities, British Standards and manufacturer's instructions. This method is often used when the subject matter is complex, important, or is likely to have some legal repercussions and requires a permanent record for reference.

Visual, sometimes called pictorial, communication takes the form of films, television, slides, posters, graphs, charts, works programmes and drawings. The presentation of information in these forms has a greater impact than a large amount of written information particularly in connection with numerical data. Where the message is less complex this form of communication is most effective.

Oral communication is often the best method because feedback is instant, attitudes, behaviour and action can be observed. The face to face confrontation is advisable when the subject matter may be disagreeable or difficult. It should also be used for simple, informal and less important situations such as giving orders to subordinates.

It would be quite wrong to think of one method of communication as totally adequate for any situation. Therefore, drawings are supplemented by specification notes, orders to workmen by sketches, safety posters by lectures and accident reports, and oral instructions are often confirmed in writing.

Communications may appeal to all the senses. The stylised signs of public conveniences, drawings with standard symbols, appeal to the sense of sight. The aural sense or hearing is used in oral communication and great use should be made of tone, loudness, excitement, temper and facial expression in speech, in order to achieve an objective. The sense of touch is often used in quality control, touching a sample often helps in communicating a standard of finish required.

Finally, smell can be important particularly in cases where fuel is not marked to indicate type. Rarely will only one sense be appealed to when communicating, it will usually be a combination of two or three senses.

1.5 BARRIERS TO COMMUNICATION

If an organisation is suffering from bad morale and lacks confidence in its future, communication problems are increased. There is sometimes a lack of will to communicate in that managers fail to see that subordinates need to know something of management affairs. However, nearly all barriers can be classified under three headings: **Physical, psychological** and **intellectual.**

The physical barriers are probably the most obvious. There may be a disability on the part of the receiver such as deafness or blindness. There are the difficulties of noise particularly on site. Similarly, bad telephone connections can be a physical barrier to communication.

Those problems of distance are probably best illustrated by the tower crane operator and slinger communication problem. There are also problems with size; information has to be passed between layer and layer of management and between different functional departments. This leads to distortion and inaccuracy and, indeed, non-arrival, which, in turn, leads to more reliance being placed on written communication than oral, thus reducing the effectiveness of communication.

The psychological barrier is probably the biggest cause of communication breakdown. The attitudes, feelings and emotions of the receiver will affect the quality of information that is transferred. Generally, people hear what they expect to hear, preconceived ideas are used to interpret what is said in a different way. There is also a tendency to ignore any information that conflicts with ones beliefs.

Attitude to the transmitter will mean that the receiver's evaluation of the information will be affected, and the feelings and emotions of the receiver influence the ability to receive the true message. When worried the receiver feels threatened; when angry the information is rejected. If argument is present the information is not understood or is badly distorted.

The intellectual barriers should be obvious but assumptions about intellectual ability should not be made without evidence. The fault may lie in the quality of transmission, the excessive use of jargon or the problem of semantics. Words mean different things to different people. Words such as profits, closed shop or union activities convey different impressions to management and employees.

Concepts are built up over a lifetime and will influence an individuals perception and thinking about the information transmitted.

1 6 CONCLUSIONS

There is a need to ensure that communications are effective through all the stages of the contract. This is particularly important at the pre-tender and pre-contract stage; the relationships established at this time affect the quality of communication throughout the contract.

Effective communication in all aspects of production is essential to ensure that productivity and competitiveness are maintained. The benefits to be achieved with good communication are those which are necessary for any efficient organisation:

Better understanding of company policy;
Improved co-operation between departments;
Improved morale and motivation of employees;
Better control over operations;
Greater personal co-operation between individuals;
More precise orders and instructions issued;
Beneficial changes in attitudes;
Reduction in unofficial sources of information.

The basic principles of good communication which have been outlined in this chapter should be applied when using any of the techniques which may be included in the following chapters. The following questions, together with those at the end of other chapters, should be answered using the principles which have been noted here.

1.7 QUESTIONS ON COMMUNICATIONS

MULTI-CHOICE QUESTIONS

1   The basic objective of communication is:
    (a) encourage social activity;
    (b) control the workforce;
    (c) to pass information;
    (d) to complicate situations.

2 Effective communication should be:
   (a) clear, concise and easily understood;
   (b) detailed, complex and exact;
   (c) jargon, long-winded and logical;
   (d) infinitely explanatory and sequential.

3 Positive feedback is indicated by:
   (a) questions from the receiver;
   (b) expected action or change of attitude;
   (c) argument as to the action to be taken;
   (d) silence and inaction.

4 The three basic methods of communication are:
   (a) verbal, pictorial and reports;
   (b) letters, notices and books;
   (c) written, visual and oral;
   (d) bills of quantities, specifications and Architect's instructions.

SHORT ANSWER QUESTIONS (15-20 minutes)

1 Briefly describe three methods of communication and give examples of the use of each method in the construction industry.

2 Outline the stages of preparation to be followed to ensure effective communication.

3 List the barriers to communication and give *two* examples of each.

4 Write a letter to an employee, who is to be warned about persistent lateness for work on site. Explain how the objective is fulfilled.

5 Select methods and forms of communication for the following situations:
   (a) instructing a labourer how to operate a concrete mixer;
   (b) giving orders to a trade foreman as to his next weeks work;
   (c) communicating the progress of the work to Head Office;
   (d) requesting further details of construction from the Architect.

QUESTIONS REQUIRING LONGER ANSWERS (30-45 minutes)

1 'Too much paper information leads to less communication' — discuss.

2 'The more levels of management between the Board of Directors and the site workforce, the greater the problems of communication' — discuss.

3 'A site manager spends more time communicating than anything else. Success depends on his ability to acquire, store, interpret and transmit information.' Discuss this statement using examples to illustrate your arguments.

4 Examine the problems of communication on site and suggest methods which may lead to their reduction or solution.

5 Describe the communications system which is involved in the production of a building, commenting on its effectiveness.

2 Site layout

2.1 GENERAL REQUIREMENTS

Site layout is the planning and organisation of the site area around the proposed building to accommodate the resources necessary to erect that building.

The need for site layout and organisation is determined by the methods of production. The uniqueness of each site requires that the 'factory' be set up at every new location. The main consideration must be that the layout provides the most efficient and economic methods of production.

The main considerations are those activities which must go on during the contract. This will mean space for erected scaffold, working plant, reinforcement bending, concrete mixing, small workshops, unloading materials and contract administration.

The next consideration should be the maintenance of stocks to ensure sufficient material is available for continuous production. Following these points a number of other considerations such as improved access, site movement, extra storage and car parking can be taken into account.

The factors that will influence the site layout should be determined in a logical sequence similar to the following order:

Ascertain contract requirements;
Determine statutory requirements;
Request sub-contractor requirements;
Conduct a site investigation;
Define and secure site boundaries;
Ascertain requirements for temporary works and services;
Study safety aspects of the methods of work;
Quantify office and administrative buildings;
Quantify materials storage requirements;
Locate static plant and plant parks;
Plan the site layout;
Communicate the plan and layout.

The best method of ensuring the effective organisation of a site is by a number of checklists. These can cover the small hand tools, tapes, pegs etc. necessary to set up a site or a list of all statutory bodies the site manager is required to contact. Similarly, all the points to be covered in the contractors site investigation could be listed.

2.2 CONTRACT REQUIREMENTS

These may already be known if the layout is being considered at the pre-contract stage. However, site layouts are also prepared at the pre-tender stage to determine the basic requirements and therefore the contract will have to be studied.

The first requirement will be to ascertain the size and complexity of the project and the unused area of the site. This information can then be supplemented by any restrictions contained in the contract such as loading or unloading. Restrictions may also be placed on working hours, for example when the site is next to a Church then Sunday working may be prohibited.

Other matters to be ascertained will be the contract period, starting, completion and site handover date. There may also be a phased schedule of completion which will require a change of layout. Also, any proposal to use the partially completed building as offices may be restricted.

The Bills of Quantities, specifications and drawings should be studied in detail, to ascertain if any methods of construction are forbidden. Similarly the constructional sequence should be decided and some discussion should take place on a safe system of work.

2.3 STATUTORY REQUIREMENTS

These requirements are mandatory and should be listed meticulously to ensure no breach of the law occurs.

The Construction (Health and Welfare) Regulations require the provision of facilities for employees on site. They are briefly:

A messroom when a contractor has more than ten men on site. The room must have means of heating food unless hot food is available elsewhere. Hot and cold water should be provided. Shelter accommodation for use when work is interrupted by bad weather. Storage for protective clothing when not in use. Drying rooms are also required for wet clothes.

Sanitary conveniences at the rate of one for every 25 persons. Separate facilities for men and women.

Provide first aid facilities according to the number of men on site. The provision of a first aid room is necessary when over 250 employees are on site.

The Offices, Shops and Railway Premises Act applies to Site Offices if moveable offices are to remain for six months or more. If the offices are fixed this period is reduced to six weeks. The Act requires:

Each office worker to have 3.7 m^2 floor space. A room temperature maintained around 16°C. The actual temperature has been varied to assist fuel economy.

Provide adequate sanitary conveniences, washing facilities, with warm water soap and towels.

A supply of drinking water and a drinking vessel.

The Food Hygiene (General) Regulations 1970 deals with the provision of canteens on site. They must be clean and be provided with hot and cold water for food handling. The canteen should not connect to a room in which there is a sanitary convenience.

Provision must be made for the removal and storage of outdoor clothing and footwear.

There are various statutes which require adequate **fire prevention** and fire-fighting measures to be taken on site. In general, these statutes do not provide for specific equipment, but require adequate and reasonable action. The best method of ensuring safety is to consult with the local Fire Prevention Branch. Generally the following are necessary:

Tresspassers should be deterred by adequate site fencing or fencing to compounds.
Temporary buildings should preferably be placed 6.1 m apart.
Storage stacks should also be spaced out using non-combustile materials between the inflammable stacks to prevent the spread of fire. Rubbish should not be allowed to accumulate on site.
Storage of inflammable liquids in the prescribed amounts should be in non-combustible sheds or in the open at least 6.1 m away from other huts. The sheds must be locked or the open storage areas fenced and secured.
Provision must also be made for suitable access for a fire engine. This should be a minimum of 3.1 m wide and 3.7 m high.

The Construction (Working Places) Regulations require that the place of work is kept clear and safe. The points which may affect the site layout are:

A safe route must be provided to and from every workplace.
Loads on scaffolds must not be too heavy for the platform. This will vary with the type or design used. Loose and unwanted material should be cleared away as soon as possible.

There are a number of other statutes which will influence site layout. **The Highways Act** requires permission to change or alter the highway and police permission must be sought for temporary exits and entrances. This Act also sets out a need for the separation of works from the highway, and therefore, the erection of some kind of hoarding.

Similarly, the Act requires that dirt is not deposited on the road and therefore the wheels of wagons leaving the site should be clean. Rubbish skips should not be placed on highways if it can be avoided.

The Local Government (Miscellaneous Provisions) Act requires that licences are needed for scaffolding, hoardings, gantries or any other temporary works on the highway.

The Control of Pollution Act sets the noise levels which are permitted to emit from sites.

Finally, **The Occupiers' Liability Act** makes the occupier of the site liable for any personal injury to, or damage to property of, a visitor. A visitor is almost anyone who is not a tresspasser; however, in the case of children a greater duty of care is owed because it is expected that they will be irresponsible.

There are a number of notices which must be displayed on site, these should be in a prominent position near to the activity to which it may be related. They are:

Building Operations Form F3 Abstract
Construction Regulation (General Provisions) Placard
Construction Regulations (Lifting Operations) Placard
Construction Regulations (Health and Welfare) Placard
Construction Regulations (Working Places) Placard
Electricity Regulations Form F954
Electric Shock Notice
Lead Paint Regulations F996
Abrasive Wheels Regulations Form F2345
Asbestos Regulations Form F2358
Highly Flammable Liquids Form F2440

Offices Shops and Railway Premises Act Form OSR9
Certificate of Insurance
Emergency Service Notice

Other registers should also be kept, the main ones being:

Building Operations General Register F36, Parts 2 and 4
Site Inspection Registers for Scaffold
Excavators and cranes (Parts I and II) F91
Lead Paint Register of Persons F92
Abrasive Wheels appointment of Mounters
Accident Book BI 501
Notice of accident or dangerous occurrence F2508 and F2509
Welfare Certificate of Shared Arrangements F2202

When considering statutory requirements and notices reference should always be made to the up to date legislation.

2.4 SUB-CONTRACTOR REQUIREMENTS

The sub-contractor(s) should be requested to provide details of the space, buildings and facilities necessary for the work to be carried out.

The first request should be for the duration of the period or periods to be spent on site. Further information will indicate when the period will be and should also detail any special provisions required for access or unusual working hours.

The amount of office space required should be expressed either as a size of hut or minimum space requirement. The maximum number of men on site should also be forecast.

The sub-contractor must indicate how the statutory requirements for welfare facilities are to be met or indicate the need for shared arrangements and the necessary certificate.

The requirements, with regard to materials, should be specified giving information as to the loading and unloading facilities, size and weights of items, amounts of material to be stored, space required for storage and any special storage or security arrangements that may be necessary.

The use of standing scaffold or other items of equipment and plant may be required. Details of these should be submitted to enable the decisions as to length of time on site and location to be made.

Finally, the services required by the sub-contractor should be listed. These include power requirements, including any special loadings or equipment; and details of use for water, drainage and rubbish disposal.

2.5 SITE INVESTIGATION

Site investigation is part of an overall enquiry into the site conditions, and this subsection will deal specifically with those matters relating to site layout. A checklist is given in *Fig 2.1*.

Under the heading of **location and personnel** the general points should be given including the names of contacts. Under the sub-heading **Local Authority,** The Borough Surveyor, Chief Building Control Officer and any other person who may be involved in the contract should be listed.

SITE INVESTIGATION CHECK LIST				SOSAT CONSTRUCTION LTD.			

Contract title _____

Contract no _____ Date of visit _____

Item	Applicable or N/A	In progress	Complete	Item	Applicable or N/A	In progress	Complete
1. LOCATION AND PERSONNEL *Record addresses and names of local contacts as necessary* County Town Villages Map Reference Roads and Routes Distances Local Authorities Police Gas Board Electricity Board Water Board Telecom Office Post Office Fire Service Health & Safety Insp. Railway Station **2. LOCATION OF SERVICES** *Record the exact location and any local contacts not in Section 1.* Water Main Electricity Cable Soil Drainage S.W. Drainage Gas Main Telephone Cable Public Telephone Rubbish Tip Petrol Supply Diesel Supply LP Gas Supply Paraffin Supply Take Away Food Est. Restaurant or Cafe Hospital Doctor **3. SUB-CONTRACTORS & SUPPLIERS** *Record locations, addresses, contacts and assessment of potential.* Local Builders				Local Services — Electric S/C's Plumbing S/C's Heat & Vent. S/C's Plasterers S/C's Flooring S/C's Roofing S/C's Scaffolding Gen. Builders Merchants Timber Merchants Quarries Sand & Gravel Brickworks Joinery Workshops Ready Mix Concrete Plant Hire Security Services Labour Lodgings. **4. SITE CONDITIONS** *Record all aspects which affect access, temporary works and production.* Access to Boundary Road Widths Bridges Difficult Corners Access on to Site Pavements, Etc. Site Boundaries, North Site Boundaries, South Site Boundaries, East Site Boundaries, West Adjacent Buildings Existing Features on Site Roads Buildings Depressions Trees Shrubs Slopes Natural Drainage Water Courses Sub-soil Water Surface Conditions Vandalism Potential			

Fig 2.1 Site investigation check list

Under **services location** the actual positions should be recorded in descriptive form and reference made to a location drawing. The names and locations of garages and cafes should also be noted; this can effect site layout as to the need for a fuel store or a canteen. Similarly, all the items should be recorded so that the provision of facilities is the most economical in the circumstances of that particular site.

The location and detailed information of sub-contractors and suppliers is also required to ascertain the need for site storage. It is often more economical to have stocks held by suppliers and sub-contractors rather than the problems of storing them on site. The list is not exhaustive but the requirements will differ according to the type of building and method of construction.

The section of the checklist relating to site conditions is the most important. The information recorded here will indicate the extent of temporary works and security required. It should also indicate the most suitable areas for the location of administration offices and other buildings.

The site investigation is likely to be a single visit and therefore it is essential that all the relevant information is obtained at this time. Great inconvenience can often be caused by this omission. A systematic approach and attention to detail are the prerequisites of a successful report. The final document should clearly communicate the information to enable the site layout to be completed.

2.6. SITE BOUNDARIES

The determination of site boundaries is important. Encroachment on adjacent property can lead to lengthy and costly legal disputes.

The boundaries should be determined by reference to site drawings and the 'setting out' should be as accurate as possible. The recording of the state of adjacent buildings should be by photographs accompanied by adequate descriptive records. The proposed building and other works should be laid out within the 'setting out' grid and the position checked. Any discrepancies between the drawings and actual physical measurements should be raised with the Architect.

The necessary security will be indicated by the site investigation report which will have ascertained the problems in the area. The main reasons for security are to guard against trespass, protect the works and plant and materials from damage, satisfy the statutory duty of care, protect people and property adjacent to the site, prevent the theft of material, and to safeguard the environment within and around the site.

The method normally used to secure the site boundary is a barrier about 2 m high; this may be either a fence or hoarding. The fence may be chain link having an overhang with barbed wire. A hoarding may be constructed from corrugated sheeting, boarding or plywood. In the latter case it would probably be 2.4 m high this being the standard size of sheet. Hoardings should have access for fire-fighting hoses in the form of 250 mm square holes at 10 m centres throughout its length. The structural stability of any fence or hoarding should be considered. The worst loading condition is likely to occur with a solid hoarding in a windy location.

The posts should be set in the ground one third of the fence height. Some bracing should also be provided, particularly on long lengths of fence facing the open countryside. Impact loads at access gates and points close to the working areas should be considered. The fence or hoarding should be erected in such a way as to discourage burrowing under or climbing over in order to force an entry.

2.7 TEMPORARY WORKS AND SERVICES

This is a most important aspect of site layout for without adequate access production will be severely hampered or stopped. The need to keep the site in production should be the primary consideration.

Space for access is determined by the flow of traffic and the sizes of vehicle to be unloaded. The methods of unloading, duration of stay, and the vehicle turning circle will also have to be considered. Full car parking may or may not be provided depending on space available, however, a limited amount of parking space will be necessary for essential transport.

Access for plant must be considered including the high loadings which may occur. It may not be necessary to provide a semi-permanent access as the use of navvy-mats may be sufficient. Hardstandings for cranes should take account of the crane's fully blocked area and clearance for the swivel of the jib and tail.

Provision should be made for movement around the site. Sizes of dumpers, fork lifts, ready-mix trucks or other vehicles which must be directly off-loaded should be considered.

Access across the highway will require police approval and a local authority licence. Details of location and construction will have to be submitted for approval. Consideration must be given to pedestrian traffic by the provision of fans, protected walkways or gantries.

Services will require the location of the nearest drainage terminus to provide temporary sanitary conveniences and the location and connection of a temporary water supply. Unless generators are used, an electricity supply will have to be provided by the local electricity board.

The size of drainage and number of conveniences will be ascertained from the number of persons on site, their gender, and the statutory requirements. The water requirement falls into two categories, that required for health purposes and the amount required for construction purposes. Some calculation of maximum demand should be made in order to ensure an adequate storage and distribution system. Power requirements will take account of office lighting and heating, security floodlighting, power tools, workplace lighting, cooking and finally major electric powered items such as tower cranes. The major power users may need separate means of supply.

Telephones will be required for the main contractor. The number of telephones will generally be one per member of the site management team, excluding supervisory posts. The telephone may be a single number with one or two extensions or, depending on the size of site, could incorporate a small exchange. The provision of a payphone will meet the needs of subcontractors and private individual requirements.

2.8 SAFETY ASPECTS

The employer owes a duty of care to everyone in his employ or legally on the site. The duty of every employee is to take reasonable care not to cause danger to others and to co-operate with the employer on safety matters. This requires an early approach to safety problems during the preparation of a site layout. The layout of the site should contribute towards, rather than against, a safe method of work.

An essential factor in the **demolition** of buildings is to ensure understanding and co-operation between the contractor and local authority. It is also a prerequisite that a competent person is appointed to supervise all operations. The following points should be considered:

Before deciding method
Age of structure;
Method of construction;
State of preservation;
Ground type and conditions;
Gas, water, electricity and other services;
Creation of public nuisances;
Location and condition of adjacent buildings.

Before work starts on site
All statutory notices sent and approvals obtained;
Ensure all necessary hoardings and warning notices are erected;
Remove window sashes and glass;
Board-up windows and doors including doors to lift shafts, stairwells or unboarded floors;
Ensure the provision of adequate shoring and temporary supports;
Remove all loose or projecting parts before main work starts;
Ensure any scaffold is free-standing;
Ensure all platforms used to support loads are adequate;
Check that all stairs used for access are safe;
Keep all access routes clear of debris;
Ensure all services are cut off or removed;
Remove all projecting nails etc. from timber taken out during demolition;
Provide control for all burning on site;
Issue adequate protective clothing for: poisonous fumes; chemical dust; harmful materials (blue asbestos); inflammable liquids and radio-active matter; falling debris;
Provide safety belts and harnesses if men are likely to fall;
Water against dust;
Insulate against noise;
Maintain all plant in a safe working condition;
Regularly check steel wire ropes;
Keep out all trespassers, especially after cessation of work, by adequate security;
Arrange for the adequate disposal of all rubbish;
Ensure that procedures are pre-arranged for warnings of collapses and other safety hazards.

A safe method of work in **excavation** commences at the setting out stage and continues after completion. The following points are important safety aspects in excavation:

The marking of all existing services;
The guarding of the excavation by lights and barriers;
Emergency facilities in the case of an unexpected occurrence;
Adequate and efficient excavation plant;
Properly trained and safety conscious plant operatives;
Suitable haulage vehicles properly loaded;
A safe method of support to prevent collapse;
Keep excavation free from water;
Satisfactory access to and from the excavation for vehicles and pedestrians;
Proper vehicle access across site and to the highway;

No dirt or mud on the highway;
Proper vehicle control where workmen are close by;
Organised loading and turnaround system;
Spoil areas should be properly located and controlled;
Keep the site tidy by removing surplus spoil;
Ensure exposed services are adequately supported;
Ensure lights, notices and barriers remain in position once the excavation is completed;
Backfill as soon as possible;
Ensure access ladders, crossovers, etc are maintained for follow-up work.

Foundation work is similar in safety precautions with regard to working below ground level. This type of work is, however, more likely to involve the use of cranage and materials. The general points listed above should be applied to foundations and the following additional precautions are necessary for a safe method of work.

Ensure stable and adequate formwork;
Provide adequate support for forms;
Ensure reinforcement is fixed immediately and not left scattered on site;
Provide a safe access for concrete delivery;
Delivery by vehicle should be by properly trained operator and driver;
Delivery by crane requires efficient operation, inspection and maintenance;
Crane signalling system must be effective;
Delivery vessel must not be overloaded or liable to spillage and should have a suitable discharge method;
Compaction equipment should be properly maintained and operated;
Completed but unstable work should carry warning notices;
Remove formwork and supports off site immediately on striking;
Ensure new concrete is not prematurely loaded.

A safe method of work for the **erection of structural frames** will depend on the material used and its method of jointing. *In situ* concrete will follow the same pattern as the foundations in the previous paragraph with some modification for relevant factors from this section. However, the use of precast concrete members or steel components should require the method of work to comply with the following points.

Ensure all lifting gear is properly operated and safe;
Calculate loading with the necessary safety factor;
Design slinging arrangements to lift loads in the fixing position;
Lifting points should be incorporated in all loads;
Preliminary stacking and storage should be safe and facilitate easy slinging and movement;
Keep the area under the load traverse free from pedestrians;
Ensure that work platforms are adequate and safe for the actual fixing operations;
Provide safety nets to platforms for difficult operations;
Provide all necessary tools and materials for immediate fixing;
Devise an efficient signalling system between, crane operator, slingers and fixers;
Incorporate a method of fine adjustment when placing heavier components;
Ensure that each fixing operation contains no risk for the operative;
Provide temporary supports for all components until fully fixed;
Ensure adequate overall stability bracing during erection until the structural frame is complete;

Provide a well-planned erection procedure with organised component delivery;
Take every precaution for the prevention of falling from heights.

2.9 OFFICES AND ADMINISTRATIVE PROVISION

The minimum requirements are designated under statutory requirements. The most effective contract administration will result from the provision of a proper working environment.

The site management structure should be agreed and the number of persons requiring offices should be known. The maximum number of men and women who will be on site should also be ascertained.

Offices should take account of the inter-relationship between members of the site management team. Similarly, regard should be given to the need for privacy and the status of the occupant. The need for each office worker is 3.7 m^2 of floor space. The offices should also have separate sanitary conveniences for each sex at the rate of one per twenty-five and washing facilities should also be available. Provision should be made for adequate fire escape routes and first aid. There will be a requirement for an office to accommodate the Clerk of Works and a conference room on larger sites. Adequate provision should be made for a table and one chair per member who may attend a site meeting. The minimum requirement is 600 mm of table edge per person and 1 m clearance around the table. The storage of drawings should be considered as a great deal of space can be taken up by plan-chests. Modern hanging storage is usually less bulky. The utilisation of the conference room or other offices for drawing storage is usually advisable.

Sanitary conveniences and washing facilities should be provided for every worker on site. Sanitary conveniences are, again, one per every twenty-five persons. Washing facility requirements are more complex but generally one for every five persons up to twenty plus one for every extra twenty-five persons should meet the requirements. The facilities should include hot and cold water plus towels and soap. The need can be met by washbasins, troughs or buckets.

The provision of a shelter or mess-room should be on the basis of a chair at a table. This again can be based on 600 linear mm of table to each person with the necessary space surrounding the table. Provision should also be made in this room for heating food and washing up dishes, i.e. a large sink and draining board. The heating of food will depend on requirements but a large domestic cooker will be adequate if canteen facilities are not provided. A water-boiler with a discharge tap and a capacity of a half litre per person should also be installed. This room should not be connected to the sanitary convenience room.

Drying rooms and lockers should be provided for the drying and storage of clothing. These are usually in the same room with provision for heating during spells of inclement weather. The size of the room should be adequate for a 300 mm wide locker, deep enough for clothes for each person to be hung on a coat hanger. These lockers should be placed in the centre of the room with the seats and wall coat hooks around the perimeter. Adequate space is needed to enable people to put on and remove protective clothing.

All the site buildings should have provision for safe access, preferably by a properly constructed path. The location of each unit should be within an easily supervised area to ensure adequate cleanliness.

2.10 MATERIAL STORAGE

There is a need for three types of storage. Firstly, **a secure store** for valuable items which may be pilfered and therefore require strict control. Secondly, **a weatherproof store** for materials which may deteriorate due to the affects of weather. Thirdly, storage for materials in the **open.** Stocks must be adequate to maintain production schedules.

The storage of materials will require some control. Usually, a time-keeper doubles as a storeman and therefore some small provision for an office and issue counter may be needed. For control purposes this should be provided close to the site entrance but not if it leads to uneconomic activity due to that location.

The items to be placed in secure storage should be enumerated. This will indicate the quantity of items which will then be allocated shelf or bin space. Once the shelf space area is known the size of the secure store hut can be calculated.

Those materials required to receive protection from the weather will include items such as cement, timber components and plasterboard. They may be placed in an open barn or in a locked full-sided shed. The access to such material must be adequate to enable a 'first in-first out' policy to be practised. Should mechanised handling be used then space must be provided for loading.

Materials to be stored in the open such as bricks, drainage goods and other material may require a sheet covering. It should be determined whether the materials should be placed in a compound or stored on site at the place of work. The latter method means single handling but probably more waste, whilst the former means double handling and more control, which should lead to a reduction in waste.

The requirement for bulk storage is a matter of size of component and height of storage. Once the floor space required is established the access lanes can be allowed for giving the total storage required. A number of materials require racking unless the site has unlimited space. The two main materials are scaffolding and reinforcement which should be racked and carefully controlled.

2.11 LOCATION OF PLANT

The siting of static plant and the parking of mobile plant should be given careful consideration.

Static plant such as hoists or tower cranes should be sited so that maximum utilisation is achieved. The radius of the crane should be used to cover the maximum area of the site. The crane should have access to the major materials storage area, the vehicle unloading area and any other location in which its loads may lie. The heavier loads should be stored close to the mast because the capacity of a crane diminishes with the operation radius.

The hoist is static and needs materials delivered to it across the horizontal plane. It is essential that adequate access and loading space is provided at the foot and each delivery point of the hoist.

The other major piece of static plant is the concrete and mortar mixing equipment. Even where most of the concrete is ready-mixed a small mortar mixing area is required. The main item to be considered is the storage of aggregates. These take up quite a large area and temporary works are required for the mixer base and to retain these materials, and if necessary for bulk cement storage.

Mobile plant is always an attraction to vandals and damage to this expensive equipment can lead to large losses in output. There is a need to immobilise the plant and if possible to secure the vehicles in a compound under the scrutiny of a watchman. Any parking should be near other security areas in order to simplify control.

2.12 PLANNING THE LAYOUT

The layout will depend on size of proposed building and the space to be left about that building. The main principles should be, to avoid any area where building is to eventually take place, any underground services, any area which may interfere with production, particularly sub-structure excavation.

Hutments should be placed on an unused area which may only require landscaping, near to the entrance of the site and a reasonable distance from the actual works. Distance can be expensive, the wasted time involved in walking to and from toilets, mess-room and stores can amount to 5% of one person's total working hours.

On congested sites, the site offices may be doubled to two storeys or, when gantries over roads are used, offices may be placed above them. The phasing of the contract can be used so that offices are placed on areas where work will commence late and are then moved into the partially completed phase of the building before the later work starts. Alternatively, it is sometimes possible to rent adjacent land or offices to ease the problem.

The sequence of planning should be production orientated and therefore the first priority is to site static plant. This should be followed by developing the access roads and spaces. Next, any work area such as small workshops or bar bending compounds should be set out. Finally, adequate stocks of materials and offices should be positioned. It is unlikely that all the criteria will be met and therefore the layout is likely to be a compromise.

The objective of the site layout should be clearly stated as 'To provide the best working environment and conditions which will lead to safe, efficient and economic production'. This objective should provide the basis for all decisions when planning the layout.

2.13 COMMUNICATING THE LAYOUT

This involves informing all the parties concerned as to the use of space and the need to confine stocks to a minimum. The advantages of a clean and tidy site should not be overlooked. The layout involves the physical use of space and the timing of its use and reuse.

The sequence of setting up the site should be carefully considered. The works should probably be as follows:

Provide access;
Ensure security;
Develop health and welfare facilities;
Carry out temporary works other than access;
Erect static plant;
Commence excavation work;

Excavation work can be very disruptive and may require a clear site. In this case it would be the first task after providing the access. Similarly, the erection of static plant near to excavations may have to be delayed.

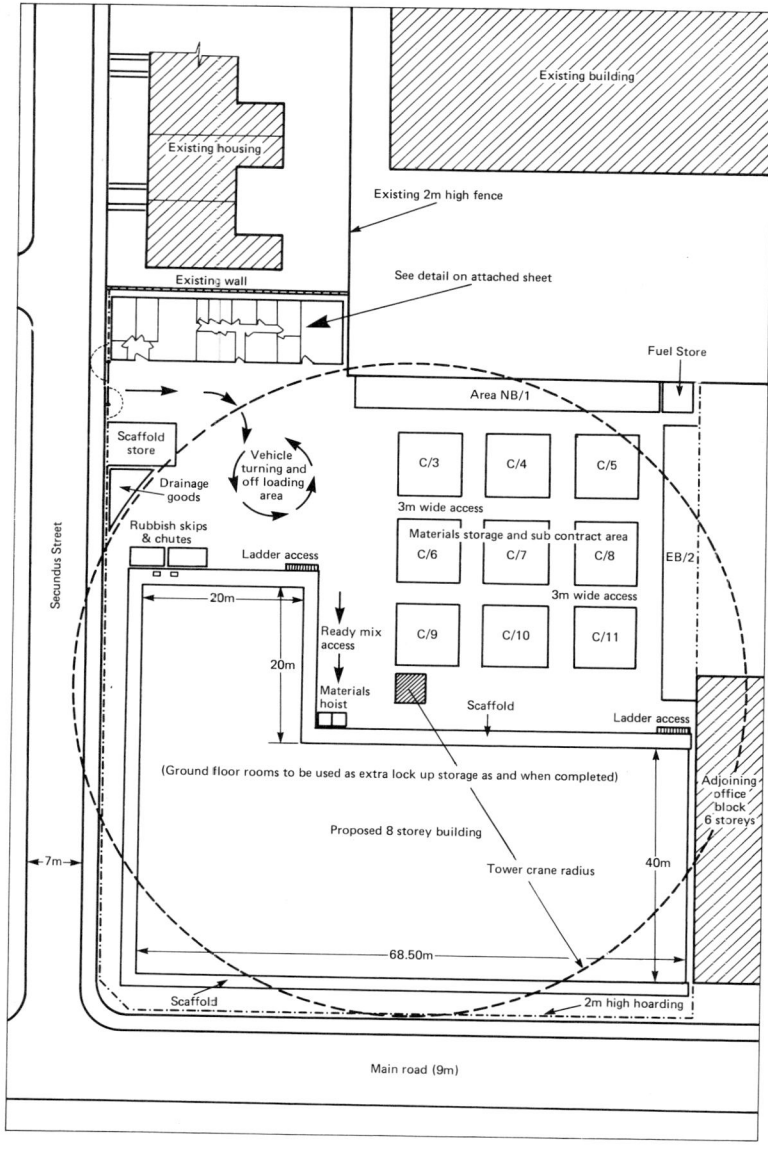

Fig 2.2 Site layout

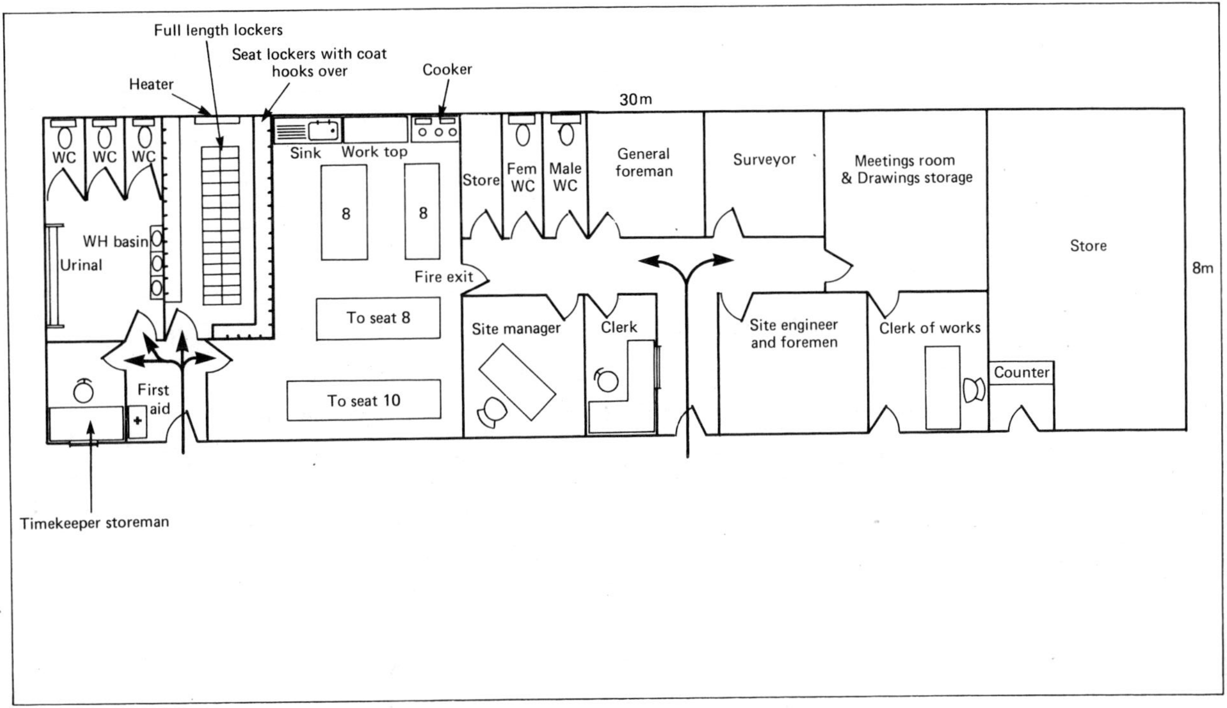

Fig 2.2a Detail of offices in Fig 2.2

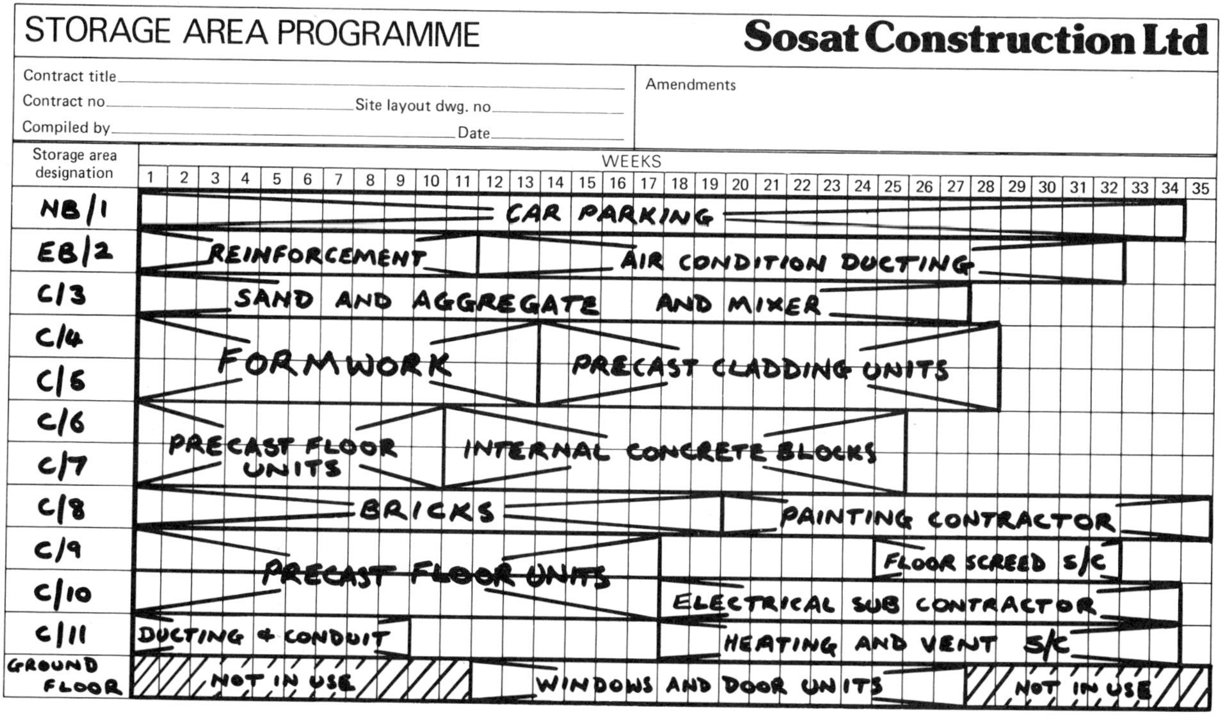

STORAGE AREA PROGRAMME — Sosat Construction Ltd

Contract title _____
Contract no _____ Site layout dwg. no _____ Amendments
Compiled by _____ Date _____

Storage area designation	WEEKS 1–35
NB/1	Car parking (weeks 14–19)
EB/2	Reinforcement (3–11); Air condition ducting (17–27)
C/3	Sand and aggregate (5–14); and mixer (15–21)
C/4	Formwork (6–13); Precast cladding units (17–25)
C/5	Precast floor units (3–7); Internal concrete blocks (13–22)
C/6	
C/7	Bricks (8–13)
C/8	Precast floor units (6–11); Painting contractor (22–32)
C/9	Electrical sub contractor (18–26); Floor screed s/c (25–29)
C/10	Ducting + conduit (1–8); Heating and vent s/c (19–26)
C/11	Not in use (1–6); Windows and door units (13–20); Not in use (29–35)
Ground floor	

Fig 2.3 Storage area programme (see site layout)

The layout should be drawn out to scale with all buildings, access roads and static plant and equipment clearly marked. Other areas should be designated as storage or sub-contractor areas and should be allocated on a time basis using a bar chart. An example of this technique is shown in *Figs 2.2* and *2.3*.

These documents should be sent to the site with copies for the storekeeper, 'setting-out' engineer, agent and general foreman. A copy should also be placed on the notice-board for information. Sub-contractors should be supplied with a copy and their attention should be drawn to the sections of the documents which apply to them. The 'setting out' engineer should mark all areas so that each space is clearly identifiable. Changes in plan should also be notified the instant it occurs.

2.14 QUESTIONS ON SITE LAYOUT

MULTI-CHOICE QUESTIONS

1. Which of the following forms would you use to indicate a shared welfare arrangement:
    (a) SWA 4;
    (b) OSR 27;
    (c) B.I. 510;
    (d) F 2202.

2. Notifiable Accidents and notifiable dangerous occurrences to be reported on F2508 are those which:
    (a) Concern young persons under 18 years;
    (b) Occur on site at any time;
    (c) Result in major injury, death or involves a dangerous occurrence;
    (d) Result in 2 weeks off work or death.

3. Sanitary conveniences should be provided at the rate of one for every:
    (a) 15;
    (b) 25;
    (c) 10;
    (d) 100.

4. The following floor area is recommended as reasonable for each office worker under the OSRP Act:
    (a) 3.7 m^2;
    (b) 6.8 m^2;
    (c) 10.2 m^2;
    (d) 1.1 m^2.

5. The objective of planning the site layout is:
    (a) Ensure the site is clean and tidy;
    (b) Provide comfortable working conditions for Site Management;
    (c) To enable the Architects to visit and tour the site;
    (d) Provide the conditions for effective production.

6. The primary consideration of site layout is:
    (a) Good access to the production site;
    (b) Storage for all materials;
    (c) Provision of good office accommodation;
    (d) To provide facilities for the Clerk of Works.

SHORT ANSWER QUESTIONS (15-20 minutes)

1 Describe a safe method of work for *one* of the following site operations on the building shown on Drawing Number . . . .
   (a) Demolition;
   (b) Excavation;
   (c) Foundations;
   (d) Erection of the structural frame.

2 Sketch the layout of the offices and buildings to meet the statutory requirements for a site with fifty-five operatives and the following management staff:
Site Manager
General Foreman
Bonus Surveyor
Engineer
Quantity Surveyor
There is also a resident Clerk of Works

3 Prepare a checklist which would be suitable to quantify the small tools to be used on any site.

4 Discuss the factors which would influence the siting of static plant.

5 Prepare a list of notifications and contacts which should be made by an efficient site manager prior to commencing work on site.

QUESTIONS REQUIRING LONGER ANSWERS (30-45 minutes)

1 Discuss the factors that influence the allocation of space to the storage of materials when planning a site layout.

2 Discuss those aspects of safety which may alter the approach to site layout planning.

3 Prepare a layout for the site shown on Drawing Number . . . . . . The maximum number of operatives employed is . . . . . . and the management staff numbers . . . . . . Give reasons for, the siting of buildings, security provision, siting and choice of plant, areas and location of access.

4 Describe in detail the procedures to be followed and provisions to be made with regard to the occurrence of accidents and their prevention for the following sites:
   (a) With a maximum of 300 employees;
   (b) With a maximum of 90 employeess;
   (c) With a maximum of 20 employees.

5 Discuss the differences in approach, which may be adopted to a site investigation (for site layout purposes) when considering a site in a conjested city centre and a green field site 5 km from a provincial town.

3 Site administration

3.1 REPORTS

Reports fall into two categories, firstly those which are made on standardised forms, such as a progress report or even a site investigation report. The second type are those written reports which are commissioned for the investigation and examination of a particular problem. Generally, the latter will convey information, describe an analysis of that information, and be followed by conclusions and recommendations. The standardised type of report will be dealt with in the sections most appropriate to their use.

The production of a report usually follows a standard format. This consists of:
Title Page
Contents
Summary
Introduction
Information and analysis
Conclusions
Recommendations
Appendices

The summary appears at the start of the report as it provides a very short edition of the main report which can be easily read by managers with insufficient time to scrutinise the full contents. If reports are only one or two pages then the contents, summary and other formalities may be discarded. The analysis or recommendations should include some cost evaluation exercise which would indicate the possible savings or extra expenditure required.

The title page of the report is often the section which sets the standard of presentation. A well prepared title page creates the right impression which may assist in the acceptance of the report. Besides the title, the page should also give the author's name and date of publication. It may also be used to display the copy number, if the report is to be restricted in any way. The reverse side of the title page should contain the terms of reference or the authority by which the report is produced. This entry should also be dated which indicates the time the work was authorised to start.

The contents is a list of the major sections giving the page numbers on which they commence. The page number on which the sections end may also be included, thus indicating the length of the sections.

The introduction follows, which should set the scene, relating the circumstances appertaining at the time and the reasons behind the enquiry. The methods of investigation and other factors which may influence the interpretation of the information should also be explained at this point.

The information section, sometimes called the body of the report, will contain all the evidence, information, facts and statistics which are relevant to the investigation. This information may contain views and opinions. Before continuing to the next phase, careful consideration should be given to the sources and reasons for the information volunteered under this category. The validation of all information is essential at this gathering stage. Any information which is contained in separate documents or drawings, and which is essential to include in full, should be attached to the report as an Appendix.

The most important part of the report is the analysis of the information. This may require the production of tables or graphs to present the information in a clearer and more concise form. Quite often the cost-benefit analysis may be included at this stage. Conclusions are reached on the basis of the analysis section and, quite often, in short reports they are combined. It is sometimes difficult to separate the stages but a logical approach to problem solving is essential. These conclusions should be the identification of the problem and the causal relationships with other factors.

The recommendations should offer solutions to remedy the causes of the problem. In cases where there are a number of remedies then all should be mentioned, but a choice should be made giving reasons for that choice. Suggestions may also be made as to the action needed to be taken and by whom. The actions required and recommendations should be written in emphatic and unqualified statements so that the reader is assured that the report is a thorough and decisive document.

The report writer should bear in mind the principles contained in the first chapter. The report must be easily understood, achieve its objective, include all information, develop the subject logically, and reach its conclusions on the basis of the best information available.

Report writing enables all the managers of a firm to benefit from the experience of a single problem. It enables discussion to be carried on about the causes of, and remedies to, problems. Such an information exchange relating to site production activities should lead to improved procedures, improvements in production methodology, better technological information exchange and more standardised and efficient production methods.

3.2 EXTERNAL ADMINISTRATION

The communications links between site and the external members of the building team are shown in *Fig 3.1*. These communications are concerned with legally enforceable contracts and are conducted between the parties or agents. They should be much more formal than those conducted within the internal organisation of the firm. Generally all communications to external parties are routed through the contractors head office.

All communications between the external participants should be characterised by:

Accuracy
Clarity
Adequate descriptions
Proper referencing to documents
Objectivity
Specific information
Timeliness

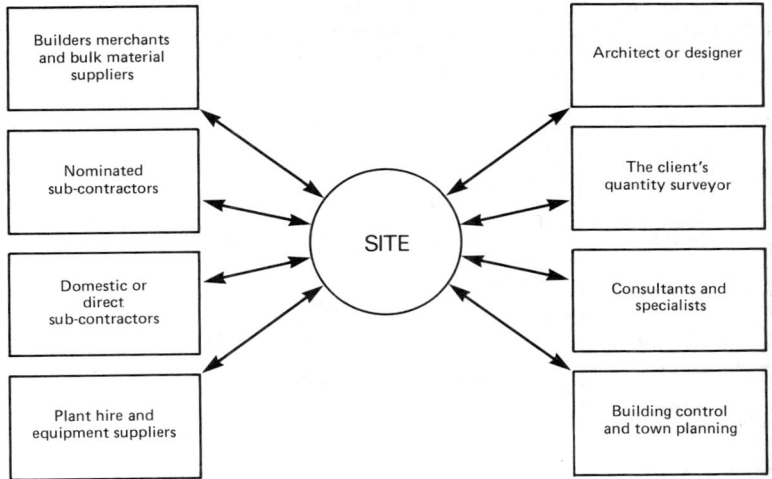

Fig 3.1 External communication links

The information system should enable all these characteristics to be present and enable a record to be kept that will be of use in the settlement of disputes.

The telephone may be used in order to fulfil urgency. The conversation should be confirmed in writing to the other party as soon as possible afterwards making reference to the time, date and content. The letter should also offer an opportunity for the recipient to disagree with its contents. There is a tendency to believe that only those conversations considered important should be recorded. The problem here is that importance is a factor which often only becomes apparent at a later date. The safest procedure is to confirm all communications in writing.

In order that communications between parties are effective each letter should contain three major sections. The first section should introduce the subject so that the reader knows what the following text will be about. The second section should convey the information that it is wished to transfer. This may mean that it is a simple request for a drawing, or information regarding a claim running to several pages. The last section should always be a request for action, such as 'Forward the drawing to this site by . . .', or 'please confirm the receipt of this claim on the attached proforma'.

To maintain correspondence and records in a logical sequence some filing system should be devised. It is also necessary that copies of all correspondence initiated by the site should go to Head Office and vice versa. The filing system will depend on the size of the contract and therefore the paperwork it is likely to generate. Smaller sites could probably cope with a file for each of the eight parties shown in *Fig 3.1* but larger sites may require further breakdown to individual firms, and sub-contractors, and in the case of the Architect and others by subject matter.

3.3 INTERNAL ADMINISTRATION

The internal system of communication should have the single objective of assisting productivity on site. If this involves procedures which may not appear to warrant the effort involved then some kind of cost-benefit analysis should be carried out. Information systems do not exist solely for themselves nor to exercise control, they exist to improve the production of the firm as a whole. The internal communication links are shown in *Fig 3.2*.

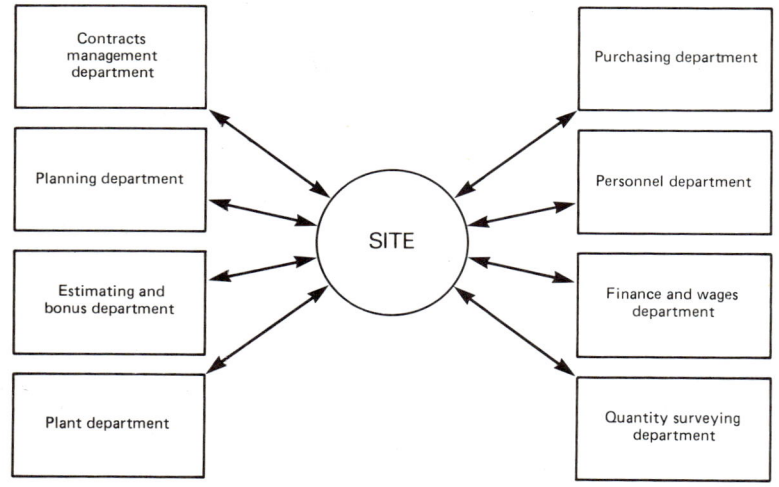

Fig 3.2 Internal communication links

Effective internal communications are characterised by the same factors as the external system. The exception is that the methods employed are usually much more informal. Greater use is made of oral communication particularly the telephone. Therefore in addition to the factors listed on page 26 the internal system should be based on:
Good organisation structure;
Effective job descriptions;
Trust between communicators;
Defined objectives;
Cooperation and coordination.

The methods of communication used may be a reflection of the presence of the characteristics listed above. Telephone conversation and face-to-face discussion will predominate in a firm with the right 'atmosphere'. Memoranda and letter writing will be the usual way where trust and respect are in doubt. To ensure coordination use is made of standard operating procedures. These standardised instructions may apply to the receipt of ready-mixed concrete, the engagement of labour or procedure in the case of a serious accident and other occurrences.

The need for internal communication leads to standardised reports and the major item to be used is the site diary. This daily record is shown in *Fig 3.3*. It should be completed promptly and should be contained in a bound book with the pages numbered so that pages cannot be removed or replaced. The reverse of the page should be lined to enable more detailed explanation of problems referred to on the front. It acts as a comprehensive record of both the internal and external

SOSAT CONSTRUCTION LTD

Page 14

DAILY DIARY	......day.............
WEATHER CONDITIONS	TEMPERATURE °C overnight minimum _ _ _ _ _ _ _ 0800 _ _ _ _ _ _ _ _ _ _ _ _ _ 1600 _ _ _ _ _ _ _ _ _ _ _ _ _ 0200 _ _ _ _ _ _ _ _ _ _ _ _ _
ORAL OR WRITTEN INSTRUCTIONS	GIVEN BY
DRAWINGS RECEIVED	NUMBER
VARIATION ORDERS RECEIVED	NUMBER
DAYWORK: DESCRIPTION AND REASON	SHEET No
LOST TIME AND REASON	LABOUR | On site | Req'd
DELAYS AND REASON	
URGENT REQUIREMENTS ORDERED	VISITORS TO SITE
Clk of Wks labour return attached by:	Signature: Date:
Further details, referenced above, are continued overleaf, please initial.	

Fig 3.3 Daily site diary

SOSAT CONSTRUCTION LTD. SITE ______________________ SHEET No ______

INCOME RECEIVED £	INCOME RECEIVED p	DATE YEAR 1981 MONTH	DATE DAY	DESCRIPTION OF ITEMS	VOUCHER No.	EXPENDITURE Postage £	Postage p	Cleaning Materials £	Cleaning Materials p	Travelling £	Travelling p	£	p	£	p	£	p	RUNNING BALANCE £	RUNNING BALANCE p
25	00	JAN	3	Cash from Finance Office	–													b/f 1	50
		JAN	5	Postage stamps	01	0	72												
		JAN	6	JONES General Hardware	02			3	64										
		JAN	8	Bus fare	03					0	84								
TOTAL INCOME -------		TOTAL EXPENDITURE -------		BALANCE -------	TOTALS													c/f	

Fig 3.4 Petty cash account

communications system. It can also become acceptable as legal evidence in court should a dispute reach that stage.

Another aspect of the site administration is the petty cash account which must be run in a proper manner. The petty cash must be accounted for and items charged to the correct accounts. A petty cash account is shown in *Fig 3.4*.

3.4 LABOUR ADMINISTRATION

This type of administration on site will be concerned with time sheets, labour allocation, application for days off, reporting of absences, sick notes, warning of misconduct and the engagement and dismissal of labour. Some of these aspects will be dealt with by other departments in the larger firms but some smaller firms delegate these functions to site management.

Time sheets are the record of attendance on site and each operative should check in on arrival on site. The time of arrival and departure from site is recorded. This information is eventually transferred to a wage and bonus sheet.

The labour allocation is usually required daily by the Clerk of Works as part of the contract administration. A typical allocation sheet is shown in *Fig 3.5*. Two copies are normally made, one for the Clerk of Works and one for records. On smaller jobs the site diary will contain the allocation and it will be copied as required for the client.

The application for days off and the reporting of absences are an essential part of labour administration. The forms should be as simple as possible indicating the facts as known. Prompt despatch to the Personnel Department will ensure an effective follow up.

Warnings as to an operative's conduct may become necessary during the employment period. It is essential that oral and written warnings are given prior to dismissal. Two warnings are necessary, firstly an oral warning with the right of appeal. These warnings do not mean that dismissal is mandatory at the next episode of misconduct. All warnings should be dated and timed and should be accurate in every detail. Standardised phraseology is sometimes used for the more common offences such as lateness or contravening safety regulations.

Dismissal usually follows warnings for misconduct although some serious offences can be liable to instant dismissal. In such cases the person must have been forewarned that this offence could lead to instant dismissal and, of course, that the dismissal must be a 'reasonable' response in the view of the court. Sometimes it is necessary to suspend workers who may be incapable of performing their duties on site. In this, a procedure must be laid down so that the suspended worker does not become a nuisance to others.

The engagement of labour is a legally enforceable contract and whilst the site manager may be the best qualified to interview and examine the suitability of the applicant, the actual engagement should be conducted by the personnel department. Terms of employment, conditions of contract, travelling and other allowances are all agreed prior to the engagement. The worker can of course be placed on probation for a 'reasonable' period of time in order to judge his suitability for the position.

3.5 MATERIALS ADMINISTRATION

This type of administration is important to prevent fraud and pilfering. It should be a continuous procedure from the ordering of materials to the settlement of the

Sosat Construction Ltd
DAILY LABOUR ALLOCATION SHEET

Contract_____

Contract number_____

Supervisor_____

Section of site_____

Lost time_____

Sheet_____ of _____

Day_____ Date_____

Cost code

Description of work

Total site hours

Overtime hours

Works no	Name	Trade									

SUB CONTRACT LABOUR (enter number of operatives under each trade)

Name of Firm	Trade									

Fig 3.5 Daily labour allocation sheet

SOSAT CONSTRUCTION LTD. MATERIALS SCHEDULE

DATE PREPARED: _____ **PREPARED BY:** _____ **APPROVED BY:** _____ **CONTRACT NUMBER:** _____ **SHEET N⁰** ___ **OF** ___

ITEM N°	MATERIAL DESCRIPTION	UNIT	QUANTITY	PACKAGING	METHOD OF UNLOADING	SUPPLIER AND CONTACT INFORMATION	ORDER N° AND DATE	DATE ORDER CONFIRMED	ARRIVAL DATE DEL. NOTE N°	DATE AND QTY REQ'D ON SITE	REMARKS
22	Crockford Red Rustic Facing Bricks BS 3921 (DD 34)	N°	104,000	1 tonne loads on pallets (450)	Fork Lift Truck	J H Crockford Ltd. Brickworks Factory Lane Claytown Contact John Common Tel N° Claytown 7478 92	N° 00147823 5 Feb 81	20 Feb 81		30 Apr 81 30,000 / 13 May 81 30,000 / 30 May 81 20,000 / 7 June 81 20,000	Stored on pallets protected by polythene sheeting

Fig 3.6 The material schedule

DELIVERY NOTE			N° 019038
GOODS SUPPLIED BY.......	**J. H. CROCKFORD LTD.** **BRICKWORKS** **FACTORY LANE** **CLAYTOWN**		DATE 30th April 81 VEH. NO BGW 001 Z DRIVER J. JONES
GOODS CONSIGNED TO.....	SOSAT CONSTRUCTION LTD. New Hospital Site Peacehaven Road Prestham		ORDER N° 00147823 DATE OF ORDER 5-2-81 DETAILS Part of Order 70,000 to follow
QUANTITY	UNIT	MATERIAL DESCRIPTION	
30,000	N°	Crockford Red Rustic Facing bricks	
CERTIFIED THAT THE GOODS DESCRIBED ABOVE HAVE BEEN EXAMINED AND RECEIVED IN A SATISFACTORY CONDITION.		NAME W. H. EVANS USE BLOCK CAPITALS POSITION Storekeeper SIGNATURE WH Evans DATE 30 April 81	

Fig 3.7 A typical delivery note

invoice. The actual quantifying of materials and the preparation of the materials schedule is described in chapter 5. The materials schedule is shown in *Fig 3.6*.

The materials schedule will have a description of the material and the order numbers placed alongside in the appropriate column. A copy of the schedule will be held in the purchasing office and copies of orders placed are sent to the site. In some cases, orders are placed for bulk quantities and the site management staff are authorised to call off smaller quantities as and when required. Some components, i.e. door and windows, may be placed on separate schedules. However they may be included in less detail on the general schedule.

The delivery note shown in *Fig 3.7* gives brief details of the load. The actual load should be checked against the delivery note and this should be checked against the order and the quantity delivered entered on the schedule. The delivery note number, material and quantity should then be entered on the materials return shown in *Fig 3.8*. This return is sent to the Contract Office for entering on their materials schedule. The return is then passed to the Purchasing Office who on receipt of the invoice can check against receipts and forward the invoice to finance for payment. The whole procedure is illustrated in *Fig 3.9*.

SOSAT CONSTRUCTION LTD.			WEEK ENDING _____			
WEEKLY MATERIALS RETURN (GOODS RECEIVED)						
SITE _____			SERIAL No _____			
CONTRACT No _____			COMPILED BY _____			
MATERIALS SCHEDULE NUMBER	ORDER NUMBER	DELIVERY NOTE No	MATERIALS DESCRIPTION	FOR OFFICE USE ONLY		
				£	p	INITIAL

ALL DELIVERY NOTES SHOULD BE ATTACHED. THE RETURNS SHOULD BE COMPLETED AND FORWARDED TO THE CONTRACTS DEPARTMENT ON THE FIRST WORKING DAY OF THE WEEK FOLLOWING THE DELIVERY. NIL RETURNS ARE REQUIRED

Fig 3.8 Weekly materials received report

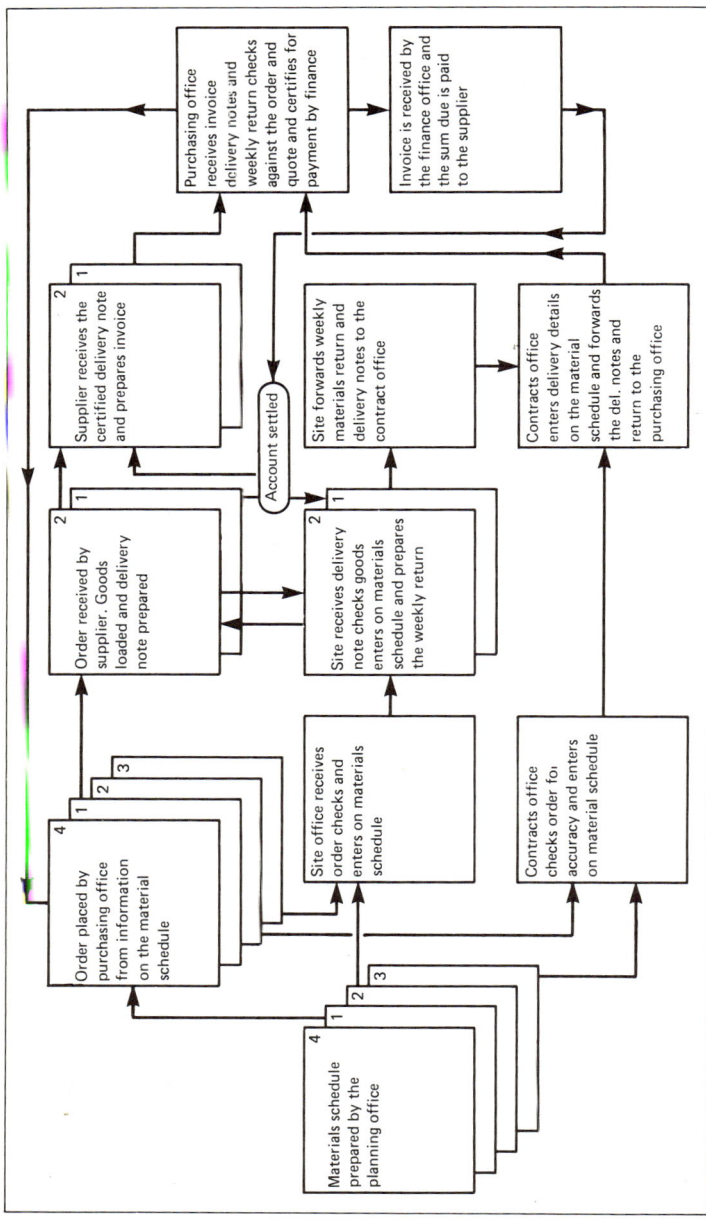

Fig 3.9 Material administration procedure

3.6 DRAWINGS ADMINISTRATION

The register of drawings and their control will depend on the organisation of the firm. If all drawings are sent initially to the site then the register will be kept there. If they are sent to the Head Office they may be registered, a copy retained and sent to the site. It is, in any case, essential that the drawings are again registered on site.

The procedure for the receipt and checking of drawings is shown in *Fig 3.10.* It is based on four copies being produced and sent to Head Office. It is also assumed that the Site Engineer is responsible for the registration and control of drawings. This may differ depending on the size of the site and the system generally employed.

The drawing should be registered on site and on receipt can be date/time stamped to authenticate actual arrival time. An example of a drawing register system using cards which are approximately 100 mm × 75 mm is shown in *Fig 3.11* (Front of Card) and *Fig 3.12* (Reverse of Card). Drawings should always be checked to ensure that they are correct and no discrepancies exist. Any mistake should be reported to the originator immediately. The drawing register cards should be in a lockable holder to prevent removal or loss.

To aid retrieval of the information contained on the drawings a suitable system of storage should be used. The first step in this system is the entry of the location of the drawing on its register card. This could be Plan Chest 3, Drawer 5. Plan chests are not the easiest method of storage as the drawers tend to be overloaded making the removal and return of drawings difficult. A vertical hanging system takes less space and provides for easier retrieval.

In order to ensure that drawings are up-dated by amendments it is necessary to have a procedure to prevent errors occurring. A system of rubber stamping is probably the easiest. Initially, drawings may be issued which are preliminary drawings, these should be stamped 'PRELIMINARY—NOT A WORKING DRAWING. Drawings are also altered by the issue of smaller drawings giving amended details. The drawing should again be stamped in red close to the amended detail, with a stamp 'THIS DETAIL HAS BEEN AMENDED SEE DWG . . .'' The drawing number can then be inserted and, if possible, the drawing stapled to the original. The other method of amendment is to issue an entirely new drawing, usually with a letter after the drawing number. Once new amended drawings are issued, the old drawings must be recalled hence the drawing issues side of the card. When these drawings are returned they should be stamped over the drawing title block and on another conspicuous place, in red, with the words 'THIS DRAWING HAS BEEN SUPERSEDED—DO NOT USE''.

One of the greatest problems in the maintenance of buildings is the location of services and the knowledge of hidden details of construction. These are often altered and amended throughout the contract and each time the changes should be recorded on the drawing by the setting out engineer or trade foreman concerned. These should be initialled so that the person can be traced later if the amendment is not clear. As drawings are returned with that portion of the work completed, 'as built' drawings should be produced by the responsible party as indicated in the contract. At the end of the contract a full set of 'as built' drawings should then be available.

3.7 ARCHITECT'S INSTRUCTIONS

An architect shall issue instructions for any extra work and other matters, such as extensions of time or omissions. These instructions must conform with the

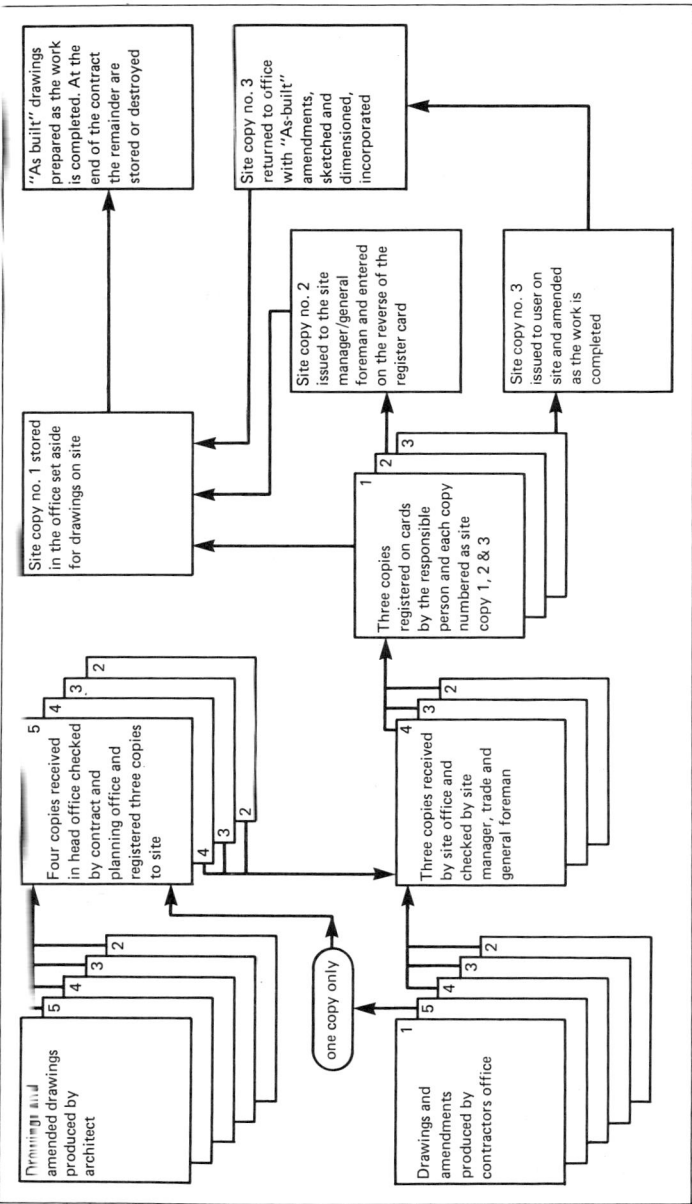

Fig 3.10 Drawings administration procedure

DRAWING ISSUES		NAME AND POSITION OF RECEIVER											
TOTAL NUMBER OF COPIES ________ NUMBER OF COPIES IN OFFICE ________ (USE PENCIL)													
DATE	SITE COPY NUMBER	ISSUED INITIAL	DATE RETURNED	RECEIVED INITIAL	ISSUED INITIAL	DATE RETURNED	RECEIVED INITIAL	ISSUED INITIAL	DATE RETURNED	RECEIVED INITIAL	ISSUED INITIAL	DATE RETURNED	RECEIVED INITIAL

THE RECEIVER OF THE COPY OF THE DRAWING SHOULD INITIAL, TO ACKNOWLEDGE RECEIPT, IN THE FIRST COLUMN. ON THE RETURN OF THE COPY THE PERSON RESPONSIBLE FOR THE REGISTER SHOULD DATE AND INITIAL IN THE OTHER COLUMNS, AND ALTER THE "COPIES IN OFFICE" FIGURE.

Fig 3.11 Front of drawing register card

SOSAT CONSTRUCTION LTD. CARD N° ________

DRAWING REGISTER CARD

DRAWING N° ____________________ DATE ____________

TITLE ____

____

ISSUED BY ____________________ MAIN SCALE ____________

LOCATION OF DRAWING ____________________ N° OF COPIES ____________

AMENDMENTS	MAIN SCALE	NUMBER OF COPIES	DISPOSAL OF PREVIOUS COPIES

ENTER THE ARRANGEMENTS FOR THE FINAL DISPOSAL OF THE DRAWINGS AT THE COMPLETION OF THE CONTRACT	

Fig 3.12 Reverse of drawing register card

architect's responsibility as indicated in the conditions of the contract. The responsibility for compliance is removed from the contractor if the architect exceeds his powers.

Only the architect is empowered to issue instructions, although the Clerk of Works does issue oral instructions to be confirmed in writing by the Architect. The contractor is not bound to comply with these oral instructions until they are confirmed. However, the relationship on site is never quite as formal between the parties and in cases where a good relationship exists, oral instructions are quite often acted upon. In the case of a dispute the claim, made by the contractor for

DESIGN AND ART PARTNERSHIP CHARTERED ARCHITECTS BOURNE AVENUE PRESTHAM PH7 OLD	ARCHITECTS INSTRUCTION NUMBER 27 DATE 3rd Feb 81 CONTRACT Prestham Hospital JOB NUMBER 748
To... SOSAT CONSTRUCTION LTD 111 GREENWOOD ROAD PRESTHAM PH 21 7LH	COPIES To.. CONTRACTOR. QUANTITY SURVEYOR CLERK OF WORKS FILE

SERIAL NUMBER	STATUS* O/A/C/D	ITEM
27/1	O	Door N° IN/F/749 Omit door entrance to vegetable preparation room from corridor as shown on Dwg. N° 748/396/2
27/2	A	Add Door type IN/F/D/750 to vegetable preparation room as shown on Drawing N° 748/27/2A. Door schedule amendment will follow. Enclosed 4 copies Dwg N° 748/27/2A

O = OMISSION A = ADDITION C = CHANGE D = DAYWORK* ANY INSTRUCTION WHICH THE CONTRACTOR DISPUTES, FOR ANY REASON, SHOULD BE NOTIFIED TO THE ARCHITECT IN WRITING WITHIN 7 (SEVEN) DAYS OF RECEIPT.	SHEET NUMBER / OF / SIGNED A J Drawer POSITION Job Architect. DATE 3/2/81

Fig 3.13 Typical architect's instruction

work done under oral instruction, is not bound to be accepted. An Architect's Instruction will look similar to the form shown in *Fig 3.13*.

If action on the Clerk of Works oral instructions is urgent, a request for them to be put in writing should be made. It helps if a pad of instruction sheets is held by the contractor for the Clerk of Works to complete. Some government departments have their own site works order forms which are completed by the site officer. This form is shown in *Fig 3.14*. Similarly, if defects are discovered either in drawings or in other documents or descriptions of work are unclear, some procedure must be adopted for submitting the problems to the architect. A letter may be used but as the problems are usually quite numerous a 'Q' sheet as shown in *Fig 3.15* should be used; These may be in pads with the original and two copies. The original and a copy are sent to the architect and one copy is retained for a record. The architect returns one copy with the answer. These sheets are eventually consolidated into an architect's instruction or form the basis of claims.

```
┌─────────────────────────────┬──────────────────────────────┐
│ SITE INSTRUCTION TO         │ SOSAT CONSTRUCTION LTD.      │
│                             │ III, GREENWOOD ROAD          │
│ SERIAL N°_____     │ PRESTHAM                     │
│ DATE_____      │ PH 21  7LH                   │
├─────────────────────────────┴──────────────────────────────┤
│ CONTRACT_____  │
│ ISSUED BY_____   │
│ ON BEHALF OF_____   │
│ AUTHORITY_____   │
├────────────────────────────────────────────────────────────┤
│ THE WORK SHOULD BE DESCRIBED IN AS MUCH DETAIL AS POSSIBLE │
│ GIVING APPROXIMATE QUANTITIES WHERE POSSIBLE. THIS SITE    │
│ ORDER SHOULD BE SUPPORTED BY AN ARCHITECTS INSTRUCTION     │
│ ISSUED WITHIN 7(SEVEN) DAYS.                               │
├────────────────────────────────────────────────────────────┤
│ Please carry out the following work:-                      │
│                                                            │
│                                                            │
│                                                            │
│                                                            │
│                                                            │
│                                                            │
│                                                            │
├─────────────────────────┬──────────────────────────────────┤
│                         │ SIGNED ON                        │
│ DATE._____  │ BEHALF OF CLIENT._____  │
│                         │ INSTRUCTION                      │
│ TIME._____  │ RECEIVED BY._____  │
└─────────────────────────┴──────────────────────────────────┘
```

Fig 3.14 A site instruction sheet

QUERY SHEET

N° ________________

FROM: SOSAT CONSTRUCTION LTD.
111 GREENWOOD ROAD,
PRESTHAM
PH 21 7LH

TO: ______________________

CONTRACT TITLE ______________________________
CONTRACT N° ______________ DATE ____________ SHEET N° ___ of ___

ITEM NUMBER	QUERY	ARCHITECTS REPLY

LATEST DATE INFORMATION
E REQUIRED BY :— ________
SIGNED ______________________
DATE ______________________

AUTHORISING
ARCHITECT
SIGNED ______________________
DATE ______________________

Fig 3.15 Contractor's query sheet

3.8 DELAY RECORDS

Delay records are required by a contracting firm to substantiate the loss sustained by various causes. These delays may not become apparent immediately as the full consequences of an act or omission may not be appreciated for a number of weeks. It is therefore, essential that full records are kept, mainly in the Daily Site Diary. The accurate recording of any minor failure should be carried out in order to set the time and dates of the first awareness of the problem.

Delays may be due to a number of reasons and almost all parties can be responsible in some way or another. A major cause of delay is often lack of information. This may arise through indecision by the client, failure to produce drawings by the designer, details not available from manufacturers, calculations and approval awaited from a consultant or notification by the builder of a problem. Many causes of delay are disputed as to whether details supplied are inadequate or whether problems should be recognised and notified. These disputes are subject to interpretation as to what is reasonable under the law and each individual circumstance will result in a different conclusion. These are all major causes which require a record of an initial request for information, all subsequent requests and the final arrival of that information. At the same time the consequences should be spelled out and latest dates for information should be noted and recorded and where possible agreed by the Clerk of Works.

Delays are also occasioned by parties outside the contract. This occurs due to non-delivery of materials, transport strikes and inclement weather. The recording of inclement weather is a matter of continuous records at all times. A weekly weather record chart is shown in *Fig 3.16* which allows for temperature to be recorded in figures and general conditions and rain in code. The codes and extent of information could be further developed but simplicity is esential if the records are to be kept. Notes of snow or fog could be made in the remarks column. The Clerk of Works should sign the sheet and it would be preferable for each day to be initialled.

The system for notifying delays, receipt of oral instructions, A.I.s and amendments to drawings must be such that the Architect and the contractors' representatives are aware of the problem created. The facts are recorded in the site diary but notification should be made to the Q.S., Clerk of Works, Contracts Manager and Architect on the form shown in *Fig 3.17*. As time is usually very important this form should be filled out immediately and sent to those concerned as soon as possible. If telephone calls are necessary reference should be made to them on the form. Five copies of the form are required for full distribution but in some cases it will not be necessary to inform the Architect or Clerk of Works.

The delays caused by the performance of nominated sub-contractors and suppliers are of particular importance. Similarly, delays in other suppliers due to materials shortages and transport problems should also be notified. The most important part is to record the effect on site production. It may mean moving labour from one task to another — this may only mean the loss of one hour in the reorganisation but it also influences the smooth running of the site. From such changes in task allocation, disputes over bonus payments and an increase in absenteeism can result. In the long term these delays may mean that stocks of materials held on site are remaining too long, require added protection and cause the postponement of delivery of other items because of lack of space. Lack of space may even cause a new storage area to be used or hired with consequent expensive double handling.

SITE WEATHER RECORD   SASAT CONSTRUCTION LTD   SERIAL N°

SITE .... CONTRACT N° .... WEEK ENDING ....

MONTH		CONDITIONS ON SITE AT											total hours rain during the day	total hours when temp. below 5°C.	REMARKS
		0800			1100			1400			1700				
DAY	DATE	temp °C	intensity of rain	general conditions	temp °C	intensity of rain	general conditions	temp °C	intensity of rain	general conditions	temp °C	intensity of rain	general conditions			
MONDAY																
TUESDAY																
WEDNESDAY																
THURSDAY																
FRIDAY																
SATURDAY																
SUNDAY																

KEY:
RAIN
A no rain
B drizzle
C showers
D normal rain
E downpour

GENERAL CONDITIONS:
A sunny
B normal
C cloudy
D dull
E windy

SITE MANAGER ....
DATE ....

CLERK OF WORKS ....
DATE ....

Fig 3.16 Weekly weather chart

```
┌─────────────────────────────────────────────────────────────────┐
│ SOSAT CONSTRUCTION LTD.              SERIAL N°_ _ _ _ _ _ _ _   │
├─────────────────────────────────────────────────────────────────┤
│        NOTIFICATION OF DELAYS AND VARIATIONS                    │
│                   TO THE CONTRACT                               │
├─────────────────────────────────────────────────────────────────┤
│ FROM: _ _ _ _ _ _ _ _ _ _ _ _ _ _   TO*: CONTRACTS MANAGER _ _  │
│ SITE _ _ _ _ _ _ _ _ _ _ _ _ _ _ _       ARCHITECT _ _ _ _ _ _  │
│ _ _ _ _ _ _ _ _ _ _ _ _ _ _ _ _ _        QUANTITY SURVEYOR _ _  │
│ *DELETE AS APPLICABLE _ _ _ _ _ _         CLERK OF WORKS_ _ _ _ │
├─────────────────────────────────────────────────────────────────┤
│ I have today received the following instructions/amendment/    │
│                                         request/notice*        │
│                                                                 │
│   (ruled lines for entry)                                       │
│                                                                 │
├─────────────────────────────────────┬───────────────────────────┤
│ NAME OF PERSON                      │ INFORMATION RECEIVED AT   │
│ INFORMATION RECEIVED FROM: _ _ _ _  │ TIME: _ _ _ DATE: _ _ _   │
│ NAME OF PERSON                      │                           │
│ RECEIVING THE INFORMATION: _ _ _ _  │ SIGNED_ _ _ _ _ _ _ _ _   │
├─────────────────────────────────────┴───────────────────────────┤
│ THIS INFORMATION IS LIKELY TO CAUSE A DELAY OF _ _ _ *HRS/DAYS. │
│ SEE DETAILS OVERLEAF                                            │
└─────────────────────────────────────────────────────────────────┘
```

Fig 3.17 Information receipt record

3.9 DAYWORKS

These are works which may be completed by the contractor and when no fair basis of remuneration can be found within the price structure of the Bills of Quantities. The works are therefore carried out on a cost plus basis. This system requires an agreement on wage and plant rates and a site on-cost percentage usually at the tender stage. Materials and plant hire invoices will be required as proof of other expenditure.

A typical daywork record sheet is shown in *Fig 3.18*. Again it ideally should comprise of 5 copies and distributed to all the parties concerned. The sheets are usually completed weekly and are the result of an architect's instruction. Some works may last less than a week and would obviously be submitted immediately the work is completed. Some government agencies provide their own forms to be completed by the contractor.

DAYWORK RECORD — SOSAT CONSTRUCTION LTD.

CONTRACT No _____ A.I. NO _____
SITE _____
WEEK ENDING SUNDAY _____ WEEK No _____
SHEET No _____ PREVIOUS SHEET Nos _____

DESCRIPTION OF WORK.

LABOUR

NAME	TRADE	M	T	W	T	F	S	S	TOTAL	RATE	£	p
									TOTAL			
									% ON COST			

PLANT & TRANSPORT

DESCRIPTION	M	T	W	T	F	S	S	TOTAL	RATE	£	p
DAILY CERTIFICATION INITIAL FOR LABOUR PLANT & TRANSPORT								TOTAL			
								% ON COST			

MATERIALS

DESCRIPTION	QUANT	RATE	£	p
OTHER CHARGES:	TOTAL			
	% ON COST			
			£	
			£	

Signed .... Site Supervisor   Date ....
Signed .... on behalf of Client Date ....

Fig 3.18 Daywork record sheet

Contractual disputes may arise over the amount of labour and other resources used on the work so the client's representative should be informed of any change in the agreed or usual method of work. It is often valuable to have the daywork sheet initialled by the Clerk of Works daily. Provision is made for this at the bottom of the daily plant columns.

The actual figure recorded in the columns is to be the actual site working time only. It should not include any supervision as this will be included in the percentage on-cost added to each of the sections. The dayworks sheet will be passed to both quantity surveyors and payment for such works will be included in the interim valuations, or stage payments made within the contract.

3.10 QUESTIONS ON SITE ADMINISTRATION

MULTI-CHOICE QUESTIONS

1. Daywork sheets should include time costs for:
   (a) all site working time for plant, labour and supervision;
   (b) only site working time plus non-productive overtime;
   (c) site working time only for labour and plant;
   (d) every hour labour and plant is on site including lunch and wet weather time.

2. If the contractor disagrees with the contents of an architects instruction he must notify the architect:
   (a) within three days by telephone;
   (b) before work commences through the Clerk of Works;
   (c) within seven days in writing;
   (d) by 'Q' sheet within 48 hours.

3. A site manager can dismiss an employee after a persistant offence because:
   (a) he doesn't like him;
   (b) he has continually had to reprimand him;
   (c) the operative is inefficient and lazy;
   (d) he has given him at least two previous warnings for the same offence.

4. Written reports are generally used for:
   (a) occupying underworked management;
   (b) investigating and examining a problem;
   (c) submitting routine information to head office;
   (d) identifying problems for top management.

5. Delivery notes should be signed:
   (a) by the materials controller after a thorough check;
   (b) at the gate by the timekeeper;
   (c) after unloading and a count of packages;
   (d) by any manager and endorsed 'unchecked'.

SHORT-ANSWER QUESTIONS (15-20 minutes)

1. Describe *two* examples of delays which may be typical of those caused by members of the Building Team. Discuss the action you would take, as Site Manager, in each case.

2. Describe the process that should be followed on the receipt of an amended drawing.

3. Illustrate a page from a site diary which may be used by a medium-sized contractor.

4. Draw up a checklist of the returns that a site would have to complete at the end of each week for submission to head office.

5   Prepare a list of files that would be kept by the Site Manager for a Local Authority Contract, lasting 2 years, to build 250 two-storey dwellings.

QUESTIONS REQUIRING LONGER ANSWERS (30-45 minutes)

1   You are a manager in a firm which usually has between 10 and 15 sites in operation at any one time. The materials control is fairly lax and has resulted in pilfering and excessive wastage due to poor quality and defective material being delivered. Prepare a report for top management proposing an effective system for the receipt, storage and control of materials.

2   Discuss the objective of site administration and its importance to site productivity.

3   Describe a suitable system for the receipt and circulation of all mail on a large site with thirty staff accommodated in close proximity in a single building.

4   Vital information is contained in drawings. Describe a suitable control procedure for drawings and discuss methods by which the content of drawings can be checked and problems raised with the Architect.

5   Delays and variations are important aspects of contract administration. Discuss the principles involved and describe a system of recording the receipt of such information.

4 Meetings

4.1 TYPES OF SITE MEETING

A number of types of site meeting are held on site with different representatives at each. Every meeting has a function to perform and that function will be directly or indirectly related to site production. The effectiveness of these meetings will be measured by the contribution they make to the productivity on site. The types of meeting are shown in *Fig 4.1* and are grouped as follows:

Type 1 — Internal control meetings
Type 2 — Subcontractor/supplier control meetings
Type 3 — Employee meetings
Type 4 — Contract administration meetings.

TYPE 1

The first type of site meeting includes those meetings which are used for exercising internal control of the project. These meetings are usually at two levels, one involving management personnel from head office, the second, site supervisory staff.

The meetings between head office and site staff will be used to review progress on the contract and discuss problems which may arise. They are also a preparation for the monthly site meeting with the building team.

The meeting with supervisory staff is usually held weekly and will include all the trade supervisors and the general and services foreman. The meeting is generally conducted by the site manager. It is likely to be very informal and will review progress over the last week and then plan the next weeks work.

TYPE 2

The sub-contractor/supplier control meetings will be between those parties concerned with the issues to be discussed. There are three main types see *Fig 4.1*.

First the initial meeting with sub-contractors. This meeting will involve a number of the main and sub-contractor's staff. It will be used to ascertain information prior to the commencement of work on site and will involve only one sub-contractor. (This subject will be more fully discussed in the section dealing with sub-contractors on page 90.) This meeting will involve only one sub-contractor.

The second meeting is the sub-contractors progress meeting. This will be chaired by the site manager and will include all the sub-contractors working on the site and may include those about to start work. The main discussions will be about

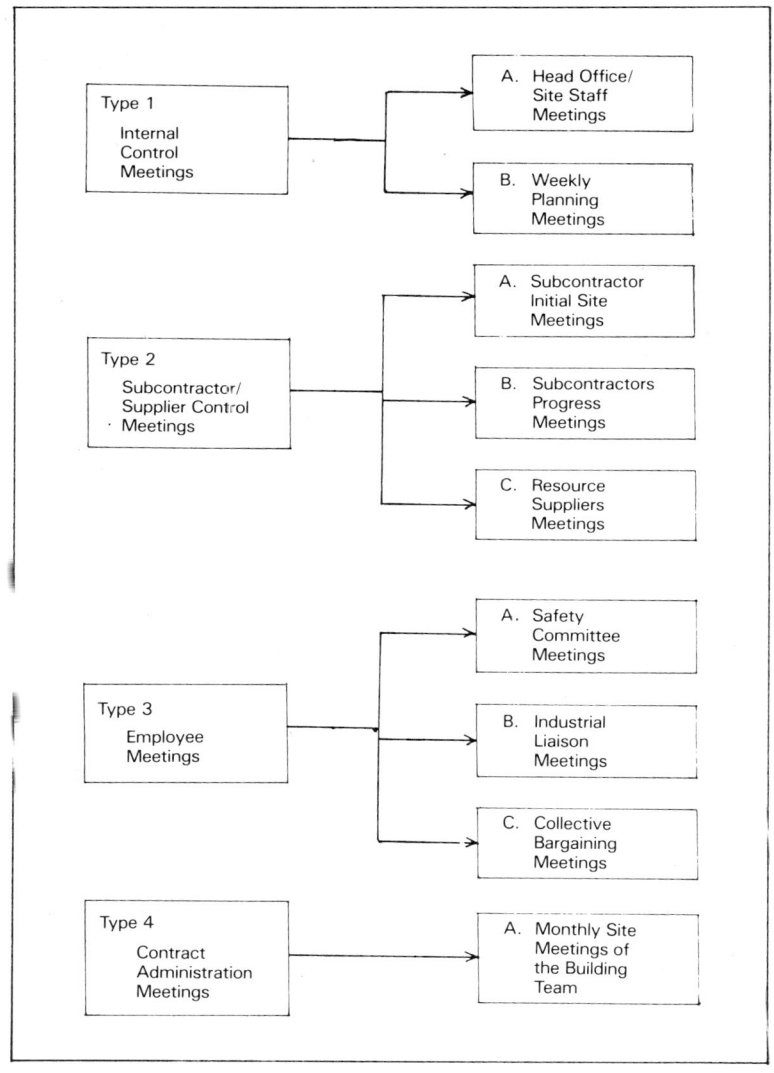

Fig 4.1 Types of site meetings

progress, attendance and coordination. On a site with a large number of sub-contracts the meeting will take place weekly but may only be called at irregular intervals on sites with less sub-contractors, or whose contracts are less technically demanding.

Another meeting under this heading is between resource suppliers and the main contractor. The resource suppliers may be either the main material supplier, the ready mix concrete firm or the plant hire company. Meetings are particularly useful initially but successive meetings may be rare in practice and probably will only take place when problems and disputes arise. However, the benefits of meetings as a contribution to co-ordination should be borne in mind.

TYPE 3

The third type of meeting are those meetings between management and employees. These are used to discuss a wide range of issues such as safety, health, welfare, pay, conditions of employment, bonus schemes and holidays. The safety committee meetings must be held if safety representatives request them but the other types are usually the result of problems which arise on site.

The industrial relations policy is negotiated nationally by a council representing employers and employees. The site meetings will be called to solve particular local disputes. Such disputes may include grievances or unfair dismissals, pay during inclement weather, working of a bonus scheme, or lack of a welfare facility. The management may also use them to pass information to their employees as to company performance, future policy or other company news.

TYPE 4

The fourth type of meeting and the most formal is the contract administration meeting. This is usually held once a month but may be more frequent if the need arises. The people who attend will be members of the building team. The latter generally fall into two groups, those representing the client or employer and those representing the production team.

The client's group will include the architect, quantity surveyor, consultant engineer and clerk of works. The production team will include the main contractors representatives, namely the contracts manager, site manager, and services engineer, and the major sub-contractor's representatives. Those attending are not usually strictly limited and any organisation which may be able to contribute is usually invited to send a representative.

4.2. PURPOSE OF MEETING

A meeting can be called for a variety of purposes and the manner in which it is conducted will be related to the purpose for that meeting. Some meetings have a different purpose for every item on the agenda and this creates difficulty in the conduct of the meeting. These meetings are less successful than a series of meetings under the classification of each purpose.

INFORMATION MEETINGS

The first kind of purpose is to **pass information.** This type of meeting is not intended to allow discussion but is meant to convey a decision which has already been taken. This meeting will usually be conducted in autocratic fashion and, whilst it may be possible to ask questions and receive explanations, it is unlikely that the decision will be altered. Quite often meetings are given the opportunity to discuss proposals even though the decision has already been made. This is an attempt by the decision makers to validate the decision by the consent of the meeting, but leads to doubts by some members as to the effectiveness of such meetings.

An example of the information type of meeting would be when a firm's management decided to issue all car owners with passes and those without passes would be unable to enter and park on sites. Questions would be allowed as to the reasons for this policy decision but no change would be made to that decision.

CONSULTATION MEETINGS

The second purpose is a meeting called to **consult.** In this meeting a decision has not already been taken but a problem is put forward for discussion. In this way the expert knowledge and different experience of those attending the meeting can be called upon to offer solutions to the problem. Generally, a satisfactory and agreed solution is sought and can often be found. A good Chairman is essential to this type of meeting and in order to make the meeting effective all those present should be able to put their views so that the discussion is not dominated by those with the strongest personality.

An example of this would be a meeting of the production staff to review a construction method being used. Should the formwork system be causing problems leading to delays then some other system of applying the resources should be decided.

DECISION MEETINGS

Meetings are also called where the purpose is to **make a decision.** These are often called committee meetings where the result is meant to be binding on all those present. They can lead to a requirement for a member to support and abide by a decision when opposed to it during the committee deliberations. This type of meeting is generally held when there are a number of solutions which may give rise to a number of different consequences. The solutions are usually surrounded by uncertainty and each course of action may be subject to expenditure which is difficult to forecast.

An example of such a meeting would be between the building team to discuss a course of action to solve a difficult excavation problem. A typical problem is running sand where a number of solutions may be possible but the extent of the problem and the resultant expenditure is unknown. Once a course of action is decided then the contractor must carry out the work as agreed and the architect and quantity surveyor must agree to certify payment for the work involved.

PERSUASION MEETINGS

Finally, there are meetings convened for the purpose of **persuasion.** This type meeting is called in order that a member can put a proposal that he thinks the meeting should adopt. In this situation it is clearly the intent of the proposer to persuade members of the meeting to accept the proposition.

An example of this type of meeting could arise with a material supplier. If a product is suddenly unavailable due to industrial problems or lack of imported raw materials then an alternative must be found. Assuming the problem is the supply of copper pipe the local builder's merchant or sales representative may try to persuade the meeting to use stainless steel tubing. Similarly, shortages in plasterboard may lead to replacement products being advocated.

CHAIRMANSHIP

These four types of meeting require a different approach by the chairman. Some require an autocratic approach, some democratic, others need a sympathetic chairman whilst others may require decision-making ability and leadership.

When each item on an agenda requires a different approach the chairman will be unable to be consistent. The perception of members is likely to view this inconsistency as unfair, inequitable and devious. It may be impossible for every item on the agenda to require one approach but in assessing the effectiveness of meetings the purpose of the meeting should be considered.

4.3 PLANNING A MEETING

Every time a meeting is called the site management and other members attending the meeting are called away from their tasks. This is a costly procedure, and every effort should be made to ensure that a meeting is the best method of achieving the objective.

Assuming that a meeting is the best method then everything should be done to enable the objective to be met in the shortest time. Planning a meeting requires a number of distinct actions to achieve maximum effectiveness. These are outlined in the following paragraphs.

THE OBJECTIVE

There must be an **objective** which is to be achieved. Before calling a meeting it should be ascertained that a meeting is the best way to tackle the situation. Having set the objective and deciding that a meeting is the best way of reaching the goal the planning can proceed.

WHO SHOULD ATTEND

The next step is to decide **who should attend.** Obviously all those concerned and who may have some point of view to contribute should be invited. The number will depend on the purpose of the meeting. If it is purely to inform, the meeting could be attended by hundreds, most of whom will only receive information. If the purpose of the meeting is consultation then ten members may be the maximum number before the control necessary reduces the value of the discussion.

DATE, TIME AND PLACE

Having decided who should attend, the decision as to **date, time and place** should be taken. Quite often it is necessary for an organisation to hold meetings at different levels on different days. Therefore it may be decided that board meetings will be on Tuesdays, head office meetings on Wednesdays, site meetings on Thursdays and contract administration meetings on Fridays. Such arrangements can also be supplemented by the site meetings being in the first week of a month, the head office meetings in the second week and board meetings in the third week.

This tends to enable meetings to be used as a filter process and to be regularly spaced so that managers are not taken away from tasks for a long time.

The next task is to summon the members to a meeting usually by using an agenda. If it is a regular review meeting it may be necessary to request items for the agenda and having received them, prepare the agenda before issuing it and the summons to the meeting.

The important point to remember is that the agenda is used to enable the participants to prepare for the meeting so that its effectiveness is maximised and its duration curtailed. If necessary, information papers covering the agenda items should be prepared and distributed.

Once the agenda is prepared and the place selected, the arrangements for the meeting should continue. The minutes will also have to be taken or a record made in some way. Some meetings which are totally informal do not require any record. Group pressure to abide by the decision is often sufficient to ensure the meeting was effective. These points are further discussed in the following paragraphs.

4.4 PREPARING THE AGENDA

The agenda of a meeting should be specifically designed to meet the objective of the meeting. It should contain items whose purpose is the same, that is, to inform or to persuade or to consult or decide. However, it would appear to be impossible to work within these limits and quite often standardised agendas are used for regular meetings.

When meetings are not regular they should have an agenda prepared to meet the objective. This will mean that the person calling the meeting will also prepare the agenda. The specific aim should be to assist the chairman in receiving a logical order of discussion and consideration of the business. The agenda can be used to limit the discussion to the actual points and to enable the meeting to progress from point to point. The skilful compilation of agenda items, allied with good chairmanship, will enable the meeting to be effective.

In a regular review meeting it may be necessary to call for items from the regular members of the committee. If this is not done a number of items are raised under 'any other business'. This creates problems because there is no forewarning of the items and some members are not fully prepared. When agenda items which are requested are returned they should be studied and those of a similar nature amalgamated. The supporting material for each item should be collected and then the whole document issued with the meeting invitation.

Agenda items to inform should be framed under a general heading such as 'Main-contractors Reports'. Those items which seek to persuade, or that need to be discussed, should be put in the form of a proposition or a number of propositions. This enables the actual proposition to be discussed and where a choice has to be made all have had time to consider the proposals. This will enable the chairman to use the agenda to keep the meeting on course to meet the objective.

The standardised agenda is very popular particularly when used with monthly contract administration meetings. It has all the short-comings which have been mentioned in that it does not aid the chairman to control or curtail discussion, practically any subject can be brought up under any item. The preparation and planning are usually inadequate due to a lack of knowledge of what will be discussed and who will be present. It is quite often part of the tactics to introduce

```
Sketch & Draw, F.R.I.B.A.,                    1st December, 1981
Chartered Architects,
1-10 Scale Street,
Blackburn.
```

AGENDA for SITE MEETING to be held on 10th December, 1981 at 2.00 p.m.

Contract - High Place Hospital.   Contract Number 4896.

1) Apologies for absence

2) Acceptance of minutes of previous meeting

3) Matters arising from the minutes

4) Main Contractors progress report

5) Sub-Contractors progress report

6) Nominated Suppliers progress report

7) Architect's report - quality and workmanship

8) Quantity Surveyors report - claims, variations and payments

9) Resources report - Labour

10)   "   "   Materials

11)   "   "   Plant

12)   "   "   Information

13) Daywork reports

14) Safety report

15) General communications problems

16) Construction Problems

17) Any other urgent business

18) Notice of special agenda items for next meeting

19) Date, time and venue of next meeting

```
Distribution:   Employer (client)            1
                Quantity Surveyor            1
                Structural Consultants       1
                Services Consultants         1
                Contractor                   3
                Electrical sub-contractor    1
                H & V sub-contractor         1
                Nominated supplier           1
                Internal : Job Architect     1
                           Clerk of Works    1
                           File              1
                           Spare             2        (15 copies)
```

Fig 4.2 Standardised agenda

items which require some decision on the part of some other party. This ploy is intended to catch the party off-guard in the hope of gaining an undeserved concession. The content of standardised agendas should be detailed so that only standard reports can be made, all other non-standard items should be notified one week earlier. A standardised agenda is shown in *Fig 4.2*. The contents should be detailed to match the actual contract so that each firm is named.

4.5 ARRANGING MEETINGS

Site managers will often be involved in organising meetings. Each meeting will have a degree of formality and to some degree a status. The status accorded to a meeting will depend on whether the organisers wish to impress those attending. A meeting with trade foreman to discuss the next week's production will be accorded lower status than the monthly site meeting. This does not indicate that the planning and preparation should be any less thorough, only that the arrangements may be less luxurious.

There are a number of preliminary questions which must be answered. Firstly how many are attending and what is the most appropriate seating plan. For the monthly site meeting the long table or hollow square is usually the best arrangement. Secondly, how much time will the meeting take and will this involve catering. As a minimum coffee and biscuits may be required. Thirdly any meeting may require visual aids or equipment and these need to be arranged. They may include the proper display of drawings, overhead projectors, tape recorder, blackboard and for larger meetings a microphone. Finally, the likelihood of a visit to the location of a work problem should be considered.

The next step is to consider the administration for the meeting. The staff to set up the meeting room must be briefed as to their duties. The catering must be arranged and the time for the break to occur agreed, along with the signal to call in the refreshments.

If the meeting requires a telephone then one should be arranged. On the other hand it may be preferable for all calls to be stopped so as not to disturb the meeting. If services such as typing or photocopying are required they should be available. Finally, ensure that electric sockets and other power facilities are available.

The meeting room should be checked as suitable for the status of the meeting. Its size and shape should be suitable for the numbers attending and the seating layout. It should also be adequate for the use of any equipment such as overhead projector or blackboard. The decoration should be bright and the lighting at a comfortable level. The room should have adequate heating and ventilation. Every attempt should be made to limit noise, particularly when meetings are taking place close to the production area of the site. Every possible source of distraction should be removed; seating should be comfortable and noiseless. Finally, toilet and washing facilities should be available.

Consider what material is required for the meeting. Initially the requirement may be ashtrays, glasses and waterjugs. Other items may be included such as paper and pencils. Spare copies of the agenda may also be necessary. The use of place cards giving the name and position of those attending are useful particularly at the initial site meeting. Other items which may be provided are drawings, blackboard, chalk and duster, felt pens for the overhead projector. Should the presentation equipment be essential, spare fuses or spare equipment should be available.

4.6 CHAIRING THE MEETING

The chairman of a meeting has a number of roles to play. Firstly, he is the representative of the organisation to which he belongs. Secondly, he is usually leader of the group and has to act to coordinate and motivate others to meet the objectives of the organisation or project. Thirdly, he is chairman and as such in charge of the conduct of the meeting.

In order to carry out the duties of chairman the person appointed should have, above all, authority. This should permit him to be positive in his actions. Allied to this is the need for him to be knowledgeable about the objective of the meeting, as well as the rules for running the meeting. The chairman must not conduct the meeting in a dictatorial manner so he must also be tolerant, tactful, a good listener with an understanding of people.

The chairman's responsibilities involve the preparation of the agenda, the arranging of the meeting, the conduct of the meeting and the recording of its business. The duty of preparing the agenda and minutes and arranging the meeting may be delegated to others.

The conduct of the meeting should be strictly in accordance with the agenda. The minutes of the last meeting should be agreed as a true record. Once that is achieved then matters arising from the minutes should be reported. Care should be taken that matters arising and other agenda items do not overlap. The next agenda item should be introduced by the chairman. This introduction should make the data clear or set the parameters on which he will allow discussion to proceed. The main contributor should then be asked to speak on the agenda item. The chairman should ensure that he keeps within the parameters set and curtails any tendency to make a lengthy speech.

The chairman should then invite other comments giving everyone an opportunity to speak. The discussion should be summarised, by the chairman, giving the main points. The minute should then be put to the meeting for approval and it should contain specific reference about who is to take action and if necessary by what date. All discussion should be directed through the chair. Other **do's** and **don't's** are given in *Fig 4.3*.

The final items should be any other urgent business and any notifications for the next meeting. Only urgent business should be allowed under any further business.

4.7 MINUTES OF MEETINGS

The minutes of a meeting are the follow up and as such are vital to the effectiveness of the meeting. The minutes must ensure that the collective views of the meeting are given coherent expression in writing so that they are meaningful and clear as to where responsibility for further action lies.

A competent minute taker should be appointed by the meeting. The secretary should have the ability to ensure that the minutes are an accurate record of the meeting; and should also appreciate the objective and purpose of the meeting. The minutes may be required to convey a decision, record views, present information or initiate action. They have more than one function.

The minutes should commence with the title of the meeting, giving the time date and place of the meeting. There should follow a list of those present and the organisation they represent. A second list may give the apologies which have been received from those who are absent. The number of minutes should be sequential.

DO'S
1. Prepare an adequate agenda
2. Establish rules of procedure
3. Open the meeting promptly
4. Introduce each item crisply giving parameters
5. Be tactful and ensure all views are expressed
6. Curtail lengthy speeches by interrupting during pauses and summarising the speakers main points
7. Encourage creativity and free speculation
8. Always be a careful and judicious listener
9. Use every member of the meeting
10. Keep interest and activity high by your example
11. In conflict emphasise 'common ground' and points of agreement
12. Limit discussion to the relevant subject
13. Guide members back to the agenda if the meeting becomes disjointed
14. Handle incorrect views delicately
15. Close the discussion after adequate exploration
16. Always repeat the minute or resolution before adoption

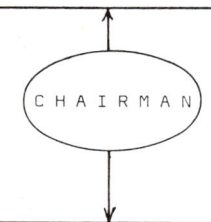

DON'T'S
1. Embarass other members of the meeting
2. Lose your temper or be sarcastic
3. Take sides in any discussion
4. Attempt to impose your own view
5. Allow discussion to ramble
6. Exercise power to inhibit alternatives or new ideas
7. Compete with other members
8. Permit any member to be placed on the defensive
9. Try to manipulate the meeting
10. Solve the problem for the members
11. Allow discussion across the meeting

Fig 4.3 Do's and Don'ts for the chairman

They may be numbered giving the year first and then the minute number, e.g. 81/1, 81/2. At the start of the new year the numbering is changed starting again at one. On a contract it may be preferable to prefix the minute with letters or job number indicating the building followed by sequential numbers which will continue to the end of the contract, as shown in *Fig 4.4*.

The minutes should be as brief as completeness and accuracy will allow. It should include the major points of discussion, particularly those which are opposed. At the end of the discussion some resolution or decision as regards to

Minutes of the HIGH PLACE HOSPITAL site meeting held at the Site Office on the 10th December, 1981 at 2.00 p.m.

Present: Apologies :

J. A. Sketch	Architect	A. Deflection	Structure Con.
I. M. Tape	Quantity Surveyor	A. Spark	Services Con.
T. Joint	H.V. Contractor		
I. Build	Contracts Manager		
A. Product	Site Manager		
A. Merchant	H. & V. Supplies		
I.A. Look	Clerk of Works		
A. Livewire	Elec.Sub/cont.		

Minute No.		Action By
HPH/28	**Minutes** The minutes of the last meeting were accepted as a true record.	
HPH/29	**Matters Arising** Nil	
HPH/30	**Main Contractors Report** The progress report was accepted with the exception of excavation of the south wing. The contractor undertook to apply extra resources during the next month.	Site Manager
HPH/31	**H.V. Sub Contractors Report** Mr. T.Joint explained that progress was delayed due to difficulties with the manufacture of specials. H. & V. Supplies explained the delay was due to lack of information from the Architect. The Architect undertook to produce drawing details by 18th December. H. & V. Supplies would manufacture and deliver to H.V. Contractors by the 5th Jan., 1982.	Architect H.V. Supplies H.V. Contractors
HPH/42	**Any Other Business** Nil	
HPH/43	**Notices for Agenda** Nil	
HPH/44	Next Meeting will be held on 12th January at 2 p.m. in the site office	Chairman Secretary

Fig 4.4 Typical minutes of a meeting

action should be recorded. The final draft of the minute should be read to the meeting before proceeding to the next item. If the discussion is difficult to follow clarification should be sought by the secretary in order that the minute is accurate.

At the end of agenda items the chairman will call for any other urgent business. These should be recorded under separate item headings, being given a separate minute number. The next item should be any notices of agenda items for the next meeting. These will only be required when meetings are held on a regular basis. Finally the meeting should agree the date and time of the next meeting.

The minutes should be prepared and typed (as shown in shortened form in *Fig 4.4*) and distributed to all those entitled to attend within a few days; a copy should be retained by the secretary and is the official record of the meetings. At the succeeding meeting these minutes should be signed by the chairman after they have been accepted as a true record. Any amendments to the previous minutes agreed by the meeting should be made and signed by the chairman. The amendments should also be recorded under the agenda item. The minutes need to be filed and retained as evidence of the conduct of those attending and, in the case of site meetings, the parties to the contract.

4.8 QUESTIONS ON MEETINGS

MULTI-CHOICE QUESTIONS:

1 The chairman should, above all, be:
 (a) authoritative;
 (b) impartial;
 (c) easy going;
 (d) humourous.

2 Meetings are held to:
 (a) achieve harmony between parties;
 (b) improve social relationships;
 (c) achieve an objective;
 (d) inconvenience those attending.

3 The principle reason for site meetings minutes is:
 (a) to record what people say;
 (b) to ensure effective follow up action;
 (c) to form a basis for future claims;
 (d) to satisfy contract requirements.

4 When arranging a meeting the organiser should consider:
 (a) the objective and purpose;
 (b) the number attending and the status;
 (c) the catering arrangements and appetites;
 (d) whether alcohol should be available.

5 The maximum number of persons invited to attend a consultation meeting should be:
 (a) unlimited;
 (b) ten or less with a point of view;
 (c) over ten but less than twenty;
 (d) two or three already in agreement.

SHORT-ANSWER QUESTIONS (15-20 minutes)

1. Describe the different types of site meeting which may take place during a building project.
2. Prepare an agenda for a site meeting of the building team for a contract valued at £1 M which has two nominated contractors and a nominated supplier among the representatives attending.
3. Meetings with employees are held to achieve a number of objectives. Describe the different subjects for which meetings may be held and suggest what might be the purpose of each meeting.
4. Prepare a list of DO's and DON'T's for a meeting chairman.
5. Discuss the production of minutes for a monthly site meeting of the building team, giving examples to illustrate your answer.

QUESTIONS REQUIRING LONGER ANSWERS (30-45 minutes)

1. Discuss the essential differences in approach, by the chairman, to meetings having the purpose of informing, persuading, consulting and deciding.
2. Describe the steps you would take in planning and arranging an initial site meeting for a £1.5 M contract on an inner-city site.
3. Discuss those qualities a chairman should possess to ensure the effectiveness of meetings. Suggest how those qualities relate to the conduct of monthly site meetings of the building team.
4. Fully describe a set of rules and procedures to be followed for the site meetings of the building team. The rules should cover all aspects from planning the meeting to distributing the minutes.
5. As site manager given the responsibility of arranging site meetings. Explain what preparations you would make and describe how you would prepare yourself for the meeting. List the type of documents you would take into the meeting.

5 Site resources

5.1 INFORMATION NEEDS

In Chapter 1 it was stated that a manager is a user of information who has no other resource to employ in the execution of his duties. It is therefore necessary that adequate information reaches the site manager regarding production activities.

The first requirement for information to be regarded as adequate is its timing. The transmitter must appreciate the need to deliver information in sufficient time for the receiver to absorb, analyse and act on the message received. *Fig 5.1* shows the stages of resource information and indicates how essential it is that the primary information is delivered at the earliest moment of the contract. This will enable key operations to be considered. The primary information is usually supplemented by more details of a secondary nature; which is not always available at the pretender stage. The later this secondary information is transmitted the greater the pressure on the production team.

The next requirement for adequate information, is quality. Design information must be easily understood by the production section of the building team. Poorly produced and uncoordinated working drawings create problems which delay activity on site and generally raise the cost of buildings. Similarly, inaccurate Bills of Quantities and unsatisfactory specifications all lead to further production problems. The receiver of design information also has a responsibility to provide feedback by asking questions and clarifying points as soon as the need arises.

The information received must also be relevant. If a shortage of information is apparent at the pre-tender stage of a contract then the consequences will be in direct relationship with its relevance to the process being carried out. At the pre-tender stage, irrelevant detail is of little use if the primary information on key operations is missing.

This problem may be aggravated by what the designer and the builder consider relevant. An example would be the nomination of sub-contractors, the architect may not perceive the implication of these nominations as a reason for delay. A contractor, however, will be unable to interpret risk, supervision and indirect cost arising out of a working relationship which is considered less than perfect.

The information will be most effective if it suits company operating procedures. The system of analysing design information received by the company must be fully understood by the site manager. When information is received on site a knowledge of how it was produced enables the site manager quickly to interpret and understand the implications more effectively. The knowledge that work has been measured off drawings, materials quantities calculated, and a percentage added for wastage will assist with all aspects of site control. A site manager, therefore, should be as familiar with the procedures used in estimating and planning as he is with production.

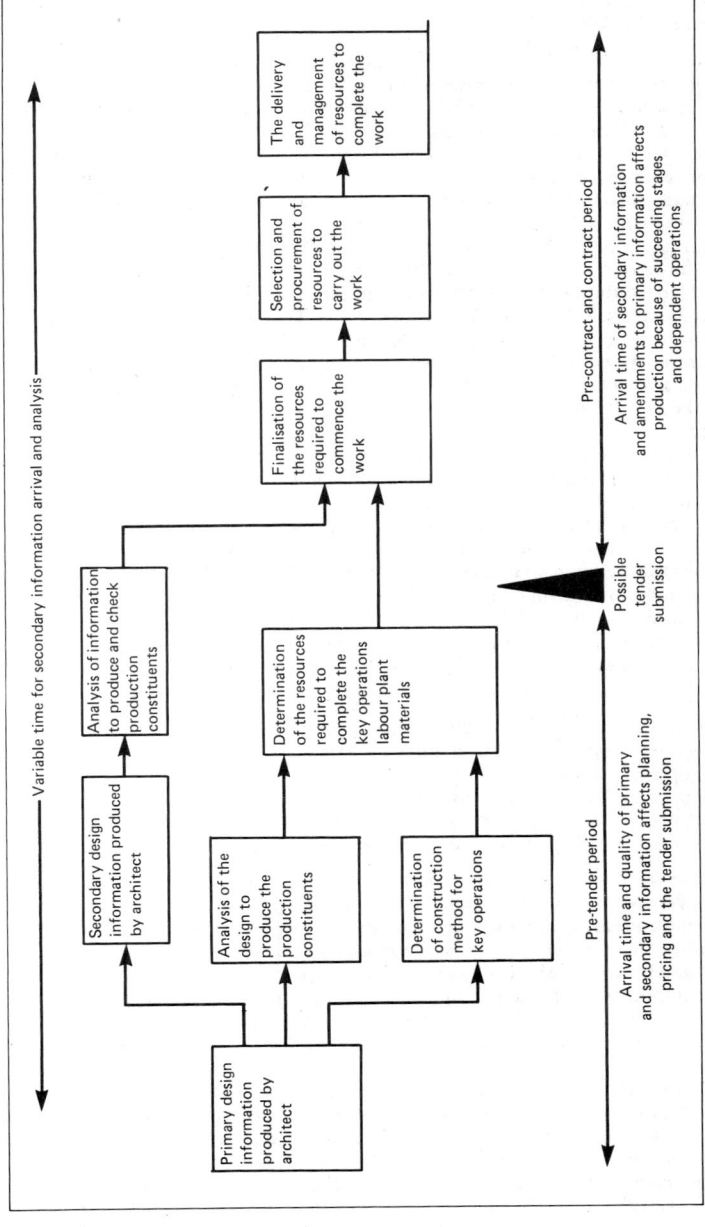

Fig 5.1 Possible delays due to arrival time of resource information

5.2 MATERIAL CONTROL

The basis of all materials control is the material schedule which is shown in *Fig 3.6* (see page 33). The schedule itemises all the materials necessary to complete a project. It will not always take the form shown but may be a combination of forms which contain, bulk items requiring call off, small items which require a single delivery, door or window schedules and schedules of precast concrete components. However, each schedule will contain the essential information for control.

The materials schedule is compiled from the information provided in the form of Bills of Quantities, specifications and drawings. The best method of calculating the quantities is by 'taking-off' the amounts from the drawings and checking them against the amounts contained in the Bill of Quantities. Major discrepancies will signify the need for a check or enquiry to the client's Q.S. The quantities should be calculated exactly. Allowances for wastage should be the absolute minimum. The amount ordered can be the exact quantity with an option for a further 5% or whatever may be considered the appropriate amount. Orders will only be placed on the option amount in the case of unforeseen problems. The actual ordering will require the specification to be re-quoted and reference made to the relevant British Standard.

Fig 3.9 (see page 36) explains the full receipt and checking procedure for materials. The control of materials on site is often the result of comparison between the cost of strict control against the cost of losses due to very little control being exercised. The losses are dependent on factors such as, the cost of items, the ease with which they can be handled and the attractiveness of the item. Materials should be classified into five categories as shown in *Fig 5.2*. A materials category number can be devised which may be, for example, B/3/iii for facing bricks.

Materials control has to be considered in conjunction with the type of storage required. This may enable stricter control to be exercised than the categories in *Fig 5.2* indicate, but it should never be used as the reason for reduced control. The type of storage required could be classed as follows:

Within a building insulated against freezing temperatures.
Within a building protected from moisture.
In the open air but protected from full sun.
In the open air but protected from moisture.
In the open air requiring a special and level surface.
In the open air with no special requirements.

Some materials may require one or more of the types of storage. Protection also has to be provided against sun, wind, traffic, fire, chemicals, dirt and mud, vermin damage and collapse of stacks.

The other factor which may affect materials control is its handling — either mechanical or manual. Manual handling does not affect control to any great extent, but mechanical handling requires provision for access, pre-packing and load sizing to make it effective. The materials handling plant available to the site manager are shown in *Fig 5.3*. The method of control to be used must take into account all these factors.

The first step in materials control is the preparation of materials checklists for the delivery inspection of key materials. These may be bricks, blocks, joinery components and precast concrete units. There may also be checklists for concrete materials and ready-mixed concrete. Such checklists are only a beginning — the next requirement will be to produce the materials information booklet shown in *Fig 5.4*. This will contain the description of materials and will refer to the category

CLASSIFICATION OF MATERIALS				
TYPE OF MATERIAL		SECURITY CLASSIFICATION		DEGREE OF CONTROL
A	SMALL ATTRACTIVE ITEMS EASILY REMOVED WITH A READY MARKET FOR RESALE OR USE.	1	TO BE PLACED UNDER LOCK AND KEY IN A BUILDING OR SECURE COMPOUND	i	METICULOUS ACCOUNTING AND STOCK CONTROL AT ALL TIMES.
B	LARGE EXPENSIVE ITEMS THAT REQUIRE A VEHICLE TO ASSIST REMOVAL	2	TO BE KEPT OUT OF SIGHT OF THE GENERAL PUBLIC WITH SOME THEFT PREVENTION MEASURES TAKEN	ii	STRICT ACCOUNTING AND CONTROL WITH DAILY CHECKS ON ESTIMATED QUANTITIES
C	LARGE ITEMS, WHICH ARE NOT ATTRACTIVE, WHICH DIFFICULT AND EXPENSIVE TO REPLACE OR REPAIR	3	MAY BE PLACED WITHIN SIGHT OF THE PUBLIC BUT SOME THEFT PREVENTION MEASURES TAKEN	iii	LESS STRINGENT ACCOUNTING WITH REGULAR VISUAL CHECKS ON STOCKS AND USAGE.
D	LESS EXPENSIVE ITEMS BUT ATTRACTIVE TO A LIMITED NUMBER OF PERSONS	4	KEPT WITHIN SIGHT OF MANAGEMENT OR SECURITY PATROL BUT NO OTHER THEFT PREVENTION MEASURES	iv	INFORMAL ACCOUNTING AND CONTROL WITH WEEKLY VISUAL CHECKS ON STOCKS AND USAGE.
E	BULK ITEMS WHICH ARE NOT EXPENSIVE AND ARE DIFFICULT TO HANDLE AND REMOVE	5	NO PARTICULAR SECURITY MEASURES TO BE TAKEN	v	NO PARTICULAR ACCOUNTING OTHER THAN AT RECEIPT, CHECKS MADE USING THE EXCEPTION RULE
CATEGORISE MATERIALS BY THE RELEVANT CLASS IN EACH COLUMN i.e. FACING BRICKS B/3/iii ENTER IN M.I.B.				

Fig 5.2 Categories of materials

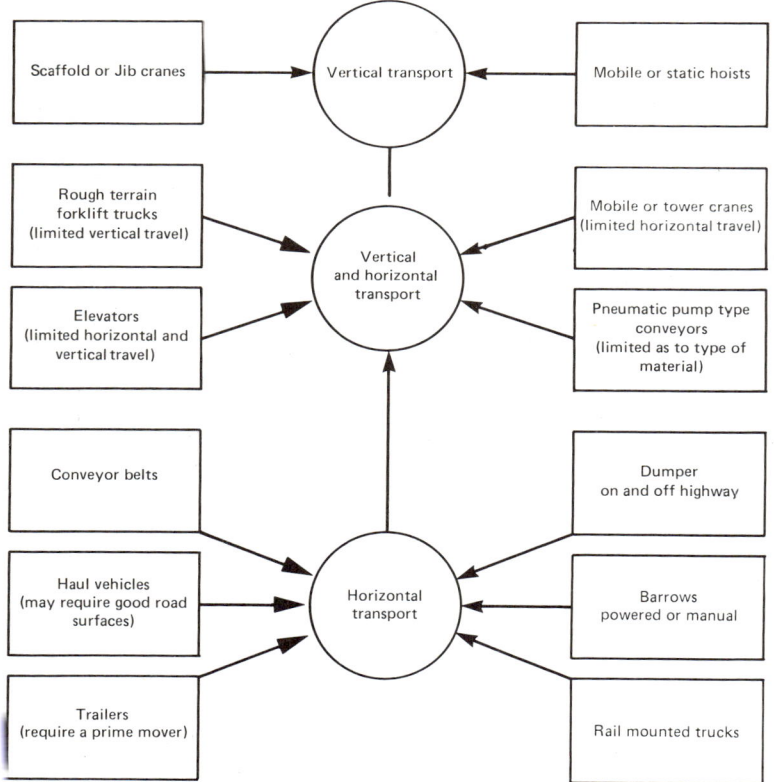

Fig 5.3 Materials handling plant available to the contractor

of each item. In the same way it will make reference to the delivery inspection checklist and the relevant British Standards. Methods of storage and other useful information should be included.

The next stage is effected by a monthly material statement an example of which is shown in *Fig 5.5*. All the columns in the figure are given a designatory letter and the source of information is from previously described documents with the exception of the monthly measure and estimate. It is essential that the wastage allowance is included as without it no control is possible. The monthly valuation measure is carried out in order to ascertain the work completed and materials on site. These materials-on-site quantities should be used for control, this emphasises the need for accuracy during that evaluation measure.

A final materials reconciliation will be carried out at the end of the project when the total materials purchased, less those returned or resold, will be compared with the actual quantities incorporated into the work. The difference will be used to evaluate the accuracy of the estimating and planning.

MIB No	MATERIAL DESCRIPTION	RELEVANT B.S. AND REFERENCES	DESIRABLE PACKAGING	LIKELY DAMAGE	EFFECTS OF WEATHER	METHODS OF STORAGE	TYPE OF PROTECTION	MATERIAL CATEGORY	REMARKS
10	Bricks Facings	B.S. 3679 3921(bb34) 4729 187 Pt 2 CP 121 Pt 1 See checklist No 40 for delivery inspection.	on small pallet 1200 × 650mm or alternatively on any pallet suitable for an R.T. forklift	corner breakages chipping on face mud splashes	frost damage saturation by rain — excessively dry	in stacks on real level ground new 1.8m high. Keep clear of ground and away from muddy areas	covered top and sides with waterproof sheeting-well secured. The completed work should be protected by waterproof for 12 hrs to at least 1m below the top course.	B/3/iii (SEE Fig.52)	Degree of security should be increased on partially completed and occupied sites

Fig 5.4 Materials information booklet

MAT'LS SCHED N°	DESCRIPTION OF MATERIAL	UNIT OF MEASURE	QUANTITY OF MATERIAL ORDERED	QUANTITY OF MATERIAL DELIVERED TO DATE	BALANCE OF MATERIAL ON ORDER-TO BE DELIVERED	QUANTITY OF MATERIAL INCORPORATED IN THE WORK	ESTIMATED QUANTITY IN STOCK ON SITE	ACTUAL STOCK ON SITE	SHORTFALL OF MATERIAL	SHORTFALL EXPRESSED AS A PERCENTAGE	ALLOWANCE FOR WASTAGE AS A PERCENTAGE
FROM M.S. SCHEDULE	FROM MATERIAL SCHEDULE	FROM MAT'S SCHEDULE	FROM MATERIAL SCHEDULE	FROM DELIVERY NOTES	$d - e$	FROM MONTHLY MEASURE	$e - g$	FROM MONTHLY MEASURE	$h - i$	$\frac{100 \times j}{e}$	FROM ESTIMATE
a	b	c	d	e	f	g	h	i	j	k	l
2.2	Bricks Facing	N°	104,000	30,000	74,000	24,310	5690	2,150	3540	11.8	7.5

Fig 5.5 Monthly material statement

5.3 MATERIALS WASTE

Wastage is that portion of the material which is unavoidable and arises during the use of the material. This is the percentage usually allowed for by the estimator. This is not what should be controlled for it is a concommittant of the type of material being used. The need for control is on waste which is avoidable.

Waste is the squandering, the misuse, the damage and avoidable losses which occur on site. However, waste is not just the responsibility of the site manager. The circumstances for waste arise in the first instance from wastage allowances; these may be 10% of the exact quantity calculated, but if in fact only 5% wastage occurs then the other 5% is still likely to become waste. The responsibilities for reducing waste are shown in *Fig 5.6.*

General management can cause waste to occur by:

Incorrect wastage allowances.
Overordering of material.
Omissions from the material schedule.
Failure to provide an effective control organisation.
Inadequate training of staff.
Poor materials handling system.
Unsatisfactory selection of suppliers.

The management of a construction firm must devise a policy which will enable its site management to act to limit the waste.

Site management may have the heaviest responsibility to reduce waste and the causes which may be dealt with by the production staff are:

Excessive material at the workplace.
Incorrectly stored materials.
Inadequate delivery inspections.
Insufficient security on site.
Poor material protection.
Inadequate handling methods.
Allowing poor workmanship.
Non-protection of completed work.
Untidy sites and poor access.
Allowing the substitution of materials.

Site managers should be prepared to take corrective action particularly on those aspects which require more effective supervision.

Waste can be classified as (a) indirect waste, and (b) direct waste.

Indirect waste is that which does not cause a direct monetary loss, i.e. when materials are used for a different purpose than that for which they were purchased. The most common example of this is when expensive bricks are used to make up parts of internal blockwork partitions. Similarly waste occurs either when excavation is a little too deep, requiring extra hardcore or the compaction of hardcore reduces levels to below that intended requiring a little more concrete than expected. It must be decided whether the extra work involved in correcting these causes of indirect waste will be a cheap as the use of substituted materials. It may be more effective and cheaper to use substitute materials in one instance but the elimination of such practices should be cheaper in the long term.

Direct waste is that which may be attributed to losses caused by dropping materials, criminal losses and quality. The dropping of materials may occur during

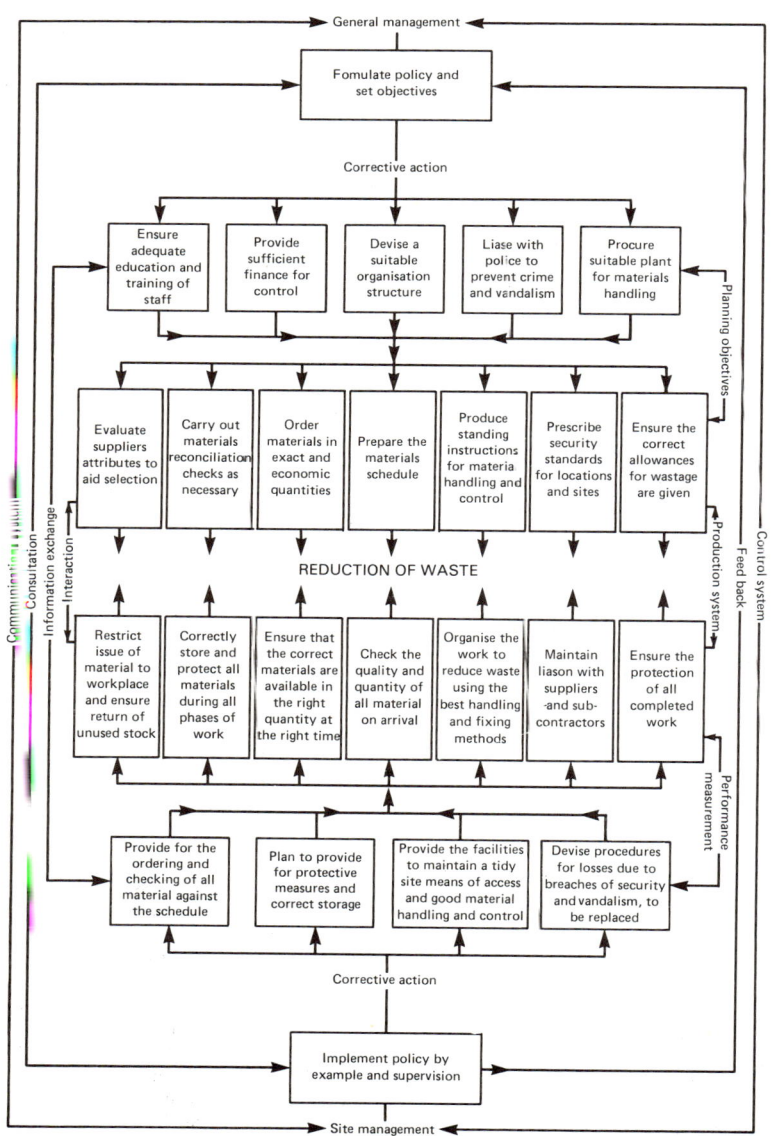

Fig E.6 Responsibilities for materials purchase, handling and control

delivery, transport around site, unloading, and fixing. Criminal losses will involve theft from site, pilfering by employees and damage such as vandalism or industrial sabotage. The waste arising under 'quality' can be from increased cutting wastage due to the need to eliminate poor quality portions. If the quality fails to meet the specification re-ordering may be necessary. Alternatively if the quality of material is too high then the increased costs may be labelled waste to be borne by the contractor.

Site cleanliness is of the utmost importance for efficient production. All waste should be placed in receptacles provided for rubbish. Any unused materials must be returned to storage areas when work is complete. There are two approaches to this problem. The first approach is to accept the difficulty of ensuring the production workers keep the site clean and tidy and to provide someone else to carry out the task. This could be one of the older operatives who would re-stack unused materials and collect rubbish. The second approach is to provide the incentive for the production operatives to carry out the work. This latter method is the best because of the need of maintaining a safe method of work and good clear access. In order to achieve the objective these requirements should be included in contracts of employment, safety policy statement and task descriptions on which bonus payments are made. A dirty and untidy work area would then lead to warnings under the contract of employment and reduction of bonus pay under the incentive scheme.

5.4 PLANT TASK DEFINITION

Before any plant can be selected and procured it is necessary to define the tasks they are to perform. This is never simple because the methods to be used are not always apparent from the information provided by the designer. It is, therefore, necessary to quantify the work to be done and this will be explained in three areas, excavation, cranage and ancillary equipment.

The definition of excavating tasks are concerned with the quantity, type of material and the situation of work. In order to obtain the quantity to be moved, the amount to be excavated, including working space and temporary works, should be calculated. To this must be added the bulking factor for the type of soil. Changes in soil types at different depths should also be noted. The exact characteristics of a soil are needed because the break out power of the excavator must be matched to the difficulty of digging. Similarly in rocky ground, alternative working methods will need to be considered. The depth of excavation should also be noted. Disposal of soil is important because the transport method will influence plant selection in respect of type of machine and dump height. The location of the work and the working space available should be considered together with any restriction on movement and the closeness of adjacent buildings.

It should be possible to obtain a task definition similar to the following:

Task:	Trench excavation
Sizes:	Width 450 mm; depth 1.5 m; length 850 m
Quantity:	Bank m^3 574. Loose m^3 746
Type of Soil:	Heavy clay
Disposal:	Part return fill; cart away 350 m^3 to tip 4 km
Restriction:	35 linear metres of trench within 1 m of building

Sketches or plans may help with more complex task definitions.

The task definition for cranes will involve deciding loads and lifting equipment. The loads themselves may be the calculation of the weight of precast concrete members, formwork, reinforcement bundles, scaffold or other material loads. For example a load of wet concrete in a skip may be calculated as follows:

Weight of 1 m^3 of concrete	2400 kg
Weight of skip	510 kg
Weight of sling and attachments	90 kg
Total	3000 kg

A further requirement is to establish the location of the pick up and deposit. In such cases it is the maximum distance horizontally and the maximum height should be recorded. These locations will eventually enable the 'outreach' and 'height under hook' of the crane to be determined. Finally, the estimated number of loads should be calculated. Similar calculations can be carried out for all loads.

The task identification for ancillary equipment may not require many calculations unless there are large operations which may not be covered by the major items of plant. The ancillary equipment will be involved in the following tasks.

Concrete mixing;
Mortar mixing;
Movement of small material lots horizontally;
Haulage of excavated material;
Compaction of surfaces;
Compaction of concrete;
Cutting and bending of reinforcement.

The list could be extended depending on the type of work involved, but the main requirement is to quantify the task content. Quite often this work will be related to the major tasks already calculated. Haulage distances, number of loads and areas to be consolidated and the number of passes of the compacting equipment should be determined.

5.5 PLANT SELECTION AND PROCUREMENT

The choice of plant is first of all limited to a number of machines capable of performing the task as defined. It may be necessary to combine tasks to ensure economic utilisation. The next stage is to actually select the particular machine from those suitable. Thirdly the source of procurement must be decided.

Before proceeding to the actual choice of plant, one other factor has to be taken into account — i.e. time. The task definition indicates types required; the planned time will indicate size and number of machines. Therefore, a decision has to be made as to the production capacity of a particular machine, the effects of inclement weather and other factors which will be detailed in section 5.6. In the case of trench excavation the task has indicated a back acter with a bucket width of 450 mm but should it be a 0.3 m^3 or 0.5 m^3 or even a 0.6 m^3 capacity? Should there be a need to complete quickly, will two machines of 0.3 m^3 capacity be better than one of 0.6 m^3? The facts can only be determined by considerations during the planning stages which is dealt with in chapter 8.

The choice of plant will be indicated by the task definition and time factor. These will provide a set of performance criteria which it is essential to meet. If, as is usual, all trench excavation has been amalgamated to provide the criteria for a single piece of plant the extreme performances for each task should be used. The biggest capacity, the greatest dump height, the deepest dig, the largest reach and the hardest ground. Care should be taken to ensure that minor sections of extreme work do not cost more overall than the short hire of a specialist machine. This analysis should provide a list of three or four machines suitable for the task which will be described by the manufacturer's trade name. All are suitable and selection can now follow.

The essential features of the chosen machines satisfy the task requirements. It is now necessary to consider which is most desirable. Therefore, it is the desirable factors and not the essential points which have to be weighed and considered. This does not mean that they are unimportant; it implies that they are not essential features required to complete the task. The major points to be considered under this section are:

Cost;
Ease of operation;
Reliability;
Adaptability;
Durability;
Availability of spare parts;
Standardisation with other equipment;
Fuel economy.

Other factors will be considered depending on the type of plant and the location of the task. The method of selection is valid for cranage, earthmoving or ancillary plant.

The selection of plant is followed by a requisition and procurement procedure. This stage cannot be separated completely from the selection process. The main consideration will be economic, in some cases this will be an overriding factor. If the ideal machine could be hired, but a less than efficient alternative is available in the plant yard of your organisation then it will often prove economical to use the machine owned by the firm. Such choices must be carefully costed including the loss of earnings due to not using the owned machine.

There are usually two main choices to be made in procurement, one is to secure the plant by purchase so that ownership passes to the firm, the second is to obtain the temporary use of the machine. The first alternative can be a purchase by cash, loans, hire purchase or lease with the option to buy. The second system involves the hiring of plant. Each method requires a complicated set of calculations which will depend on the circumstances of the firm, its cash holdings, tax position, possible government allowances and other factors. The most fundamental point is the utilisation which can be obtained and for what period of time. For short periods of high utilisation hiring may be the most economical but for long periods of normal utilisation it may be better to purchase by one of the methods outlined above.

The aspects of procurement and selection apply to any type of plant or equipment. The stages which must be followed are similar whether purchasing for one contract or for general use of a small builder. The main difference is that the task definition for general use has to be a forecast of the type of work that can be expected. The method will also be equally valuable in choosing and buying a tower crane as it would for an electric power drill. The economic return on such plant will depend on its operation.

5.6 PLANT OPERATION

In all aspects of plant operation there is a correct and economical method of performing the task. If the maximum profit is to be obtained from mechanisation then trained operators and management are essential. Such training must not be confined to specialists. Every person required to operate or supervise any machine should receive the necessary training to achieve maximum performance. The factors affecting the performance of plant are those which affect efficiency and those that affect time.

The factors which affect efficiency may be divided into the responsibilities of the plant department, site management and operator. Some are unavoidable like the nature of the ground. The factors for which the plant department are responsible are those of servicing and maintenance. Engines which are not properly tuned, loose parts, dirty filters, damaged components are all points which may reduce the productive capacity of the machine. Failure to regularly grease, fuel, top up with water, charge batteries, and other daily servicing will in the end increase the incidence of breakdown but will also reduce the machine's efficiency.

Site management are responsible for the organisation of the work-flow. Where the machine is dependent on the support of other machines or labour gangs then the organisation can decrease production dramatically. The utilisation of plant will be much reduced by this inefficiency, although this may be difficult to determine. The plant may appear to be continuously working but its output is small.

The operator of the machine has the main responsibility, as his efficiency will have the greatest effect on the capacity of the machine. Assuming that the machine has a maximum output of 40 m^3 per hour, the reduction may look like this:

Unavoidable ground conditions	5%
Maintenance and Servicing	10%
Management inefficiency	10%
Operator inefficiency	25%
Total	**50%**

Therefore output is reduced from 40 m^3 to 20 m^3 per hour. The second aspect of plant operation is time.

Plant cannot be used for the full eight hours of every day unless perfect conditions are always available. Therefore, the time that a piece of equipment works will depend on the three main participants, plus the unavoidable — e.g. bad weather. The latter will cause different machines to be inactive for different reasons. Tracked vehicles may cope with wet ground whereas tyred vehicles may be unable to work. Rain is usually considered the main cause of stoppages but tower cranes become inoperative in high winds and concrete machinery is often idle due to the difficulties of laying the material in low temperatures. The severity of the weather will vary between location and time of year. Winter in Scotland may lead to a 30% reduction whilst in Cornwall work interruptions for this reason may be minimal. On the other hand high winds are nearly always present at some time during the year in the coastal regions.

One aspect affecting time, related to the plant department, is breakdown of machinery. This is the result of the maintenance and servicing aspect but cannot be fully avoided. The time from breakdown to completion of repair depends on the efficiency of the plant department, its spares holding and the effectiveness and training of the mechanics. Site management is responsible for the allocation and planning of work. Any failure to allocate work or to set out the work leads to the plant being idle, therefore time is lost.

The final factor affecting time is the operator. The operator may be unwilling to work for the full period of time and therefore reduces the actual working time of the machine. This aspect may also be considered the responsibility of site supervision. The reduction to be applied to the 8 hours may be as follows:

Inclement weather	10%
Breakdown	8%
Management inefficiency	3%
Operator inefficiency	4%
Total	**25%**

Therefore the 8 hour day becomes 6 hours being reduced by 25%. Output for the machine at 20 m^3 per hour becomes 120 m^3 per day. Consider this with the original 40 m^3 per hour for 8 hours per day and the significance of training for all staff should be fully appreciated.

5.7 PLANT CONTROL

Control implies that the performance of plant can be monitored. If this is so then a plant system must take account of all those factors which affect performance. These factors have already been detailed in the previous section and a system will be described which should isolate costs and performance criteria. However, it must be stressed that records are only as good as the information put into them and that all systems are capable of distortion.

Almost all items of plant, no matter what the source, is subject to a rate for its hire. When a plant department supplies its own firm, it does so on the basis that the contract account will be charged a weekly or hourly rate. This will include servicing maintenance, repair and may include the operator and fuel. However, transport, erection, and in some cases other factors, will be charged direct. Whether or not the costs are itemised to a contract or site they should be recorded to enable an evaluation of the machine to be conducted when replacement is due. The method which will be explained is as simplified as possible and is capable of expansion as required.

The first basis for control is the recording of the delivery and installation of plant on site. Next any maintenance and servicing should be recorded and finally any repairs and overhauls. As all these operations require the same three resources as all other operations they can be recorded on the same type of sheet. This plant service sheet is shown in *Fig 5.7*.

So that all parts of the form are easily filled, standard descriptions and codes should be known to those who should complete the form. The costing would be carried out at the finance department. The number of copies required would be three or four depending on the system. One copy would be retained on site, one by the plant manager for the machine records, one by the finance department to

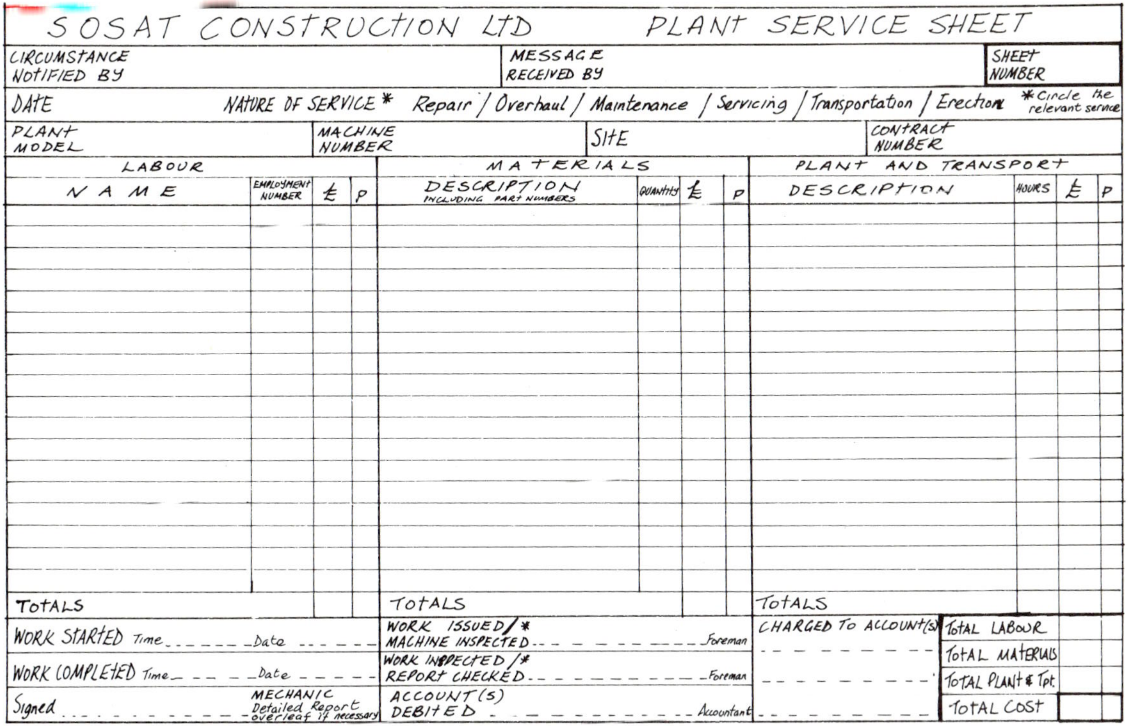

Fig 5.7 Plant service sheet

SOSAT CONSTRUCTION LTD					PLANT EMPLOYMENT SHEET					SHEET NUMBER
PLANT MODEL					MACHINE NUMBER					
OPERATORS NAME(S)					EMPLOYMENT NUMBER					
LOCATION OR SITE					CONTRACT NUMBER					
WEEK ENDING					WEEK NUMBER					
TASK DESCRIPTION						NON-EFFECTIVE TIME see code list below		TOTAL HOURS WORKED	TOTAL BONUS HOURS	TOTAL ENHANCED HOURS INCLUDING OVERTIME
COST CODE						HRS	CODE			
SUNDAY										
MONDAY										
TUESDAY										
WEDNESDAY										
THURSDAY										
FRIDAY										
SATURDAY										
TOTAL HRS WORKED										
TOTAL BONUS HOURS										
QUANTITY OF WORK										
TOTAL COST TO CODE										

SIGNED OPERATOR

SIGNED SITE MANAGER

- IM IDLE NO TASK
- IO IDLE NO OPERATOR
- IW IDLE DUE TO WEATHER
- BD BREAKDOWN
- SE BEING SERVICED
- UR UNDER REPAIR
- PY IN PLANT YARD
- TP BEING TRANSPORTED
- OT NON-PRODUCTIVE OVERTIME

Fig 5.8 Plant employment sheet (obverse)

ISSUES OF FUEL ETC													SHEET NUMBER.	
WEEK ENDING MACHINE NUMBER.	TYPE OF FUEL. Etc												ISSUED BY (INITIALS)	RECEIVED BY (INITIALS)
DAY AND DATE														
TOTALS													CONSUMPTION PER HOUR	
UNITS													TOTAL COST	
COST														

SERVICE SHEET REFERENCES								
SHEET NUMBER	COST £	P	SHEET NUMBER	COST £	P	SHEET NUMBER	COST £	P
						TOTAL SERVICE COST		
TOTAL LABOUR COST (TO INCLUDE BANKSMAN)						HOURS		
TOTAL PLANT HIRE COST (WEEKLY COST OF HIRE)						HOURS		
TOTAL INEFFECTIVE COST (SPLIT IF NECESSARY TO EACH CODE)						HOURS		
TOTAL CHARGE COSTS (TOTAL COST FOR PLANT FOR 1 WEEK)						HOURS		
COST RATIOS								
APPROVED AND CHECKED BY SITE MANAGER								
CHECKED BY PLANT MANAGER								
ENTERED IN ACCOUNTS BY FINANCE DEPT.								
CHECKED AND NOTED BY ESTIMATOR								

Fig 5.9 Plant employment sheet (reverse)

support the account and one to the estimating department to provide feedback. The site copy is not absolutely essential but the necessity for this will depend on the organisation. Details of any problems or other significant factors can be added on the reverse of the form which is lined to assist writing.

The second proforma which should be used is shown in *Figs 5.8* and *5.9*, the obverse and reverse sides respectively. The form is intended to be used to record the actual employment of the plant. It is also intended to assist in weekly planning. The obverse would be filled out with the details and the week's tasks would be entered in the space provided with cost codes to ensure correct accounting. This task would be fulfilled by the site manager or the person carrying out the weekly planning. The time spent on each task is entered against the day concerned. When the plant is not employed on production there may be a number of reasons, the codes are provided at the bottom on the form. It is essential that accurate records are provided to ensure that the feedback to the estimating department will assist the increased accuracy of pricing that should evolve from the system.

The reconciliation of resource utilisation can take place only when a task is completed although it may be possible to conduct an estimate on a weekly basis if the task is of long duration. The utilisation of plant can only be measured against historic records or the planned targets. It is therefore necessary at the planning and estimating stage to break down the plant time into productive time and non-effective time. The non-effective time should be further broken down so as to indicate areas where planned targets are not achieved. Items like inclement weather are not subject to remedial measures by management. Control is exercised in order to indicate causes of inefficiency and to enable management to assist by providing resources to correct them. Control measures should not be used to chastise staff for failure to meet targets but as a barometer to reflect the need for increased resource application.

5.8 LABOUR

The control of labour presents less of a problem than other resources. A number of controls have been present for many years. Historically labour controls and costs have been recorded from the earliest times, the changes that have been made are with regard to techniques. Incentive schemes and programming techniques are the basis of most labour control today.

Basic incentive schemes will be dealt with in Chapter 7 and programming in Chapter 8. The control of labour by using a weekly labour employment sheet similar to that for plant will be advocated. The sheet shown in *Fig 5.10* enables the next week's work to be entered on the form and the attendance of a gang and the hours worked allocated by the foreman. The bonus targets are also included and at the end of the week, space is provided for a bonus surveyor to enter the measured production. Provision must also be made for non-effective time to be recorded.

The utilisation of labour is measured by the comparison of targets set with those achieved. This can be a complicated process if all the factors of pay are not isolated. Targets should be expressed as units per hour so that the complicated wage structure is not considered; the hours are later converted into money earned by the bonus surveyor. Differences in payments for incentive bonus and spot bonus can be shown by the use of asterisks or colour, and this system may be extended to cover other differences. The total cost charge will be computed at the all in rate for each cost code. The total pay box will show the total wages paid and

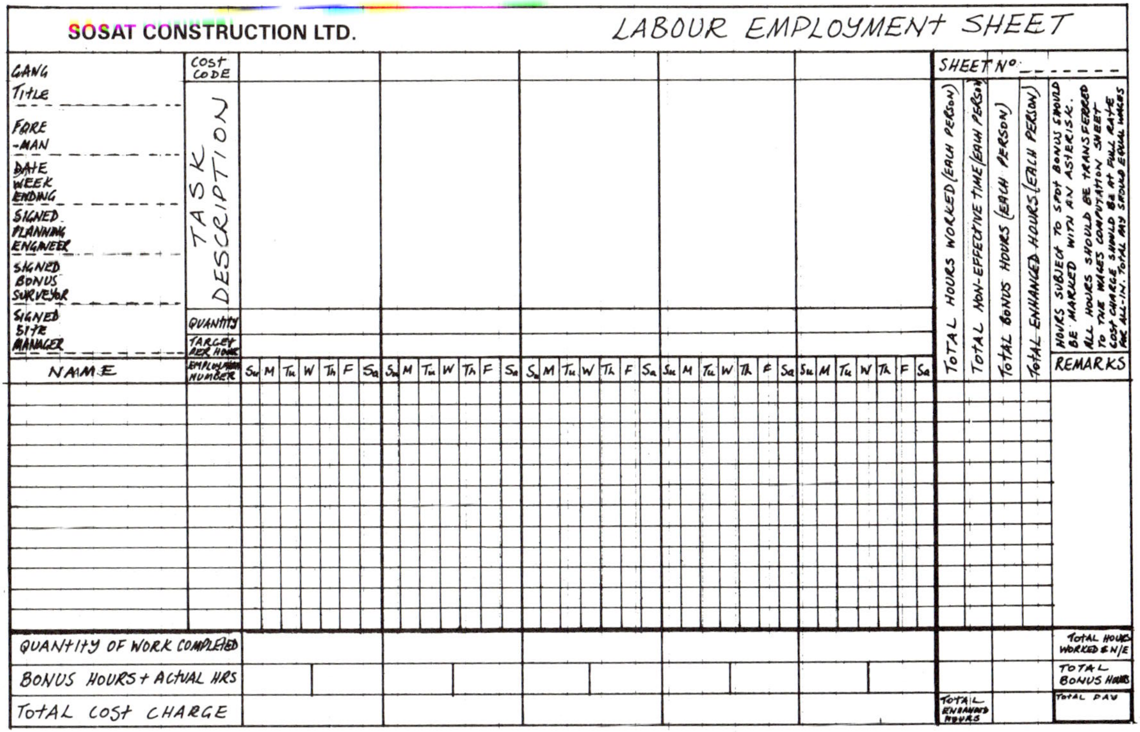

Fig. 5.10 Sheet for assessing labour utilisation

a comparison can then be made between each. Again accuracy in recording production is essential if the feedback is to bring its rewards. Three copies of the form are required, one copy to the site manager, one for the bonus surveyor and one for the estimator.

5.9 QUESTIONS ON SITE RESOURCES

MULTI-CHOICE QUESTIONS

1. The main objective of resource control is:
   (a) to apportion blame for problems;
   (b) to initiate remedial action;
   (c) to ensure site management are kept on their toes;
   (d) to keep the accounts straight.

2. The most important attributes of resource information are:
   (a) source and method of transmission;
   (b) receipt and recording;
   (c) neatness and legibility;
   (d) timing and quality.

3. Company operating procedures should be designed to:
   (a) suit the supplied information;
   (b) prevent external organisations from copying;
   (c) maintain hidden secrets and hide facts;
   (d) enable the architect to be well informed.

4. There are four main aspects which affect materials administration, they are:
   (a) storage, type, degree of control and security;
   (b) price, size, shape and weight;
   (c) cost, value, market and the effect of weather;
   (d) weather, roads, transport and attractiveness.

5. Selection of plant is based on:
   (a) essential attributes needed for the task;
   (b) desirable attributes of suitable machines;
   (c) amount of price discount available;
   (d) colour and make of machine.

6. The factors which affect the output of plant can be classified as those affecting:
   (a) efficiency and working time;
   (b) supervision and operator attendance;
   (c) management and plant maintenance;
   (d) weather and morale.

SHORT-ANSWER QUESTIONS (15-20 minutes)

1. Describe the method by which you would carry out a monthly reconciliation of materials on a housing site consisting of 150 dwellings.

2. Explain the need for early information if site management is to ensure that contracts are completed on time.

3 Explain how you would define the plant tasks for a contract using the information supplied at the pre-tender stage.

4 Describe the factors which may influence the output of either:
   (a) a hydraulic backacter excavating a trench, or
   (b) a crane delivering concrete to a 10 storey building.

5 Describe a suitable method of recording the employment and output of operatives on a site using an incentive bonus scheme.

QUESTIONS REQUIRING LONGER ANSWERS (30-45 minutes)

1 Discuss the action which may be taken by Head Office and site management to reduce material waste.

2 Compare the factors which have to be considered, and devise methods for the materials handling systems on a single storey industrial development site of 30 factory units and a multistorey office block with a two storey podium and twin towers 15 storeys high.

3 Discuss the essential factors which would affect the choice of cranes for the building shown on drawing No. . . . . and outline the desirable attributes which would influence selection.

4 Describe a suitable system for conducting labour and plant utilisation studies.

5 Discuss the reasons why items of plant are unlikely to achieve the maximum outputs listed by manufacturers in trade literature.

6 Sub-contractors

6.1 DEFINITIONS

Sub-contractors can be appointed to perform many services. They cover a multitude of trades and offer a service ranging from labour only to design and installation. A sub-contractor is a party who is

under a duty to the main contractor to carry out construction operations
or
under a duty to provide labour — his own or the labour of others
or
answerable to the main contractor for the carrying out of operations whilst under a contract or alternative arrangement with others.

The sub-contractor under a duty to the main contractor is usually termed a **domestic** or **direct sub-contractor.** This type of sub-contractor is used by all main contractors on engineering services work to provide materials and to carry out the works. Other trades are also usually provided by sub-contract, include roads and asphalt, roofing, flooring and metal windows or cladding. Under the Joint Contracts Tribunal, Standard Form of Contract agreement is required from the architect to the sub-letting of work.

The sub-contractor who is under a duty to provide labour only is also a direct sub-contractor. Opposition to the appointment of such contractors is sometimes incorporated in contracts by a specific prohibition clause. On sites where unions have a number of members, objections are likely to be raised to the appointment of labour only sub-contractors and consequently this type of sub-contractor is more often found on those sites which are speculative developments. The risk feature of these developments and the casual nature of labour-only sub-contracts allow for a rapid close-down or increase in operations depending on the market situation.

The third type of sub-contractor is not usually under contract to the main contractor but has usually been nominated by the architect. Within the sub-contractor's contract is a clause dealing with his responsibility for complying with the reasonable requirements of the main contractor, whilst the main contractor's obligations are included in the main contract. The contractor will be employed by the main contractor and is responsible for the control and payment for which he is paid a percentage of the contract sum. The nominated sub-contractor usually prepares a design and the responsibility for the design rests with the nominated sub-contractor. The main contractor must ensure that the sub-contractor's insurance covers for design defects for the whole liability period.

The authority that a main contractor has over each type of contractor differs according to the relationship between them. Authority is the right to make

decisions which require action from others, it is of a fivefold nature.
Legal That which is conferred by law;
Economic This is conferred by financial relationships;
Technical This is implicit in special skill or knowledge;
Formal That which is prescribed by the organisation structure;
Informal That conferred by personality and popularity.

It can be seen that the authority with each type of sub-contractor will be quite different. The main contractor will have little or no authoriy derived from the economic or technical nature of the relationship with a nominated sub-contractor. On the other hand the legal and formal are likely to be the weakest source in relation to the labour only sub-contractor.

6.2 SELECTION

This aspect will only apply to direct sub-contractors, although where a choice of nominations is allowed then the same principles could be followed. Time spent in ensuring effective selection can lead to benefits during the construction stage. Many qualities are required by sub-contractors and many may be particular to prevailing circumstances. The attributes of sub-contractors can be classified under a number of headings but each firm will have different factors to consider. The following is a general list.

Co-operation and service;
Price;
Financial stability of the firm;
Management expertise;
Effectiveness of on-site supervision;
Technical expertise;
Quality of materials used;
Standards of workmanship;
Industrial relations;
Safety procedures;
Punctuality — commencement and completion.

Other general factors such as the sub-contractor's main area of specialisation, previous work record, state of the current order book and the normal geographical area of operation should be considered.

The relative importance of these factors must be taken into account. Different people filling different roles in a firm will consider the relevance of each factor with a different objective in mind. It is therefore important that the completion of the sub-contract works within the time allotted is considered the overall objective. The factors should be allocated a weighting which totals 100. This has been done in the weight column of *Fig 6.1*. Price is given a large weighting because of its importance in the competitive tendering situation. However it will not always be weighted so heavily, particularly if a nominated selection is being made. There is also a case for increasing the weight of safety but the allocations here are not applied to a particular contract and therefore any particular weighting cannot be justified.

The method to be used to select the contractor is matrix analysis. It is assumed that three contractors are being considered, they are designated X, Y and Z. Each sub-contractor has now to be rated on each factor. The rating will be out of one hundred. The best contractor should be given a mark of 100 and the other two

FACTORS OR ATTRIBUTES	WEIGHT	SUB-CONTRACTORS					
		X		Y		Z	
		RATING	AWARD	RATING	AWARD	RATING	AWARD
CO-OPERATION AND SERVICE	4	100	4.0	95	3.8	90	3.6
PRICE	30	95	28.5	90	27.0	100	30.0
FINANCIAL STABILITY	6	95	5.7	100	6.0	80	4.8
MANAGEMENT EXPERTISE	10	100	10.0	95	9.5	95	9.5
ON-SITE SUPERVISION	6	90	5.4	100	6.0	90	5.4
TECHNICAL EXPERTISE	10	80	8.0	100	10.0	90	9.0
QUALITY OF MATERIALS	6	95	5.7	95	5.7	100	6.0
STANDARDS OF WORKMANSHIP	10	95	9.5	90	9.0	100	10.0
INDUSTRIAL RELATIONS	4	100	4.0	100	4.0	80	3.2
SAFETY PROCEDURES	4	100	4.0	90	3.6	80	3.2
PUNCTUALITY & COMPLETION	10	100	10.0	100	10.0	95	9.5
TOTALS	100		94.8		94.6		94.2

Fig 6.1 Matrix analysis of factors affecting sub-contractor selection

marked in relation to the best. If Z has the lowest price and is rated 100 for the £10 000 estimate then an £11 000 estimate would rate 90 and a £10 500 at 95. The same method is applied all through the list but the relative rating is more difficult for the other factors. These ratings are entered in the rating column of *Fig 6.1* and the final award is obtained by:

$$\frac{\text{Rating}}{100} \times \text{weight} = \text{award}. \quad \therefore \quad \frac{90}{100} \times 30 = 27$$

The award is calculated and entered in each column for each sub-contractor. Each award column is then totalled and from *Fig 6.1* the result is:

Sub-contractor X = 94.8
Y = 94.6
Z = 94.2

The appointment of sub-contractor X with the highest award would appear to be the most effective.

The rating of each factor is simple enough if the sub-contractor has worked for the firm before. In order to rate the firms of which the main contractor has no experience a question sheet should be sent with the tender documents, either as part of the documents or separate. This questionnaire is shown in *Fig 6.2*. It is not a complete list of questions but should indicate the sort of information which should be obtained from the other firms for whom the sub-contractor has worked. It may well be worthwhile to ask sub-contractors to obtain references from previous main contractors and their bank manager.

SOSAT CONSTRUCTION LTD	SUB-CONTRACTORS QUESTIONNAIRE.
Contract_____	Date_____
Job No_____	Tel No_____
Firm._____	

QUESTION	ANSWER (complete on additional sheets if necessary)
1. PLEASE STATE THE DATES AND CONTRACT WHEN YOU LAST WORKED WITH US.	
2. PLEASE GIVE NAMES AND ADDRESSES OF AT LEAST TWO OTHER FIRMS FOR WHOM YOU HAVE WORKED IN THE LAST TWO YEARS.	
3. HOW LONG DO YOU REQUIRE TO COMPLETE THE WHOLE WORKS.	
4. WHAT IS THE MAXIMUM NUMBER OF EMPLOYEES YOU PROPOSE TO HAVE ON THIS SITE.	
5. IN WHAT SEQUENCE DO YOU PROPOSE TO CARRY OUT THE WORK	
6. HOW MANY VISITS WILL YOU HAVE TO MAKE TO THE SITE	
7. WHAT INFORMATION IS REQUIRED BEFORE WORK STARTS ON SITE. (Drawings etc)	
8. HOW MUCH NOTICE DO YOU REQUIRE BEFORE STARTING WORK	
9. HOW SOON CAN YOU PROVIDE INFORMATION ON SIZE AND POSITIONS OF HOLES AND CHASES AND BUILDERS WORK.	
10. AT WHAT STAGE OF WORK WILL IT BE POSSIBLE FOR YOU TO TAKE THE SITE MEASUREMENTS YOU REQUIRE.	
11. WHAT DRAWINGS AND OTHER INFORMATION ARE REQUIRED FROM OTHER SPECIALISTS.	
12. WHAT ADDITIONAL INFORMATION IS REQUIRED FROM THE MAIN CONTRACTOR	
13. WHAT TYPE AND SIZE OF STORAGE SPACE IS REQUIRED AND WHEN.	
14. WHAT REQUIREMENTS DO YOU HAVE FOR OFFICE SPACE.	
15. WHAT ATTENDANCES ARE REQUIRED? LABOUR, PLANT, EQUIPMENT, WELFARE FACILITIES. ETC.	

A.	ARE YOU EXEMPT VALUE ADDED TAX. Vat Reg N°.	YES/NO
B.	ARE YOU PREPARED TO PRODUCE YOUR TAX CERTIFICATE (714) PRIOR TO COMMENCING WORK. Certificate N°._____	YES/NO
C.	ARE YOU PREPARED TO FURNISH PROOF OF INSURANCE AGAINST YOUR LIABILITIES	YES/NO
D.	ARE YOU WILLING TO GIVE 48 HRS NOTICE OF ALL MATERIALS DELIVERIES OR ALTERNATIVELY PROVIDE THE LABOUR TO UNLOAD.	YES/NO
E.	DO YOU AGREE TO SUBMIT A WEEKLY INFORMATION DEMAND AND PROGRESS REPORT ON A FORM PROVIDED BY THE MAIN CONTRACTOR	YES/NO
F.	DO YOU REQUIRE US TO PROVIDE CANTEEN FACILITIES	YES/NO

Position _____

Signature _____ Date _____

Fig 6.2 Sub-contractors' questionnaire sheet

6.3 ATTENDANCE

Attendances are generally those provided to nominated sub-contractors in that provision for payment is made in the contract documents. However, direct sub-contractors may also require attendance. Attendance is classified under two main headings, they are general and special.

General attendance is the provision of that facility which is shared or used by the sub-contractor but has already been provided by the main contractor. This usually involves the main contractor in extra expense and is included in the preliminaries under the JCT Form of Contract. The facilities which will be used by the sub-contractor are:

Temporary roads, pavings and paths;
Standing scaffold;
Standing hoists and cranes;
Temporary lighting and power;
Water supplies;
Clearing away rubbish off-site;
Space of the s/c office;
Space for storage of s/c's plant;
Space and protection for materials storage;
Welfare facilities.

Special attendance is that extra service to be provided by the main contractor. It is usually described in the Bill of Quantities giving a description of the work required in each case. The special attendance to be provided will include

Special or additional scaffolding (other than standing);
Provision of additional roads or hardstandings;
Strengthening of roads etc. for special loads;
The unloading and handling of significant items (weight and size);
The provision of covered storage (not just space);
Additional extra power supplies;
Maintenance of specific humidity or temperature levels;
Any other special attendances for works.

The best method of assembling the general and special attendance requirements is by extracting them onto the form shown in *Fig 6.3*. As much production information, in the form of quantity, weight and area, should be recorded as required to prepare an accurate estimate and plan the work.

Attendance for work is recorded as a simple yes or no on *Fig 6.3*, it is then more fully detailed on the form shown in *Fig 6.4*. Each entry should contain sufficient detail to enable the necessary resources to be acquired without further reference to the Bill of Quantities or the agreement with direct sub-contractors. These *two* forms provide the basis for enquiries to sub-contractors and for discussion at initial site meetings. They should be compiled for the general benefit of the estimator, planner, site manager and the sub-contract letting department.

Attendance can also include those general responsibilities for security and safety. The security of all the materials and property on site is the responsibility of the main contractor. It is likely that some requirement for the sub-contractor to insure against such losses will be insisted upon. However, the overall security problem remains the main contractors responsibility.

The responsibility for safety is in three distinct areas of law. Firstly, there is the responsibility under the law of contract. The parties to the contract are committed to the terms contained therein and generally reference is made to health and safety

SUB-CONTRACTORS NAME	TRADE OR OPERATION	B OF Q REFERENCE	VALUE £	GENERAL AND SPECIAL ATTENDANCE (PLEASE INSERT DETAILS WHICH WILL ASSIST ESTIMATING AND PRODUCTION)						ATTENDANCE FOR WORK REQUIRED INSERT YES/NO
				Scaffold	Power	Unloading	Storage	Protection	Access	

Fig 6.3 Abstract sheet for attendance

SUB-CONTRACTORS NAME	TRADE OR OPERATION	B OF Q REFERENCE	VALUE £	ATTENDANCE FOR WORKS (PLEASE INSERT DETAILS WHICH WILL ASSIST ESTIMATING AND PRODUCTION)				
				Holes Walls or Floors	Chases	Making good	Provision of mortar	Provision of concrete	Provision of heating	Provision of Unskilled lab.

Fig 6.4 Abstract sheet for attendance work

PROGRAMME

Main Contractor requirements
Sub-Contractor preferences
Periods of notice
Activity durations
Sequence of work
Number of visits required to site
Dependence on other sub-contractors
Actual calendar dates
Testing and handover procedures

FACILITIES

Main contractors provisions
Sub-contractors entitlements
Off-loading, transport assistance
Sub-contractor storage space
Sub-contractor office space
Welfare facilities
Setting out and other attendances
Cleanliness of the workplace
Disposal of rubbish
Safety responsibilities and inspections

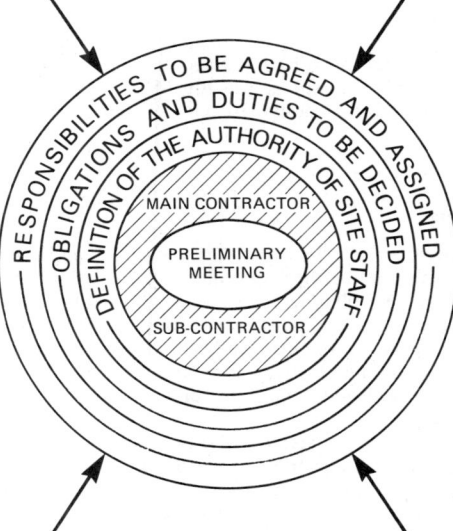

PERSONNEL

Channels of communication
Provision of information
Reporting of progress
Revisions of design
Revisions of programme
Telephone calls and use
Safety ploicy – accidents
Site instructions to sub-contractor
Communication with other
 sub-contractors
Payment and retention
Maintenance and defects liability period

INFORMATION

Main contractors management structure
Sub-contractors management structure
Sub-contractors supervision on site
Level and continuity of labour
Site hours and closures
Sub-contractors holiday arrangements
Movement of sub-contract labour
 on and off-site
Associated labour and suppliers
Availability of extra skilled labour

Fig 6.5 Subjects for a preliminary site meeting with a sub-contractor

matters. Secondly, is that responsibility under the common law. This generally imposes a duty of care upon anyone who may by their acts cause harm to someone. In matters of industrial safety the major issue is between employer and employee or indeed any other person who may be affected by their activities. Thirdly, there is statute law, these are the Factories Act, Health and Safety at Work etc. Act, and many others with all the attendant regulations which apply to the Construction Industry. Generally under this law each main and sub-contractor is responsible for the safety of the man he employs or controls and this responsibility cannot be passed to another contractor. In some cases labour only sub-contractors may be held to be employees of the main sub-contractor.

6.4 MEETINGS

The meetings between sub-contractor and main contractor are of crucial importance to the performance of both parties; their ultimate objective is the coordination and control of the sub-contractor. Meetings will depend on the complexity of the work but may be classified under four headings:

1 Preliminary;
2 Coordination;
3 Progress;
4 Problem solving.

A preliminary meetings follows soon after the selection and appointment of a sub-contractor. At this meeting the responsibilities, obligations and authority of each party are decided. A preliminary meeting is followed by a site visit nearer the starting time. The general items for discussion are shown in *Fig 6.5*.

The relative importance of each item will vary with each contract and lengthy meetings could be held on the provision of attendance alone. The duration of the meeting will very much depend on the clarity and definition already contained in the contract documents.

Coordination meetings do not seek to solve problems or check progress but are used to exercise that most important of management functions — the display of interest. The meetings are usually of a casual nature and are not concerned with the work aspect but more with the necessary social relationships on site. The casual check on progress or interest in problems would not be ignored but the primary purpose is the improvement of relationships which leads to effective coordination. The coordination of some sub-contractors such as plasterers, floor finishers on roof felters may require no other meetings than this casual visit, in which case progress and problems may be discussed.

Progress meetings would normally be held weekly and will be based on the sub-contractor's information demand and progress report which is shown in *Fig 6.6*. These meetings may be held in the site manager's office with a number of sub-contractors but should the problems of progress be the concern of only the single sub-contractor then discussion may take place with each in turn. The amount of formality will depend on the size of the project, the number of sub-contractors, the relationship between the sub-contractors themselves, and between them and the main contractor.

Monthly site meetings may be attended by sub-contractors if they have a major constribution to make. Generally it is preferable for the main contractor report on the sub-contractors' progress and explain any difficulties that arise. Major

SUB CONTRACTOR ....
WORK.. DATE ....

DRAWINGS AND DETAILS REQUIRED (give latest date)	

OTHER INFORMATION REQUIRED (give latest date)	APPROVALS AWAITED (Refer to request)

ATTENDANCE REQUIRED (labour - plant - equipment - power - etc)

MATERIALS POSITION (arrivals - stock - problems)	LABOUR POSITION (arrivals - departures - absences - problems)

LOCATION OF WORK DURING NEXT WEEK

PROGRESS REPORT WORK OR BUILDING	DATE STARTED	% LAST WEEK	% THIS WEEK	EST DATE COMPLETE	DATE COMPLETED	REMARKS

SIGNATURE .... DATE ....
to be submitted by cease work thursday

Fig 6.6 Sub-contractor's information demand and weekly report

coordination, design and progress problems may be discussed at the meeting. Generally this meeting will be concerned with delays which may be subject to a claim for an extension of time. A meeting of sub-contractors prior to the monthly site meeting of the building team may be the most effective method of acquiring the necessary information. This would be an extension of the normal weekly progress meeting.

6.5 COORDINATION

The principles of coordination are contained in *Fig 6.7*. The factors numbered 1 to 4 are essential for the effective coordination of sub-contractors.

Quite often there are fundamental differences in outlook by sub-contractors when compared with the main contractor. The sub-contractors may have a different background in engineering with vastly different experiences to the construction industry. This makes coordination doubly difficulty. The factors which may affect coordination are:

The nature of the work to be executed;
The degree of involvement of the sub-contractor in the project;
The differences in organisation of the firms;
The degree of consultation at the pre-contract stage;
The standard of information;
The number of visits necessary;
The number of contractors to be integrated;
The amount of work available during each visit;
The standard of sub-contractor supervision;
The standard of main-contractor supervision;
The regularity of meetings.

The main problems of sub-contractor coordination arise with engineering services contractors. Major contractors often find it necessary to appoint services coordinators, whose function is to organise the coordination of the engineering services sub-contractors and provide a focal point for liaison with the design team. Services coordination is to ensure that:

1 No conflict occurs between the various services during installation.

2 There is no physical interference between service elements and the structure.

3 A correct sequence of installation is established.

4 The sequence and timing is adhered to by the sub-contractors.

A similar appointment is often made on smaller sites for the coordination of finishing trades.

The selection procedure advocated earlier requires that objective records are kept. A report should be submitted on the completion of a sub-contractor's task. This report should be compiled by a number of people who have to deal with the sub-contractor; in this way a much more balanced view of his performance is likely. The report should include all those attributes which were considered at the selection stage with the exception of price and financial stability. There should be an opportunity for comments on particular members of the sub-contractor's staff to be included overleaf. It may be necessary to obtain opinions on other factors which affected performance, such as the standard of information and degree of pre-contract consultation. A typical report form is shown in *Fig 6.8*. The form should contain a brief description of the work involved in the main and sub-contracts.

Under the standard form of contract the nominated sub-contractor is paid by the client through the main contractor. The main contractor is paid a discount usually of 2½% for the administration and control of a sub-contract. The monies paid are also subject to a retention percentage up to a ceiling. The money is contained in a valuation carried out by a quantity surveyor. This valuation is processed and approved for payment usually a month in arrears. A record of such payments must be kept and a suitable form is shown in *Fig 6.9*. The architect will

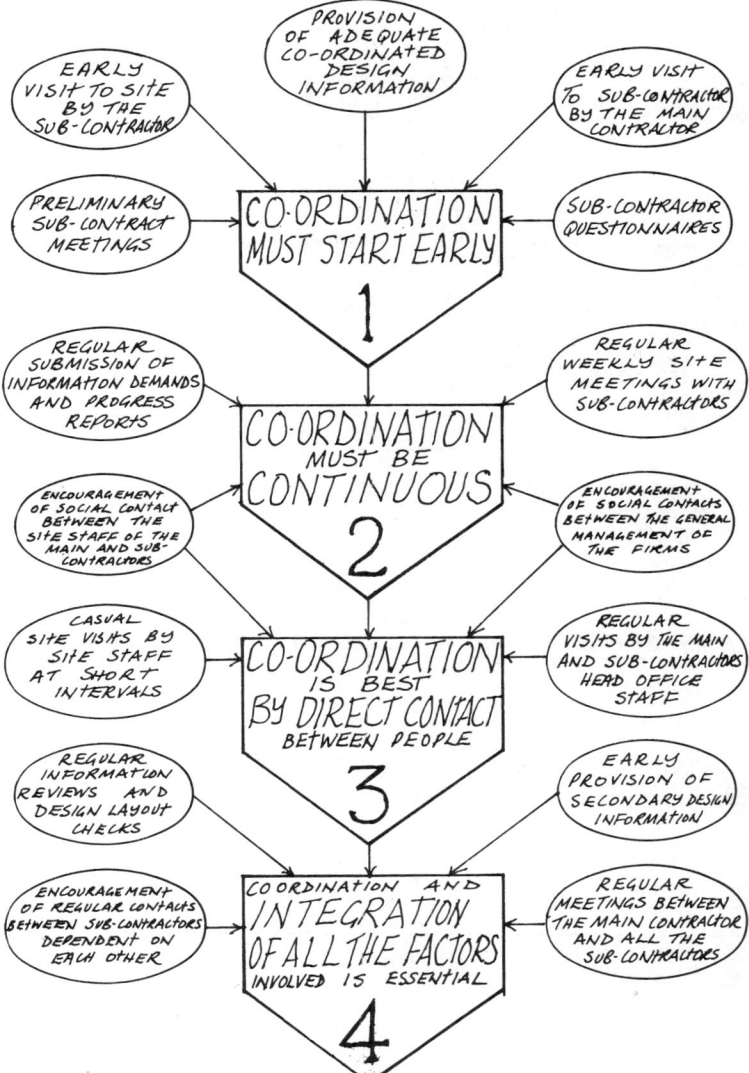

Fig 6.7 Co-ordination of sub-contractors

also inform the nominated sub-contractor of the amount due under a certificate. Payments to direct sub-contractors may have to be made weekly or monthly directly the work is completed. Such payments may be essential for a small sub-

CONFIDENTIAL

SUB-CONTRACTOR REPORT

SUB-CONTRACTOR	
	MAIN CONTRACT _ _ _ _ _ _ _ _ _ _ _ _ _
	CONTRACT Nº _ _ _ _ _ _ _ _ VALUE _ _ _ _ _
	SUB-CONTRACT _ _ _ _ _ _ _ _ _ _ _ _ _
	SUB-CONTRACT Nº _ _ _ _ _ _ _ VALUE _ _ _ _
	DURATION _ _ _ _ _ _ _ _ _ _ _ _ _ _ _
	DATE _ _ _ _ _ _ _ _ _ _ _ _ _ _ _ _ _

RATING OF SUB-CONTRACTOR

FACTORS OR ATTRIBUTES	WEIGHT	RATING BY (MARK OUT OF 100)				
		CONTRACTS MANAGER	SITE MANAGER	SERVICES COORDINATOR	QUANTITY SURVEYOR	
CO-OPERATION AND SERVICE	4					
MANAGEMENT EXPERTISE	10					
ON-SITE SUPERVISION	6					
TECHNICAL EXPERTISE	10					
QUALITY OF MATERIALS USED	6					
STANDARDS OF WORKMANSHIP	10					
INDUSTRIAL RELATIONS	4					
SAFETY PROCEDURES	4					
PUNCTUALITY AND COMPLETION	10					

DELAYS OR PROBLEMS NOT ATTRIBUTED TO THE SUB-CONTRACTOR

SITE MANAGERS REPORT

SUB-CONTRACTORS SITE STAFF	PERFORMANCE REPORT
	Signed _ _ _ _ _ _ _ _ _ _

CONTRACT MANAGERS REPORT

SUB-CONTRACTORS MANAGEMENT CONCERNED WITH THIS CONTRACT	PERFORMANCE REPORT
	Signed _ _ _ _ _ _ _ _ _

CONFIDENTIAL

Fig 6.8 Report on sub-contractor performance

FROM SOSAT CONSTRUCTION LTD.			SUB-CONTR...					
TO			CERTIFICATE No _____					
			VALUATION No _____					
			MAIN CONTRACT No _____					
			SUB-CONTRACT No _____					
	GROSS VALUATION		RETENTION		NETT VALUATION			
	£	P	£	P	£	P		
TOTAL CERTIFIED PREVIOUSLY								
VALUE ON THIS CERTIFICATE								
TOTAL TO DATE								
NOW DUE								
AMOUNT TO BE COSTED £ _____					AMOUNT OF CHEQUE £ _____			
SIGNED _____						DATE _____		

Fig 6.9 Form for payments to a sub-contractor

contractor to remain in business. These payments are the subject of much negotiation prior to the acceptance of the sub-contractor.

The coordination of sub-contractor activity can only be successful if it is started at the very earliest moment and continues to the final payment. Therefore, effective selection, accurate scheduling of tasks, detailed planning, mutual control, improved consultation and proper liaison are essential if the main and sub-contractors are to maximise profit potential.

6.6 QUESTIONS ON SUB-CONTRACTORS

MULTI-CHOICE QUESTIONS

1. A nominated sub-contractor is one who is:
   (a) Recommended by a previous employer;
   (b) Named by a friend;
   (c) Declared financially sound by the bank;
   (d) Preferred by the Architect.

2. The effective coordination of sub-contractors should be:
   (a) Prompt, pleasant, particular and profitable;
   (b) Early, continuous, direct and integrated;
   (c) Purposeful, simple, complete and wise;
   (d) Spasmodic, casual, autocratic and detailed.

3. General attendance on nominated sub-contractors is detailed in:
   (a) All parts of a Bill of Quantities;
   (b) The specification;

correspondence;
...nary section of the Bill of Quantities.

...relationship between the main and sub-contractor is as determined

...Construction Regulation, Factories Act and Health and Safety at Work etc.
...ct;
(b) Contract, common and statutory law;
(c) Architect, Factories Inspectorate and Police;
(d) Main contractor, sub-contractor and client.

5 The money paid to sub-contractors after an interim valuation should be:
   (a) The total amount for the measured work;
   (b) The gross value less retention;
   (c) The gross value less retention and discount;
   (d) The amount estimated by the sub-contractor as due.

SHORT ANSWER QUESTIONS (15-20 minutes)

1 Define attendance in relation to sub-contractors giving examples from the construction industry.

2 Describe the different types of sub-contractor and explain the relationship of each with the main contractor.

3 Prepare an agenda for a preliminary meeting between the electrical services sub-contractor and the main contractor on a multi-storey in-situ concrete framed building.

4 Describe the type of information required, and a method of obtaining it, from a sub-contractor at the pre-tender stage.

5 Problems sometimes arise with payments made to nominated sub-contractors. Outline the limitations of the main contractors authority and a method of recording payments to a nominated sub-contractor.

QUESTIONS REQUIRING LONGER ANSWERS (30-45 minutes)

1 Describe how the main contractor should incorporate the work of sub-contractors into the overall works programme to ensure the maximum benefits to site production.

2 Discuss the necessity for the exchange of progress information between the main and sub-contractor. Describe how such an exchange may be implemented.

3 Information is of crucial importance to the performance of sub-contractors. Describe how such information can be provided on a continuing basis during a contract.

4 Safety and security are important aspects of site policy. Discuss the responsibilities of the main and sub-contractors for these aspects of site policy.

5 Discuss the factors which will influence the selection of sub-contractors and describe a suitable method of evaluating the factors.

7 Work study

7.1 INTRODUCTION

Work study is a term used for a number of techniques which may be employed to study work. The techniques may be used by work study officers in large firms; in smaller building firms the principles involved should never be ignored by the site manager when seeking solutions to problems. The benefits obtained from work study are likely to be greater if fully trained work study officers are employed. The most immediate benefits may be those which derive from focusing attention on a single operation and gathering detailed information.

Work study consists of two main branches, method study and work measurement; each has a function to perform. Method study consists of techniques used to improve the layout and system of work. Work measurement is used to provide a basis to which the actual performance can be compared. Operations research takes the study of work a stage further and will be included briefly in simplified form as it is often useful on site. All the techniques are applied to resources so that the most economic and productive systems can be devised. The results enable management to improve its performance so that higher productivity is achieved. This application of work study is illustrated in *Fig 7.1*.

It is often assumed that an operation is working efficiently because there are no apparent delays or excess costs. However, the work content of any operation may contain additional work and ineffective time. The operation will always have a minimum basic work content as shown in *Fig 7.2*.

The added work may be due to design defects, including a shortage of information or poor quality materials and components. The amount of ineffective time is increased by two groups of people. Firstly by the shortcomings of management and secondly by the practices of the operatives. The causes of the excess time spent on operations and suggestions for curing the problems are contained in *Fig 7.2*.

The selection of work to be studied depends on three factors, economic, technical and human. The economic considerations will apply at all stages and at all times the question 'will this study produce an economic return for its cost?' should be asked. If the answer is 'no' then the study should not be started or continued. There are obvious reasons why operations should be chosen such as excessive costs related to previous records, bottlenecks causing delays in follow-up operations, excessive movement of material back and forth and any operations involving repetitive work. The technical considerations should take into account developments of equipment and other forms of assistance which may be applied to any work method.

Any operation which contains outdated machinery may be worth studying for economic reasons, but adequate knowledge of machine limitations is necessary to

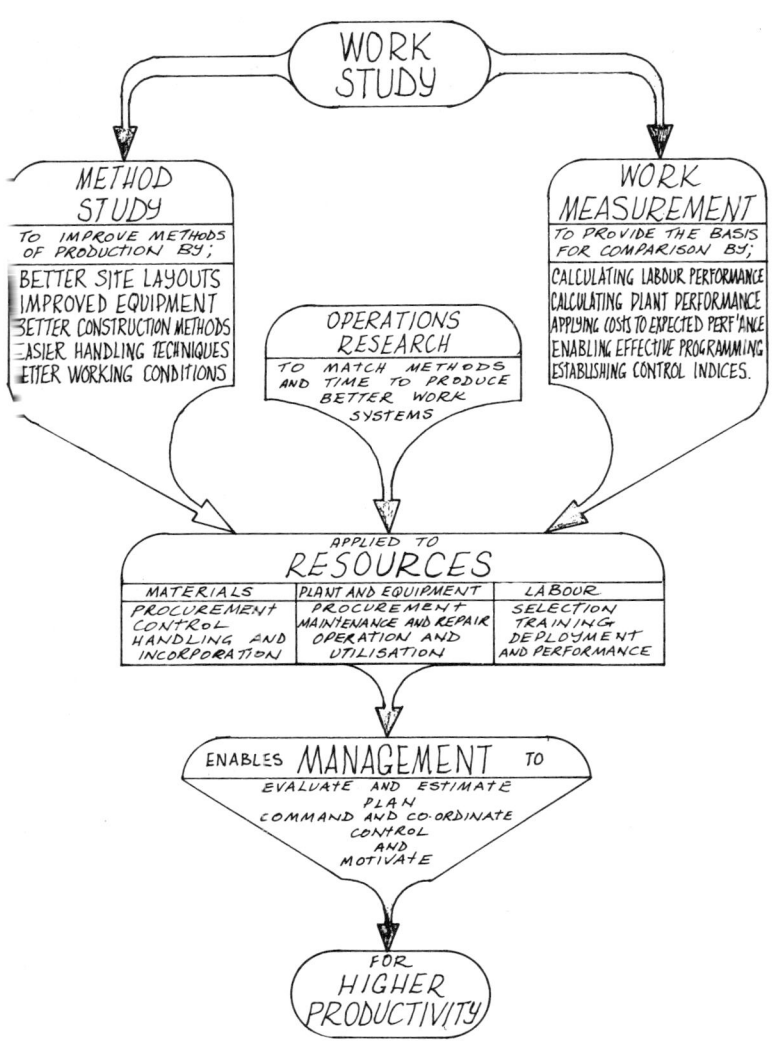

Fig 1.1 The application of work study

prevent overloading or unbalancing the work system. The human factor is the most difficult to assess and the reaction of operatives is most important to a successful study. The study of a particular operation may lead to unrest or ill feeling and even outright opposition. Therefore, the operations selected for study should be the most unpopular in terms of safety, conditions and rewards. If these

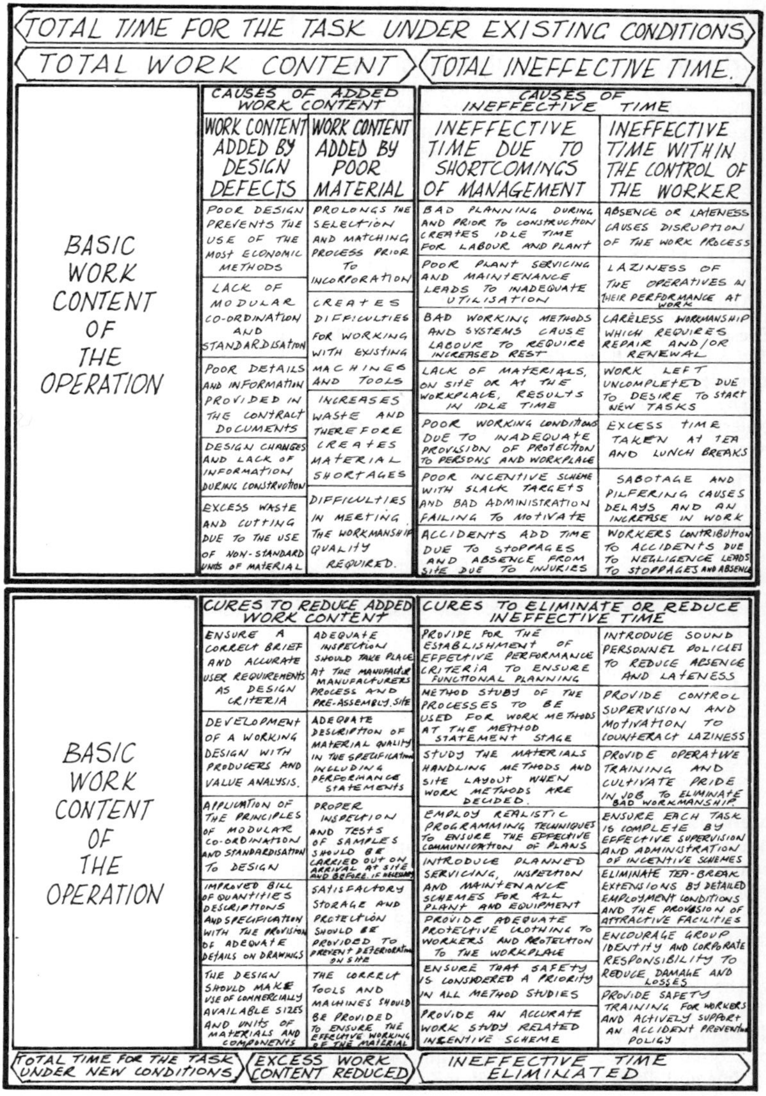
TOTAL TIME FOR THE TASK UNDER EXISTING CONDITIONS
TOTAL WORK CONTENT
TOTAL INEFFECTIVE TIME.
BASIC WORK CONTENT OF THE OPERATION
CAUSES OF ADDED WORK CONTENT
WORK CONTENT ADDED BY DESIGN DEFECTS
POOR DESIGN PREVENTS THE USE OF THE MOST ECONOMIC METHODS
LACK OF MODULAR CO-ORDINATION AND STANDARDISATION
POOR DETAILS AND INFORMATION PROVIDED IN THE CONTRACT DOCUMENTS
DESIGN CHANGES AND LACK OF INFORMATION DURING CONSTRUCTION
EXCESS WASTE AND CUTTING DUE TO THE USE OF NON-STANDARD UNITS OF MATERIAL
WORK CONTENT ADDED BY POOR MATERIAL
PROLONGS THE SELECTION AND MATCHING PROCESS PRIOR TO INCORPORATION
CREATES DIFFICULTIES FOR WORKING WITH EXISTING MACHINES AND TOOLS
INCREASES WASTE AND THEREFORE CREATES MATERIAL SHORTAGES
DIFFICULTIES IN MEETING THE WORKMANSHIP QUALITY REQUIRED.
CAUSES OF INEFFECTIVE TIME
INEFFECTIVE TIME DUE TO SHORTCOMINGS OF MANAGEMENT
BAD PLANNING DURING AND PRIOR TO CONSTRUCTION CREATES IDLE TIME FOR LABOUR AND PLANT
POOR PLANT SERVICING AND MAINTENANCE LEADS TO INADEQUATE UTILISATION
BAD WORKING METHODS AND SYSTEMS CAUSE LABOUR TO REQUIRE INCREASED REST
LACK OF MATERIALS, ON SITE OR AT THE WORKPLACE, RESULTS IN IDLE TIME
POOR WORKING CONDITIONS DUE TO INADEQUATE PROVISION OF PROTECTION TO PERSONS AND WORKPLACE
POOR INCENTIVE SCHEME WITH SLACK TARGETS AND BAD ADMINISTRATION FAILING TO MOTIVATE
ACCIDENTS ADD TIME DUE TO STOPPAGES AND ABSENCE FROM SITE DUE TO INJURIES
INEFFECTIVE TIME WITHIN THE CONTROL OF THE WORKER
ABSENCE OR LATENESS CAUSES DISRUPTION OF THE WORK PROCESS
LAZINESS OF THE OPERATIVES IN THEIR PERFORMANCE AT WORK
CARELESS WORKMANSHIP WHICH REQUIRES REPAIR AND/OR RENEWAL
WORK LEFT UNCOMPLETED DUE TO DESIRE TO START NEW TASKS
EXCESS TIME TAKEN AT TEA AND LUNCH BREAKS
SABOTAGE AND PILFERING CAUSES DELAYS AND AN INCREASE IN WORK
WORKERS CONTRIBUTION TO ACCIDENTS DUE TO NEGLIGENCE LEADS TO STOPPAGES AND ABSENCE
BASIC WORK CONTENT OF THE OPERATION
CURES TO REDUCE ADDED WORK CONTENT
ENSURE A CORRECT BRIEF AND ACCURATE USER REQUIREMENTS AS DESIGN CRITERIA
DEVELOPMENT OF A WORKING DESIGN WITH PRODUCERS AND VALUE ANALYSIS.
APPLICATION OF THE PRINCIPLES OF MODULAR CO-ORDINATION AND STANDARDISATION TO DESIGN
IMPROVED BILL OF QUANTITIES DESCRIPTIONS AND SPECIFICATION WITH THE PROVISION OF ADEQUATE DETAILS ON DRAWINGS
THE DESIGN SHOULD MAKE USE OF COMMERCIALLY AVAILABLE SIZES AND UNITS OF MATERIALS AND COMPONENTS
ADEQUATE INSPECTION SHOULD TAKE PLACE AT THE MANUFACTURERS PROCESS AND PRE-ASSEMBLY SITE
ADEQUATE DESCRIPTION OF MATERIAL QUALITY IN THE SPECIFICATION INCLUDING PERFORMANCE STATEMENTS
PROPER INSPECTION AND TESTS OF SAMPLES SHOULD BE CARRIED OUT ON ARRIVAL AT SITE AND BEFORE, IF NECESSARY
SATISFACTORY STORAGE AND PROTECTION SHOULD BE PROVIDED TO PREVENT DETERIORATION ON SITE
THE CORRECT TOOLS AND MACHINES SHOULD BE PROVIDED TO ENSURE THE EFFECTIVE WORKING OF THE MATERIAL
CURES TO ELIMINATE OR REDUCE INEFFECTIVE TIME
PROVIDE FOR THE ESTABLISHMENT OF EFFECTIVE PERFORMANCE CRITERIA TO ENSURE FUNCTIONAL PLANNING
METHOD STUDY OF THE PROCESSES TO BE USED FOR WORK METHODS AT THE METHOD STATEMENT STAGE
STUDY THE MATERIALS HANDLING METHODS AND SITE LAYOUT WHEN WORK METHODS ARE DECIDED.
EMPLOY REALISTIC PROGRAMMING TECHNIQUES TO ENSURE THE EFFECTIVE COMMUNICATION OF PLANS
INTRODUCE PLANNED SERVICING, INSPECTION AND MAINTENANCE SCHEMES FOR ALL PLANT AND EQUIPMENT
PROVIDE ADEQUATE PROTECTIVE CLOTHING TO WORKERS AND PROTECTION TO THE WORKPLACE
ENSURE THAT SAFETY IS CONSIDERED A PRIORITY IN ALL METHOD STUDIES
PROVIDE AN ACCURATE WORK STUDY RELATED INCENTIVE SCHEME
INTRODUCE SOUND PERSONNEL POLICIES TO REDUCE ABSENCE AND LATENESS
PROVIDE CONTROL SUPERVISION AND MOTIVATION TO COUNTERACT LAZINESS
PROVIDE OPERATIVE TRAINING AND CULTIVATE PRIDE IN JOB TO ELIMINATE BAD WORKMANSHIP.
ENSURE EACH TASK IS COMPLETE BY EFFECTIVE SUPERVISION AND ADMINISTRATION OF INCENTIVE SCHEMES
ELIMINATE TEA-BREAK EXTENSIONS BY DETAILED EMPLOYMENT CONDITIONS AND THE PROVISION OF ATTRACTIVE FACILITIES
ENCOURAGE GROUP IDENTITY AND CORPORATE RESPONSIBILITY TO REDUCE DAMAGE AND LOSSES
PROVIDE SAFETY TRAINING FOR WORKERS AND ACTIVELY SUPPORT AN ACCIDENT PREVENTION POLICY
TOTAL TIME FOR THE TASK UNDER NEW CONDITIONS
EXCESS WORK CONTENT REDUCED
INEFFECTIVE TIME ELIMINATED

Fig 7.2 Work content of construction tasks—causes and cures

can be improved reducing effort and fatigue, whilst increasing rewards then the study of other operations will be more acceptable.

7.2 METHOD STUDY

In relation to site production the techniques of method study are likely to prove the most useful. They should always be employed when planning the site layout and preparing the method statement. Any method study involves six very distinct stages which may be remembered by the mnemonic SREDIM which indicates the stages and the sequence to be followed:

Select
Record
Examine
Develop
Install
Maintain

These stages are further explained in *Fig 7.3*. The main aim of method study is to find out what is being done and to discover a means of improving the process to increase productivity.

The usual method of recording is by the use of symbols advocated by the American Society of Mechanical Engineers (ASME). There are five basic ASME symbols:

Operation ○
Transport ⇧
Delay D
Inspection ☐
Storage ▽

These symbols may be combined and used together and additional symbols may be devised. Examples include:

Inspection and operation ◻
Make ready for operation ⊚
Carry out the operation ○
Put away after operation ●
Temporary storage ▽
Necessary delay or queue. ⃝

Many other symbols may be developed for use in the construction industry where unique practices may require greater clarification. The problem in the use of symbols is shown when decisions have to be made as to whether an item is in storage or delayed. The temporary storage or necessary delay symbols may assist in these cases. All the techniques of method study do not use these symbols and some techniques are more useful than others. It is, therefore, intended to describe only five techniques.

The flow process chart is the simplest method of recording an operation. It uses the ASME symbols and they are linked to show the flow of the man or material depending on what is being followed. A man type chart and a material chart can be plotted for the same operation and compared. These charts have no relationship to time and distance, they merely indicate elements of the operation and may only be the first step in a series of studies using different techniques. A flow process chart showing the distribution of bricks to a dwelling plot is provided in *Fig 7.4*. Once the recording process is complete one should question, the delays, use of a barrow, the position of the main brick stack and the amount of travel.

Further information is given by a flow diagram which is drawn on a scaled plan

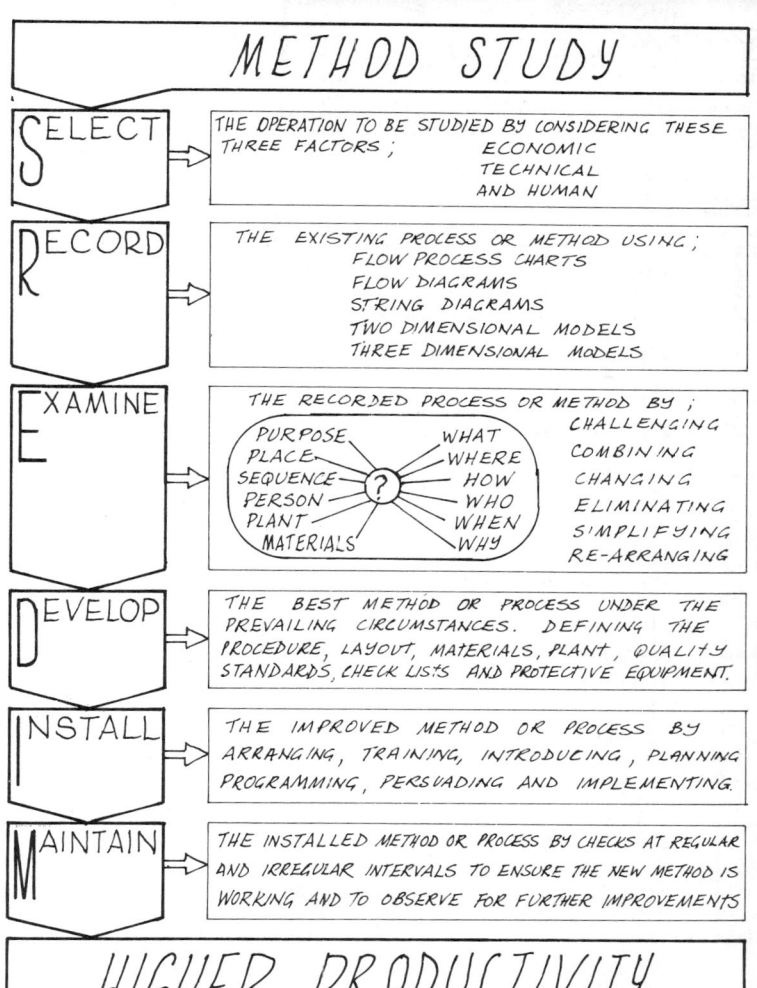

Fig 7.3 Method study for site production

of the site where the operation takes place. The flows are again either men or material and in some cases plant, but the distances are relative and therefore indicative of excess travelling and use of space. These diagrams are particularly useful in the construction industry because of the availability of scaled plans and drawing skills. The operation shown on the flow process chart would provide much more information if it had been produced as a flow diagram.

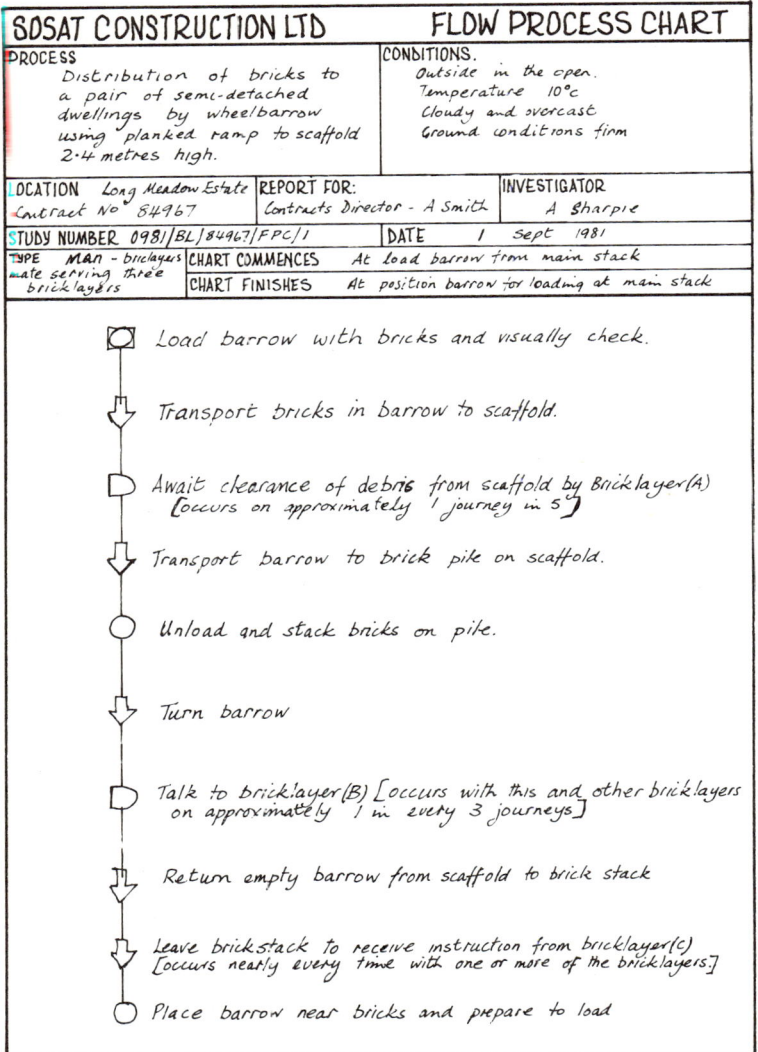

Fig 7.4 Example of a flow process chart

It has already been stated that the benefits which derive are often due to the singular purpose to which the studying officers' attention is directed. In some cases improvements become immediately apparent and the investigator is inclined to propose immediate implementation before the study is complete. This temptation should be resisted and the whole operation improved once the investigation and development of a new method are complete. Flow diagrams can be drawn to show an operation over a number of floors in a multi-storey building. An example of a material type flow diagram is given in *Fig 7.5*. Where a scale drawing is used the form may be attached as a cover sheet.

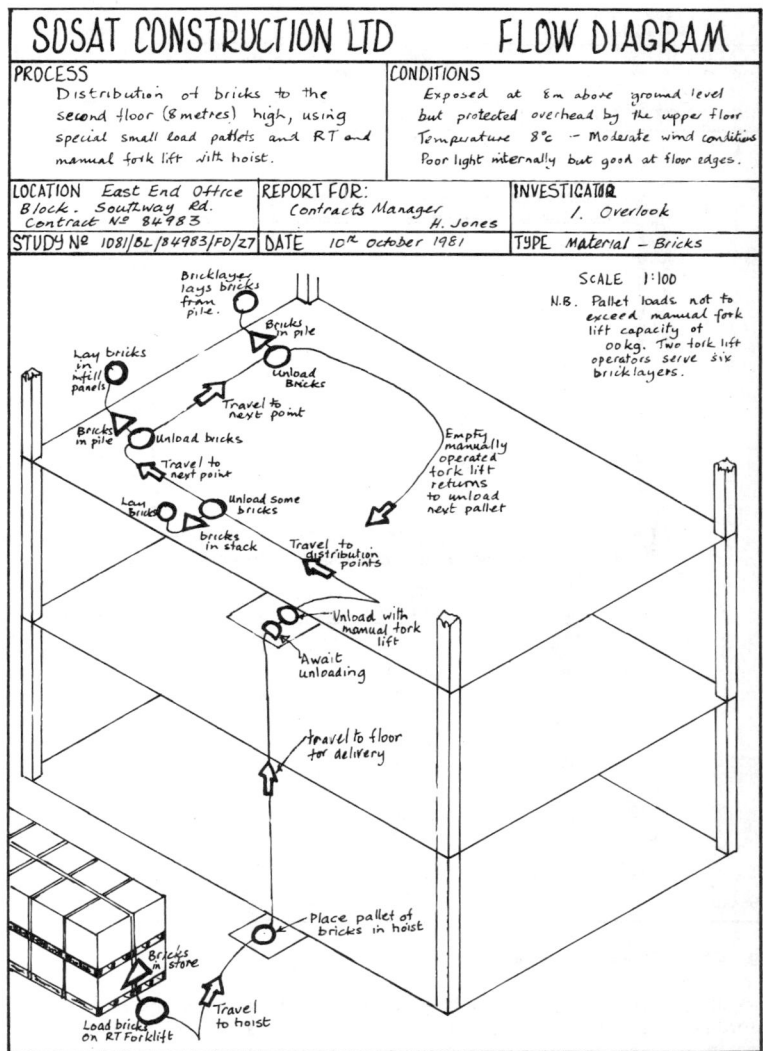

Fig 7.5 Example of a flow diagram

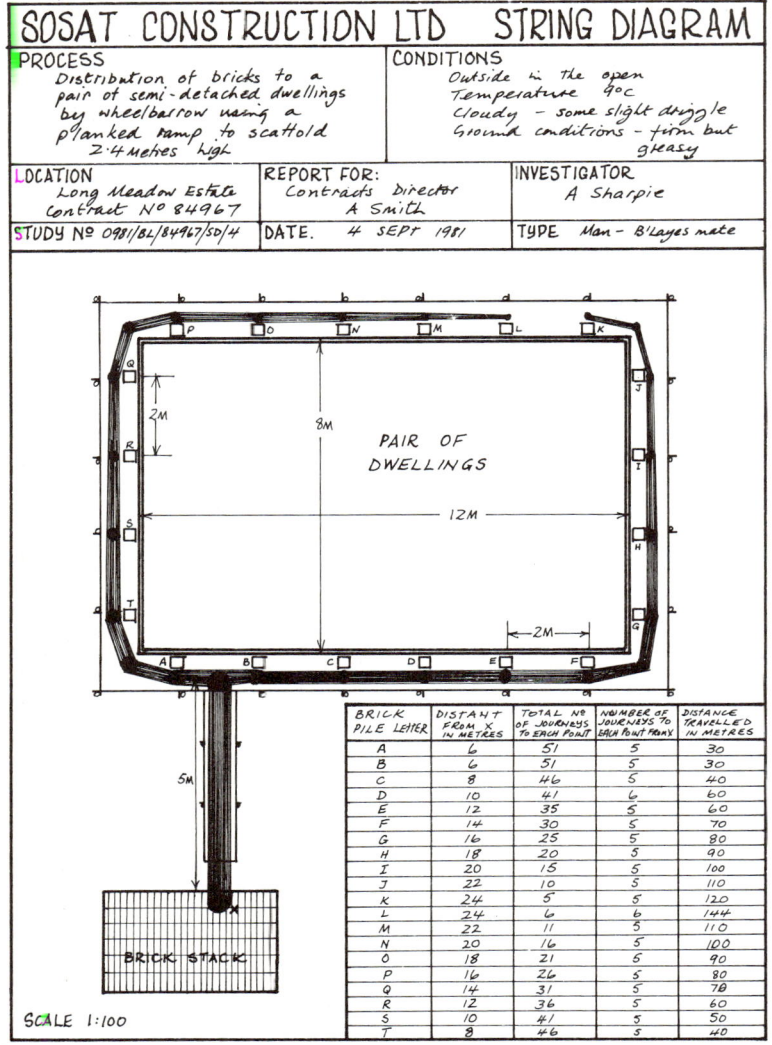

Fig 7.6 Example of a string diagram

A string diagram is very similar to a flow diagram but contains more information. This technique also involves the use of a scaled plan. The positions of machines or men are marked on a plan with a large pin or nail. A piece of string or fishing line is then wound around each nail as the man or material moves from one

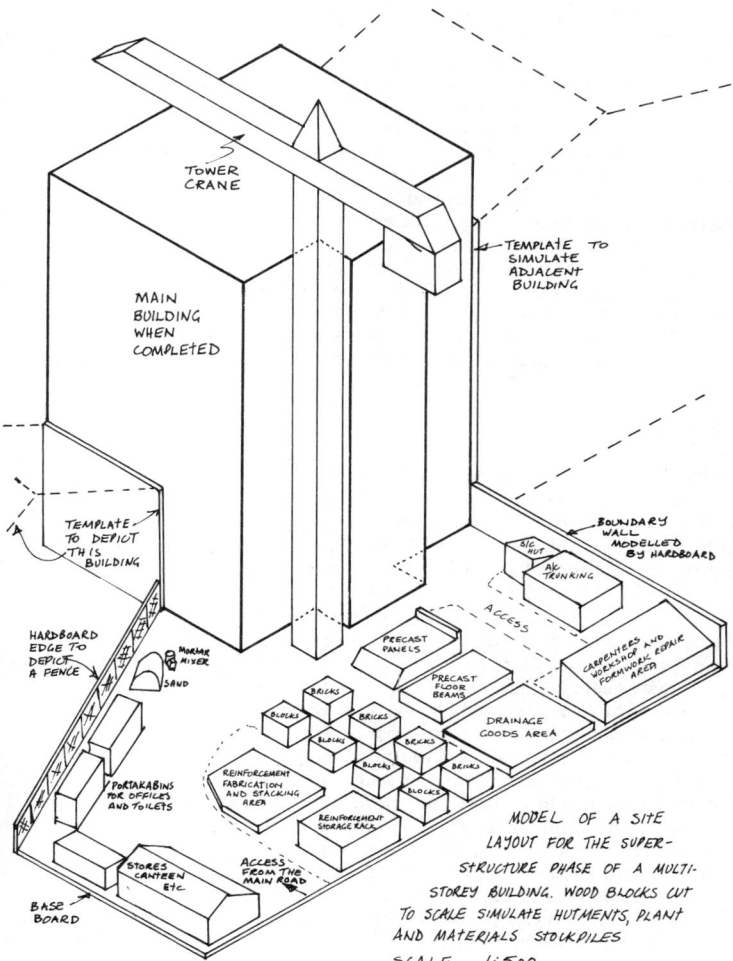

Fig 7.7 Three-dimensional modelling

station to another. This indicates the number of times a person or material travels between two points. The obvious improvement is for those with the maximum number of journeys between to be placed closest together.

A further development of the system is to use different colours to indicate the man and material on the same layout. This type of diagram is particularly useful for joinery workshops and pre-cast concrete yards. A simple string diagram is shown in *Fig 7.6*, it depicts the brick distribution system shown on the flow process chart. It can be seen that each technique conveys different information; the table in the corner of *Fig 7.6* gives the journeys and distances to each point.

The final method study technique is the use of models. The two dimensional models require paper cut-outs or templates to be placed on a scale plan. The cutouts are scaled representations of equipment or space that is to be used for different purposes. These model layouts enable trial string diagrams to be compiled to enable the optimum solution to be developed. Three-dimensional models are used where height is of critical importance. The model shown in *Fig 7.7* shows a site layout for a multi-storey building project at the superstructure stage. These layouts should be developed at the excavation and later stages so that the usage of space is most economic and practical.

The benefits from three dimensional models are much greater if scale models of vehicles and cranes are also available. When restricted sites have to be excavated then modelling will often assist in the development of the most economical method. If a firm regularly uses such techniques, sets of models depicting huts, brickstacks and other typical site plant and equipment become readily available.

7.3 TIME STUDY

This is by far the most important branch of work measurement. The Time Study is used to evaluate and quantify the operation thereby enabling comparisons to be made. Time Study measures the basic work content and is then used to produce a time which may be considered reasonable for the setting of bonus targets. The time study procedure consists of six distinct stages which can be remembered by the mnemonic STREAM which is explained in *Fig 7.8*.

The operation which is chosen to be studied will be one which is causing problems to a firm or the operatives. Outputs which vary from site to site are an indication, as will be failure to meet targets, uncompetitive prices, poor incentives and inadequate quality. Once the operation is selected it should be broken down into elements. The elements should be the smallest measurable parts of an operation. The timing should be carried out using two stop watches. The first watch should be started and allowed to run until the end of the study, this watch will measure the elapsed time. The second stopwatch should have a flyback mechanism and is used to measure each element. Some practice is needed to read the flyback watch accurately. Each study has a check in and check out time so that the two watches need not be operated whilst the study is being carried out. The total flyback times should be within ±2% of the elapsed times. The flyback times are recorded as **observed times,** as shown in *Fig 7.9*.

Whilst timing the elements of the operation, each element should be rated. The **rating** is applied to each element and using the scale shown in *Fig 7.8* where 100 equals the performance of Mr. Average. No person will fit this description perfectly but the performance will be rated to it by taking into account aptitude for the task, dexterity, skill and pace. The individual task differences will cover the range of attributes already mentioned but the patterns of work will differ. Some will work continuously and some pausing for rest whilst the time is being recorded. Care should be taken in the observation as to the reasons why the attributes vary. The conditions prevailing at the time of the study should be accurately recorded so as to indicate the allowances which should be made later. The process should also be accurately defined giving clear descriptions of the start and finish of operations.

The observed times for each element should be multiplied by the rating and divided by 100 (the standard rating) so as to produce **a basic time.** The basic time is

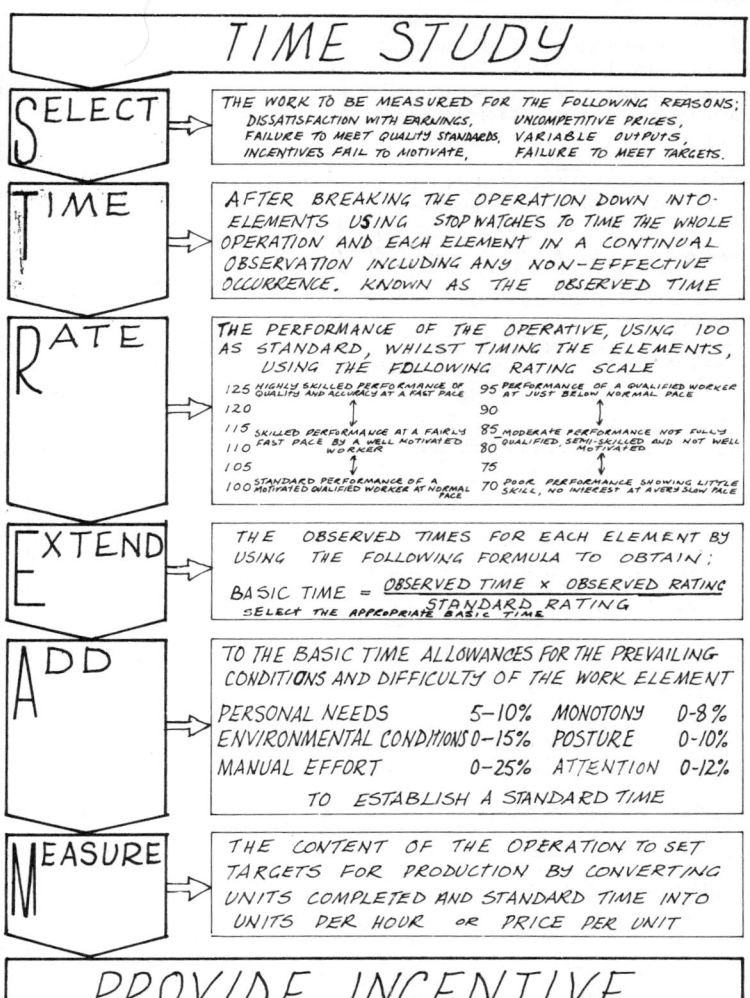

Fig 7.8 Time study procedure

then intended to represent the performance of the mythical Mr. Average. To take only one time study will produce a very unfair sample, so a number of time studies must be conducted and recorded in the same way as that shown in *Fig 7.9*. The more studies taken the more likely an accurate performance measurement will result.

The time study abstract shown in *Fig 7.10* assumes that a further nine studies have been undertaken and all ten sets of times for each element are shown in the columns headed 'basic times'. The idea is to arrive at a selected basic time. This selection is based on many factors and will depend on the practice within the work study department. In order to find the basic time a number of ways are available; a

SDSAT CONSTRUCTION LTD		TIME STUDY SHEET		
PROCESS Erection of 300×300 × 3.6m high timber column formwork with 6 steel collars and two push/pull props. Forms already cleaned and oiled and fixed to 150mm upstands. Reinforcement and spacers already in position.		CONDITIONS On fourth floor of multi storey building 16m high. Cloudy day, with fresh winds temperature 6°C. Occasional rain which leads to squall conditions with wind. Light fair. 2 Carpenters using one Hilti-gun.		
LOCATION East End Office Block Southway Rd Contract No 84983	REPORT FOR; Contracts Manager H. Jones	INVESTIGATOR 1 Overlook		
STUDY No 1181/FW/84983/TS/1	TIME STARTED 0845	TOTAL OBS. TIME 23.4 mins		
SHEET No 1 of 1	TIME FINISHED 0908	DIFFERENCE ET-OT 0.4 mins		
DATE 1 November 81	ELAPSED TIME 23 mins	VARIATION % 1.74%		
ELEMENT DESCRIPTION		OT	R	BT
Check Time in		1.75		
Pick up sides 1 and 2 of column form and tack		0.90	120	1.08
Move to and pick up side 3 bring and tack to 1 and 2		1.50	100	1.50
Ditto side 4		2.30	90	2.07
Place first 3 collars around column form adjust and tighten		3.25	110	3.58
Ditto further 3 collars		2.95	105	3.10
Bring in first push/pull prop and fix to floor and column form		2.10	115	2.42
Bring in second push/pull prop and fix ditto		2.45	95	2.33
Adjust the whole form for line and verticality		3.55	100	3.55
Pack up tools and move to next column		2.5	90	2.25
Check out time		1.90		
Totals		23.4		21.88

Fig 7.9 Example of a time study

common one is by taking the average. A refinement on this is to remove the two highest and two lowest times and average the remaining times. A more subjective method is to select the time which was produced under the 'most normal' conditions. The method of selection used on this abstract sheet is a subjective selection close to the average. The total of the column containing the selected basic times is 22.3 minutes.

The total selected basic time indicates that 'Mr. Average' will erect a set of column formwork every 22.3 minutes. This is not really possible as there would be no respite at all throughout the working day; nobody can work continuously without some rest on recovery period, or time to attend their personal needs. Therefore **allowances** must be given for such factors, and the items to be considered are given on the allowances sheet shown in *Fig 7.11*. Personal needs include going to the lavatory, smoking and satisfying a thirst. These are usually agreed between unions and management at a certain percentage, which is then allowed on all elements of all operations.

Environmental conditions are those which affect the work performance of operatives. Although very little attention is paid to this in the construction industry it has a tremendous effect particularly if you consider the likely output of a bricklayer on a windy day at very low temperatures and on a summer's day. The target performance set is often the same and if work study is applied it should not be similar. Dust in boilers, water in trenches and working in sewers are other environments which may require a large allowance.

SOSAT CONSTRUCTION LTD												TIME STUDY ABSTRACT		
PROCESS Erection of 300×300×3500 high timber column formwork with 6 steel collars and two push/pull props. Forms already cleaned and oiled and fixed to 150mm concrete upstands. Reinforcement and spacers already in position.							GENERAL OUTLINE OF CONDITIONS Fourth floor of building - open air 16m to GL. Cloudy days with fresh winds Temperature between 6-8°C. Occasional gusts with rain (about 15%) Light generally fair over the 2 days 2 carpenters using 1 Hilti gun.							
LOCATION East End Office Block Southway Rd Contract N° 84983		REPORT FOR: Contracts Manager H Jones								INVESTIGATOR 1 Overlook				
STUDY N°s 1181/FW/84983/TS 1, 2, 3, 4, 5, 6, 7, 8, 9 and 10.		ABSTRACT N° 1181/FW/84983/AB/2								UNITS N° Per column				
		ABSTRACT DATE 5/11/81								UNITS MEASURED 4.2 m²				
		VARIATION %'s 0·3 to 1·8%								TOTAL SELECTED BT 22·3 mins				
ELEMENTS	BASIC TIMES											TOTAL BASIC TIME	SELECTED BASIC TIME	UNIT
Pick up sides 1 and 2 of column forms and tack	1·08	1·50	1·40	1·74	1·30	1·42	1·12	1·18	1·14	1·43		13·31	1·35	2·1 m² form
Move to and pick up side 3 and tack to 1 and 2	1·50	2·10	2·00	1·80	1·69	1·52	1·86	1·66	1·72	1·95		17·80	1·80	1·05 m² form
Ditto side 4 and tack to other sides	2·07	2·02	2·10	2·20	2·06	2·30	2·12	2·25	2·16	2·30		21·58	2·15	1·05 m² Form
Place first 3 collars around the column form adjust and tighten	3·58	4·01	3·50	3·86	3·92	3·70	3·53	4·25	4·25	3·96		38·56	3·85	Three collars
Ditto further 3 collars	3·10	3·00	3·20	3·50	3·56	3·27	3·70	3·25	3·18	3·21		32·97	3·30	Three collars
Bring in first push/pull prop and fix to form and floor	2·42	2·20	1·99	2·10	2·12	2·14	2·18	2·30	2·42	2·35		22·22	2·20	per prop
Second push/pull prop and fix ditto	2·33	2·30	2·46	2·16	2·40	2·50	2·18	2·35	2·34	2·36		23·38	2·35	per prop
Adjust whole column form for line and verticality	3·55	1·70	1·96	2·20	3·25	2·50	2·98	2·70	3·80	4·10		28·70	3·00	per column
Pack up tools and move to next column	2·25	2·50	2·30	2·16	2·35	2·40	2·44	2·15	2·41	2·35		23·31	2·30	per column
													22·3	

Fig 7.10 Abstract of basic times

SOSAT CONSTRUCTION LTD								ALLOWANCES SHEET	
PROCESS Erection of 300×300×3500 high timber column formwork with 6 steel collars and two push/pull props. Forms already cleaned and oiled and fixed to 150mm concrete upstands. Reinforcement and spacers already in position.								**GENERAL OUTLINE OF CONDITIONS** Fourth floor of building – open air 16m to GL. Cloudy days with fresh winds. Temperature between 6–8°C. Occasional gusts of wind will rain (15%) Light generally fair over the 2 days 2 carpenters using 1 Hilti gun.	
LOCATION East End Office Block Contract N° 84983 South Ruway Rd			**REPORT FOR** Contracts Manager H Jones					**INVESTIGATOR** 1. overlook	
STUDY DATES 1/11/81 & 2/11/81		A	**PERSONAL NEEDS**		D	**MONOTONY**		**UNITS**	4.2 m²
ABSTRACT DATE 5/11/81		B	**ENVIRONMENTAL CONDITIONS**		E	**POSTURE**		**CONTINGENCY ALLOWANCE**	0.23 mins
ABSTRACT N° 1181/FW/84983/PB/2		C	**MANUAL EFFORT**		F	**ATTENTION**		**TOTAL STANDARD TIME**	27 mins

ELEMENTS	SELECTED BASIC TIME	% ALLOWANCES						TOTAL %	STANDARD TIME	UNIT
		A	B	C	D	E	F			
Pick up side 1 and 2 of column forms and tack in position	1.35	5	2	10	0	3	0	20	1.62	2/m² form
Move to and pick up side 3 and tack to side	1.80	5	2	10	0	3	0	20	2.16	1.05 m² form
Ditto side 4 and tack to other sides.	2.15	5	2	10	0	3	3	23	2.64	1.05 m² form
Place first 3 collars around the formwork – adjust and tighten	3.85	5	2	7	1	2	2	19	4.58	Three collars
Ditto further 3 collars	3.30	5	2	7	1	2	2	19	3.93	Three collars
Bring in first push/pull prop and fix to form and floor	2.20	5	2	17	0	3	0	27	2.79	per prop
Second push/pull prop and fix ditto	2.35	5	2	17	0	3	0	27	2.98	per prop
Adjust whole column form for line and verticality	3.00	5	2	3	0	1	4	15	3.45	per column
Pack up tools and move to next column location.	2.30	5	2	5	0	2	0	14	2.62	per column
							Total		26.77	

Fig 7.11 Calculation of standard time

The manual or physical effort involved should also be considered. A man swinging a pick or sledgehammer will need more recovery time than a person painting or applying mould oil to formwork. Monotony also causes people to seek relief by talking to others, so a person alone doing a repetitive task should be given the maximum allowance. Posture during work creates a need for more rest, a person bending down or working in a confined area will require a larger allowance than a person performing his task standing or walking. The allowance for attention is needed for close work which may involve some visual fatigue or extra concentration. Measuring or levelling, machining timber and other tasks attract allowances under this heading. The allowances are totalled.

The total allowances available are about 80% and it is conceivable that such a task which would attract the maximum, is possible, although it is hard to imagine this occurring in the construction industry. The total allowances are now added to the selected basic times to give **standard times** for each element. Some experts advocate the addition of a contingency allowance to the elements but it is preferable to add this to the total standard time. The contingency allowance should not be greater than 5%. The total standard time is 27 minutes and this will be used to set targets for incentives and will be more fully dealt with in section 7.6. The basic times for elements can be used by combining them with other elements from different operations to form times for operations which have not been studied. This is called synthesis and is a way of obtaining a selected basic time from the records of past studies. The allowances are added as shown in *Fig 7.11*.

7.4 ACTIVITY SAMPLING

This technique is based on statistical methods of sampling. Instead of observing an activity continuously intermittant observations are made and the activity of the whole operation is based on this sample. The reliability of the result will depend on:

The size of the sample;
The size of the element within the sample;
The degree of accuracy required.

The degree of accuracy can be found for a set number of observations or alternatively the number of observations required for a specified degree of accuracy can be determined using mathematical formulae. These are for a 95% confidence level.

$$L = \sqrt{\frac{4P(100-P)}{N}}$$

$$N = \frac{4P(100-P)}{L^2}$$

where

P = percentage size of element within the sample;
N = total number (100%) of observations in the sample;
L = degree of accuracy.

Activity sampling can be used in a number of ways to determine the amount of ineffective time in an operation.

The first technique is the field count which is used to determine the level of site activity. Careful judgement is called for when assessing the results. The example in *Fig 7.12* illustrates that 46% of the operatives were active during the period of the study. What does this indicate? Very little, unless it can be compared with a site which has regular results stating 70% active.

The nature of the work must also be considered. Two men laying concrete in a confined space under poor conditions may work hard one at a time; this situation will produce a 50% active rate. Alternatively, if a gang of two laying concrete in the open are working leisurely they will produce a 100% active result. However this should not deter management from the use of the field count as an indicator of the effectiveness of incentives or supervision.

SOSAT CONSTRUCTION LTD							FIELD COUNT SHEET	
LOCATION East End Office Block, Southway Road. 13th week 1st and 2nd floor superstructure under construction. Contract No 84983						CONDITIONS Day 1. Cloudy Temperature 8°C Day 2 Overcast - windy Temp 7°C Day 3 Some rain tho' generally dry - Temp 9°C		
STUDY No 0781/SC/84983/FCS/1 DATE 7-10th November 81				REPORT FOR: Contracts Director			INVESTIGATOR 1. Overlook	
ROUND N°	TIME	NUMBER ON SITE	OBSERVED			PERCENTAGE		REMARKS
			ACTIVE	IDLE	TOTAL	ACTIVE	IDLE	OBSERVED	
1	0810	42	20	21	41	48	50	98	
2	0820	42	20	20	40	48	48	95	
3	0827	42	19	23	42	45	55	100	
4	0835	42	15	26	41	36	62	98	
5	0845	42	25	17	42	60	40	100	
6	0903	42	22	19	41	52	45	98	
7	0920	40	20	20	40	50	50	100	2 operatives left site
102	1640	40	15	25	40	38	62	100	
103	1648	40	20	19	39	50	48	98	
104	1656	40	17	23	40	43	57	100	
TOTALS	104	3920	1802	2078	3880	46	53	99	

Fig 7.12 Typical field count sheet

The field count is taken with two mechanical or digital counters, one in each hand. All active persons are recorded on one, and all those observed to be idle on the other. The counters are read at the end of the count and entered on the form. The percentages can be worked out later. It is unlikely that all persons would be observed as some may have left site or be missed in some way. If less than 90% are recorded then the validity of that count should be questioned. The degree of accuracy for the active element can be calculated as:

$$L = \sqrt{\frac{4P(100-P)}{N}} = \sqrt{\frac{4 \times 46(100-46)}{104}} = \sqrt{\frac{184 + 54}{104}}$$

$$= \sqrt{\frac{9936}{104}} = \sqrt{95.538} = 9.774$$

The limits of accuracy are therefore ±9.8%.

If the accuracy required was ±5% then the number of observations could be calcualted as

$$N = \frac{4P(100-P)}{L^2} = \frac{184 \times 54}{25} = \frac{9936}{25} = 398$$

Therefore a further 294 observations would be required for a ±5% degree of accuracy.

SOSAT CONSTRUCTION LTD							GANG ACTIVITY SHEET		
PROCESS Lay concrete in a 200 mm thick reinforced concrete slab with forms cleaned out and reinforcement in position. Float finish followed by brush. Bay sizes 4m × 4m							**CONDITIONS** Sunny and dry but cold. Temperature 9°C. Concrete delivered by dumper - 6 men. Completed work has to be covered at the end of the day.		
LOCATION Industrial Estate New Town Contract No 84998				**REPORT FOR:** Contracts Planning Office A M Smith			**INVESTIGATOR** I M Drawing		
STUDY N° 2081/CON/84998/GA/2 **DATE** 20th Nov 1981				**CODE** S - Spread Concrete VT - Vibrate and Tamp FF - Float and Finish			J Insert and finish joints ID Idle Time		

ROUND N°	TIME	OPERATIVES								REMARKS
		A	B	C	D	E	F			
1	0830	S	S	S	ID	ID	ID			
2	0840	S	S	S	VT	VT				
3	0855	S	S	ID	VT	VT	FF			
4	0903	ID	ID	S	VT	VT	J			
5	0912	S	S	S	ID	ID	ID			
6	0920	ID	ID	ID	J	J	FF			
7	0923	S	S	S	ID	ID	ID			
8	0931	ID	S	ID	VT	VT	FF			
9	0940	S	ID	S						
				ID	VT	ID	FF			
30	1633	J	J	J	FF	FF	FF			

	TOTALS							Number	%	
Observations		30	30	30	30	30	30	180	100	
Spreading		15	16	10	—	—	—	41	23	
Vibrate + Tamp		—	—	5	12	15		32	18	
Float + Finish		—	—	—	4	2	10	16	9	
Jointing		5	7	4	8	6	7	37	20	
	Idle	10	7	11	6	7	13	54	30	
Total	Active	20	23	19	24	23	17			Active 70%
	Active %	66	77	63	80	77	57			Idle 30%

Fig 7.13 Example of gang activity sampling

The next use of activity sampling is in recording activities of particular gangs. This is done by observing a gang and recording the activity being undertaken by each member. The example shown in *Fig 7.13* is for a concreting gang. The code should be recorded and the initials placed against each member indicated by the letters at the top of the operative's columns. This is not easily executed because of the need to record the activity at the instant of observation. Any observations over a lengthy period will lead to members of the gang doing two tasks in the space of the recording. The technique is therefore limited as to the number of operatives that can be observed instantly. This number will be a maximum of ten but would be more suited to six or less.

SOSAT CONSTRUCTION LTD			SYSTEMATIC SAMPLE STUDY				
PROCESS Study of Site Managers activity on the East End Office Block Contract N° 84983 over the 14th week of the contract with the superstructure in progress. Observations were made every 10 minutes.			STUDY N° 1581/SM/84983/SSS/2				
			DATES START 15 Nov 81 FINISH 19 Nov 81				
			INVESTIGATOR I. M. Construct				
			REPORT FOR Contracts Manager				
			LOCATION Southway Rd Prestford.				
ACTIVITY	MON	TUE	WED	THU	FRI	SAT/SUN	TOTAL %
Read and answer mail complete site diary and administration	|||| |||| || (12)	|||| |||| (10)	|||| ||| (8)	|||| (4)	||||	(6)		40 / 16·6
liason with general foreman and site engineer	|||| ||| (8)	|||| || (7)	||||	(6)	||||	(6)	|||| ||| (8)		35 / 14·5
QS problems. under-measured items, hidden work and dayworks	|| (2)	||||	(6)	||||	(6)	|| (2)		(1)		17 / 7·1
formal site meeting with Architect			|||| |||| |||| ||| (18)				18 / 7·5
Weekly planning and meetings with chargehands	|||| (5)		(1)			|||| |||| || (12)		18 / 7·5
Industrial relations grievances and disciplinary problems		(1)	|| (2)		|| (2)	||| (3)		8 / 3·3
Head office queries policy, purchasing progress etc.	||| (3)		|| (2)	|||| (5)	||| (3)		13 / 5·4
Sub-contractors, supervision, liason and coordination	|| (2)	|||| (4)	||||	(6)	|| (2)	|||| ||| (8)		22 / 9·1
Clerk of works and architect queries and liason	|||| (5)	||| (3)		||||	(6)	|| (2)		16 / 6·6
On-site inspection and problem solving	|||| || (7)	|||| |||| (10)	|| (2)	|||| |||| || (12)	|||| (4)		35 / 14·5
off site duties		||||	(6)		||| (3)			9 / 3·7
safety duties, reports inspections etc.	||| (3)			|||| (6)		(1)		10 / 4·2
TOTALS	48	49	48	48	48		241

Fig 7.14 Example of a sample of a site manager's activity

The reliability of the results can be checked mathematically. If these have a degree of accuracy which is unquestionable they can be used to provide bonus targets. This technique involves removing all the idle time so that the remainder of the observations are used to calculate observed time. If the gang worked for 8 hours then the observed time would be 70% (5.6 hours) of the total because the gang had 30% idle time. The next step is to generally rate the gang as a whole, say at 95, giving a basic time of 5.32 hours. Allowances can then be made in the same way as for a time study. Assuming all the allowances added up to 25% then the standard time for the task would be 6.65 hours. This will be explained further under the incentives section of this chapter.

Activity sampling can also be used to monitor a single person's activity. This is best done systematically rather than at random intervals. Systematic samples are taken at regular intervals and can be easily recorded by the person being studied. *Fig 7.14* shows a sample of a site manager's time. An alarm or timing watch is necessary so as to prompt the observer to record his actions at the agreed time interval. The usual activities are recorded and the days of the week are also used to separate the observations as this gives a daily pattern for the week. The observations should be approximately every 10 minutes which will give nearly 50 observations in an 8 hour day. The length of the study period will depend on the cycle of work. Are the activities of the same pattern every week or are they monthly? In the case of the site manager, the cycle pattern will be monthly, and therefore a sample should take place over at least a month but preferably three months. Some account should be taken of the time of year for no matter how keen and efficient a site manager, site tours are likely to be more numerous in summer than in winter.

Activity sampling is an ideal first step to enable a manager to get an idea of what is going on, but the results should be carefully considered. Managers tend to look most closely at operations which concern them. This can result in false impressions being given leading to less effective decision making. Wherever possible observations should be made over the whole site by field counts or be concurrent observations of all the gangs working on site. When site productivity gives cause for concern and the reasons are difficult to determine, activity sampling can provide evidence as to the most ineffective operation. This will enable more detailed method and time study to be carried out where they are likely to produce the greatest benefit.

7.5 OPERATIONS RESEARCH

This branch of work study involves many mathematical techniques which are beyond the scope of this unit. There is, however, one simple method of modelling a process which is of particular use to the manager on a construction site. This is the multiple activity chart (*Fig 7.15*) which records a number of men and machines plotting their activities against a time scale. Such charts can be compiled in a number of ways.

Most operations on a construction site are not separate and independent but are reliant on other activities for their proper functioning. Therefore any increase in productivity is unlikely to arise unless all operations are integrated and matched into a whole production unit. Time studies, activity samples and method studies can all be employed to improve and compare operations but any piecemeal improvement may upset the integration and balance of the related activities. Therefore, a multiple activity chart can be used to record information from a number of studies to enable them to be examined as a whole. This type of recording using actual recorded times will indicate the areas of major imbalance between related activities. These areas will be shown as queues of material or major periods of idle time for men or machines.

The improvement of such imbalances and under-utilisation requires a method of eliminating variations in the durations of activities. Method study and time study

SOSAT CONSTRUCTION LTD — MULTIPLE ACTIVITY CHART

PROCESS
Mixing, transporting and laying concrete in a 200mm thick reinforced concrete slab. Forms cleaned out and reinforcement in position. Float finish followed by brush. Joints at 4m intervals - bay width 4m.

CONDITIONS
Overcast day - temperature 9°C. No rain - very little wind. Plant + men as shown. Ground conditions good. Completed work has to be covered at end of work.

LOCATION Industrial Estate, New Town. Contract No. 84998

REPORT FOR: Contracts Planning Office - A M Smith

INVESTIGATOR I. M Drawing.

DATE 28th NOV 1981

STUDY No 1181/CON/84998/MAC/3

TIME MINS	Concrete Mixer 600/400 litre NTR-Diesel	DUMPER A ½m³ capacity shaped body front tipping	DUMPER B ½m³ capacity shaped body all round tipper	A	B	C	D	E	F
	LOAD HOPPER								
	MIX & LOAD								
	DISCHARGE	LOAD							
5	LOAD HOPPER	TRAVEL TO SLAB							
	LOAD MIXER AND MIX	DUMP		SPREAD CONC	SPREAD CONC				
10	DISCHARGE	RETURN	LOAD						
	LOAD HOPPER	TO MIXER	TRAVEL TO SLAB						
	LOAD MIXER AND MIX		DUMP		SPREAD CONC	SPREAD CONC			
15	DISCHARGE	LOAD	RETURN TO MIXER						
	LOAD	TRAVEL TO SLAB							
	MIX	DUMP					Vibrate		
20	DISCHARGE	RETURN TO MIXER	LOAD	SPREAD CONC	SPREAD CONC				
	LOAD		TRAVEL				Tamp slab	Tamp slab	
	MIX		DUMP	Spread	Spread				
25	DISCHARGE	LOAD							
	LOAD	TRAVEL TO SLAB	RETURN			INSERT AND FINISH JOINT			INSERT AND FINISH JOINT
	MIX	DUMP							
30	DISCHARGE	RETURN TO MIXER	LOAD	Spread	Spread				
	LOAD		TRAVEL						
	MIX		DUMP		Spread	Spread		Vib	Finish and Float slab
35	DISCHARGE	LOAD	RETURN				Tamp slab	Tamp slab	
	LOAD	TRAVEL							
	MIX	DUMP		Spread	Spread				
40	DISCHARGE		LOAD						
	LOAD	RETURN	TRAVEL						
	MIX		DUMP						
45	DISCHARGE	LOAD	RETURN	Spread	Spread	Joint etc			Joint etc

Fig 7.15 The charting of a multiple resource process

tend to standardise method and time. This standardisation of activities is essential if variations in performance are to be reduced. The reduction in variety of performance enables a multiple activity chart to be drawn using standard times as in *Fig 7.15*. Note that all the identical elements are of the same duration. The concrete mixer always produces a mix every 5 minutes when in actual practice it may vary from any period between 3½ and 6½ minutes. Once such a chart is drawn the idle time can be hatched to highlight the underutilisation of resources, attempts can then be made to reduce these periods. This can be achieved by increasing or decreasing gang sizes, changing plant capacity, increasing the amount of plant or even returning to the basic processes and conducting further method studies so as to reduce these periods.

7.6 INCENTIVES

Any reward or punishment, whether financial or non-financial that encourages employees to change attitudes or take a specific course of action can be termed an incentive. Punishment is a negative incentive which is unlikely to be successful unless accompanied by an acceptable management philosophy. It will motivate employees to produce a minimum amount of work but much higher productivity is not usually the result of the threat of dismissal. The main concern of this section is financial incentives related to work study.

The role of rewards, and particularly the bonus system, in the construction industry, is illustrated in *Fig 7.16,* from which it can be seen that bonus payments alone are not the sole answer to producing a well motivated worker. All employees have similar requirements but they possess them in different degrees. An illustration of this is that young people are highly motivated by financial rewards whilst employees of greater age desire stability by way of job security, status, interpersonal relationships and other incentives. This is not to say that the older worker is uninterested in financial rewards, it is the degree by which it influences the persons actions that counts. It follows that the most effective incentive is the one designed for the individual and this in the construction industry is difficult to implement. The industry relies on casual labour and most operations require a gang rather than an individual to carry out the work. It is almost impossible to separate these operations into individual tasks. Some tasks also create problems in the setting of targets because of the unique conditions on every site. This may be the best reason for using work study, in the construction industry, to set targets.

The objectives of an incentive scheme can be briefly stated as 'an improvement in the productivity of labour'. Labour productivity may be defined as:

'the efficiency of use and the amount of labour employed by a unit of production to carry out the work tasks assigned.'

The unit of production may be an individual, group, site or firm. The greater the number of persons involved the less effective the incentive. Improvements in productivity can be brought about by the following factors:

Increases in the quantity of work;
Increased flexibity between trades;
Rationalisation of working hours (less overtime etc);
Reduction in the number of operatives;
New methods of work and changes in working practices;
Increased mechanisation;
Improvement of rewards to labour and capital;

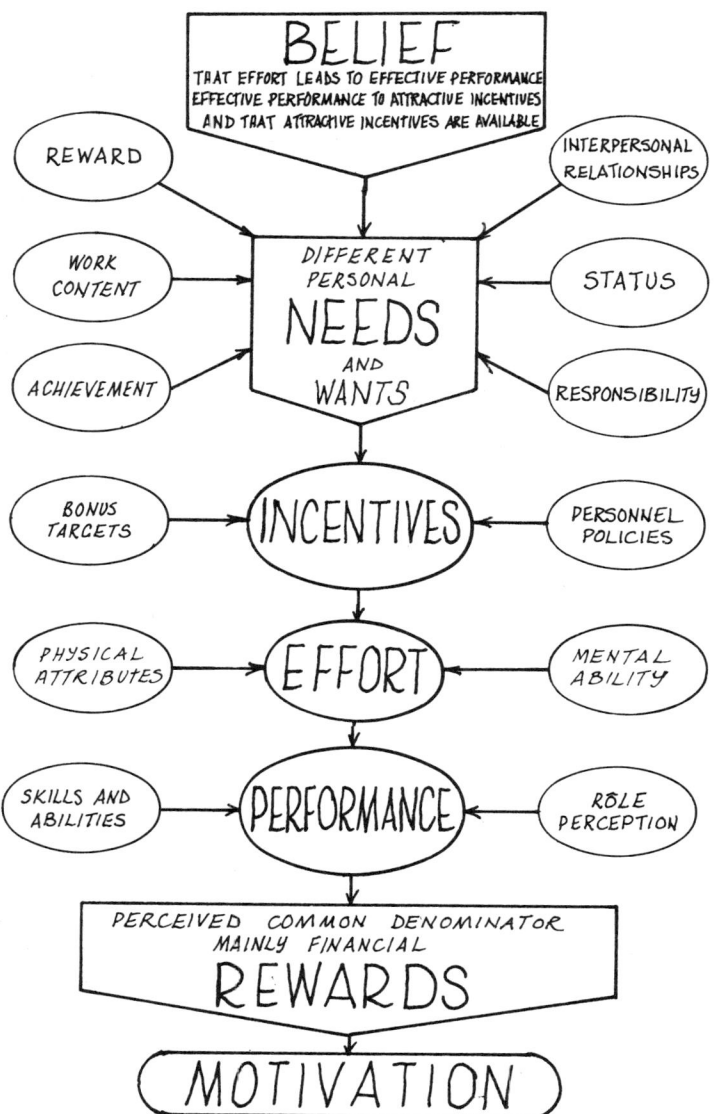

Fig 7.16 The role of rewards in motivation

Improvement in quality;
Improvement in safety;
Less waste of material;
Reduction in absenteeism;
Reduction in labour turnover;
Improved organisation structure;
Improvement in industrial relations.

These factors may be converted into more specific objectives depending on the actual operation. The incentive can be set by using not only time study, but all the techniques of work study. It must be remembered, however, that the task for which the incentive is offered should be accurately defined. The start, finish and content should be unambiguously described and recorded so as to minimise later disagreements.

Financial incentives are the most commonly used incentive because the casual nature of the workforce, and lack of regard by the public for the construction industry, tends to encourage the seeking of non-financial satisfactions away from the workplace. Money is also seen by the majority of operatives as the one common factor which will supply their different wants and needs.

The setting of these targets can be made from numerous sources but the major claim of time study is that it is based on scientific measurement under actual working conditions. It is totally flexible because the rating systems equalise the differences in human skills and the system of allowances takes account of the differences of environmental conditions. *Figs 7.17* and *7.18* show how the bonuses may be calculated from the previously illustrated time sheet and the gang activity sheet. The targets may be set as time allowed for a task or as a payment for a measured unit of work. The financial target is probably the most commonly used in the construction industry. If pay is at a level of £3.00 per hour then they can form the basis of a target except that there is some extra cost involved in setting and administering targets and in paying guaranteed bonuses for delays and inclement weather. If site management fails to provide efficient organisation direction and control of the tasks, it may lead to delays due to the following:

Shortage of materials;
Lack of coordination between trades;
Lack of information (drawings etc);
Unavailability of plant and equipment;
Poor instructions and orders;
Deployment of operatives on 'panic jobs' and emergencies;
Delays caused by sub-contractors;
Inadequate protection of the workplace during inclement weather.

These factors will reduce bonus earnings and in such circumstances most firms have arrangements to pay an agreed bonus. This may be related to previous earnings or at a standard rate per hour. The money has to be found from the contract sum to pay for the lack of production; therefore, the £3.00 per hour is reduced. This is called gearing in that the bonus is paid at only 75% or 50% of the total due. Such deductions can also occur when the targets are being set and this is shown on the bonus abstract in the column headed cost of administration and contingencies. In this case the hourly rate is reduced to £2.50 a deduction of just under 17%. The monetary targets are then set at £1.80 per column for the gang of two erecting the formwork and at £0.83 per square metre for the gang of six laying the concrete slab.

FORMWORK									
TOTAL STANDARD TIME	UNITS		NUMBER OF OPERATIVES	COST AT £3 MAN HR	COST OF ADMIN AND CONTINGENCY	MONETARY TARGETS		TARGET TIMES	
	N°	M²				PER UNIT	PER M²	PER UNIT	PER M²
27 mins or 0.45 hrs	Column	4.2 m²	2	£2.70	£0.90	£1.80 per Column	0.43p	54 mins or 0.9 hrs	12.86 mins or 0.21 hrs
150 mins or 2.5 hrs	—	10 m²	2	£15.00	£2.50	—	£1.25	—	30 mins or 0.5 hrs

Fig 7.17 Bonus abstract from a time sheet

CONCRETING									
TOTAL STANDARD TIME	UNITS		NUMBER OF OPERATIVES	COST A £3 MAN HR	COST OF ADMIN AND CONTINGENCY	MONETARY TARGETS		TARGET TIMES	
	N°	M²				PER UNIT	PER M²	PER UNIT	PER M²
6.65 HRS	24 m³	120 m²	6	£119.70	£19.95	£4.16 m³	0.83p	100 mins or 1.66 HRS per m³	20 mins or 0.33 hrs
8.75 HRS	45 m³	150 m²	6	£157.50	£26.25	£2.92 m³	0.88p	70 mins or 1.17 HRS per m³	21 mins or 0.35 HRS

Fig 7.18 Bonus abstract from a gang sheet

If the target times are used then the bonus hours would be computed and they would be paid at a reduced rate per hour so that the whole number of hours were paid at £2.50. In order to equate this with the monetary targets if 60 hours work was completed it would be as follows:

Financial Target	Pay	Time Target	Pay
£1.66 per unit		1.46 hours per unit =	
(based on £2.50 per hr)			40 hours × £3 = £120
4 completed units =		41 units = 60 hours	
			20 hrs × £1.50 = £30
Total	**£150**		**£150**

It can be seen that the targets are subject to a 50% gearing whichever type is used. However, the financial target may prove the most acceptable.

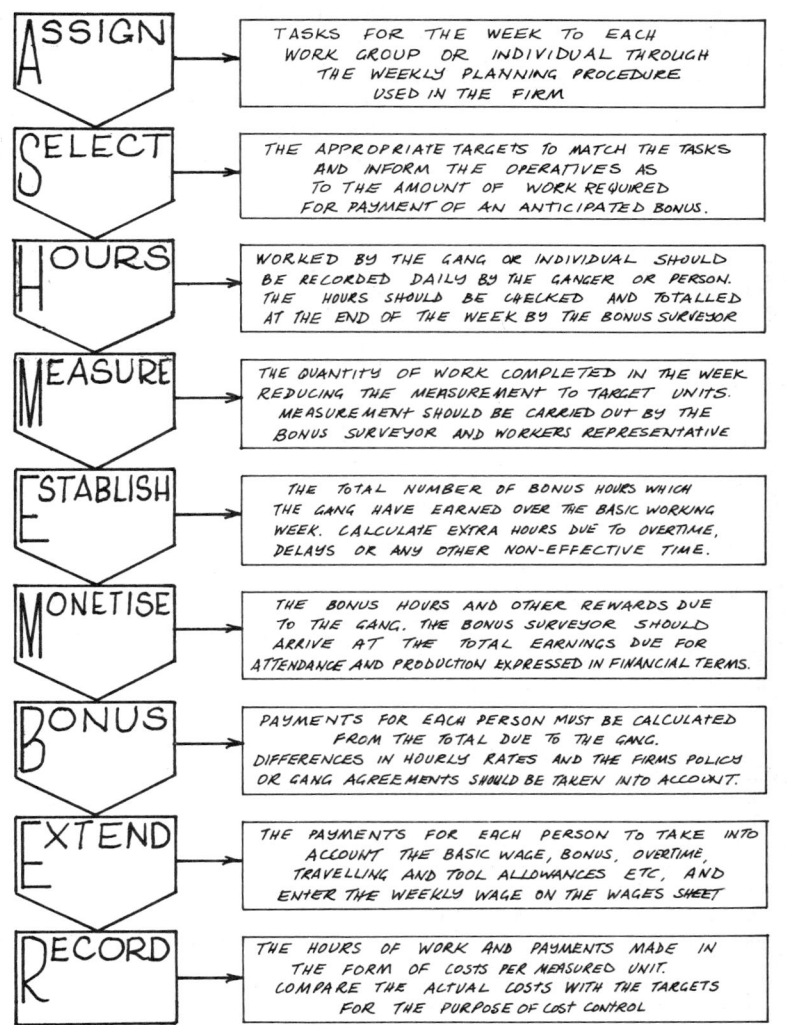

Fig 7.19 Target bonus procedure

The procedure for applying the targets should generally follow that outlined in *Fig 7.19*. The first action on the part of site management is to assign the tasks early so that each gang or individual has time to organise and prepare for the task ahead. This should be done at the end of the week prior to the actual working week. This basis of this work allocation should be the weekly planning system. The selection of the actual targets should be from past time studies and should provide a basic time to which allowances can be added, according to the prevailing conditions, so as to provide a standard time for the target. The time target can be converted to a financial target if the firm uses this system. To illustrate this a time target of 42 bricks per hour becomes a financial target of £60 per thousand using a rate of £2.50 per hour.

EXAMPLE NUMBER	BASIS OF CALCULATION TO ALLOCATE EARNINGS		PAY BRICKLAYER £3.00 PER HR		PAY LABOURER £2.50 PER HR	
1	BASIC PAY FOR 40 HRS AT BASIC RATES		120	00	100	00
	BONUS PAY FOR 20 HRS AT 50% OF BASIC RATE		30	00	25	00
	TOTAL PAY ON EXAMPLE 1		150	00	125	00
2	BASIC PAY FOR 40 HRS AT BASIC RATES		120	00	100	00
	BONUS PAY FOR 20 HRS SHARED = (2×£30)+£25 = £85÷3 =		28	33	28	33
	TOTAL PAY ON EXAMPLE 2		148	33	128	33
3	TOTAL EARNINGS SHARED = BASIC (2×£120)+£100 = £340 + BONUS (2×£30)+£25 = £85 £425÷3 = £141.66	STANDARD BASIC PAY	120	00	100	00
		BONUS TO EQUALISE PAY	21	66	41	66
	TOTAL PAY ON EXAMPLE 3		141	66	141	66

Fig 7.20 Comparison of payment methods

Depending on the targets the work is measured and converted either to establish the total hours or the total amount earned. In the latter case the 'monetise' stage can be ignored as the bonus earnings will already be expressed in financial terms. The amount earned by the gang must then be divided between them. If for example there are two bricklayers and a labourer in a gang paid at different hourly rates how is the bonus paid? There are three different calculations based on the hours system. Assuming 60 hours, each is to be paid at 50% gearing. Example 1 in *Fig 7.20* shows the bonus as it would be paid assuming the pay of tradesmen is £3 and the labourer £2.50 per hour. Example 2 shows how it would be paid if the bonus pay was to be split equally. Example 3 shows how the bonus would be paid if all the earnings were to be split equally. Assuming the total hours to be paid is 180, being 60 hours each, the result would be as shown in *Fig 7.20*. Example 3 illustrates how the bonus has to be almost doubled for the labourer to receive the same total pay as the bricklayers. Example 3 is often the preferred method of pay for labour only sub-contractors. Example 2 is often selected as the fairest method as it maintains craft differential but equalises bonus payments.

Finally the results of all the incentive schemes should be recorded and compared as a method of cost control.

7.7 QUESTIONS ON WORK STUDY

MULTI-CHOICE QUESTIONS

1. The selection of work to be studied should be based on a combination of
   (a) the discontent of operatives and management;
   (b) economic financial and production factors;
   (c) economic, technical and human factors;
   (d) costs and delays.

2. The main aim of a time study is to:
   (a) ensure the operatives are working;
   (b) provide a basis for an incentive scheme;
   (c) improve the method of work;
   (d) manipulate the wage structure.

3. A basic time is calculated from
   (a) the observed time plus allowances;
   (b) by multiplying the observed time by their rating over 100;
   (c) by adding standard time to the observed time;
   (d) by rating all the basic times and selecting the appropriate time.

4. The following formula gives the number of observations required to meet a certain degree of accuracy:

   (a) $\dfrac{Z\sqrt{P(100-P)}}{L}$;

   (b) $\dfrac{4P(100-P)}{L^2}$;

   (c) $\dfrac{P(N-L)}{L \times L}$;

   (d) $\dfrac{2^2 + (100-P)}{L}$

5. The basic reasons for an incentive are
   (a) to provide higher wages to match outside rates;
   (b) to match wages to productivity and avoid a wage freeze;
   (c) to make the pay system as attractive as other firms;
   (d) to encourage changes of attitude and/or a course of action.

SHORT-ANSWER QUESTIONS (15-20 minutes)

1. Produce a flow process chart of the process covering all the tasks from the delivery of steel reinforcement to its fixing in the formwork. Use a hypothetical situation assuming all the work is carried out on site.

2. Describe the allowances which may be added to basic time to calculate a standard time. Give examples of the allowances you would use.

3. Describe the process for taking a field count and a gang activity sample.

4 Describe how improvements in the productivity of labour can be achieved and indicate those with which work study will prove particularly helpful.

5 A gang comprising of two bricklayers and one labourer having basic rates of pay of £3.00 and £2.50 per hour respectively. Assuming that they are given the following targets for the next weeks work:

Facing bricks	30 bricks per hour
Commons	45 bricks per hour
Concrete blocks	10 blocks per hour

and that they complete the following work:

2700 facing bricks
2700 commons, and
500 concrete blocks

Calculate the weekly earnings of each gang member using a 50% geared system for the bonus hours and the bonus only is to be shared equally.

QUESTIONS REQUIRING LONGER ANSWERS (30-45 minutes)

1 The production of a firms joinery workshop has become uncompetitive. The workshop has never been re-equippped or had its layout changed since it was built 20 years ago. Describe the action you would take to produce a system which will ensure the return of the workshop to a competitive position.

2 Describe how you would conduct a time study to produce bonus targets for a concreting gang working on floor slabs, columns, beams and staircases for a multi-storey building. Discuss how much discretion the site manager should be allowed to change the allowances to match changing conditions.

3 As a site manager you have been accused of spending too much time in the office. Describe how you would sample your time and relate it to the quantity of work that you do. Specify, the period over which you would conduct the sample, the number of observations and the degree of accuracy you would require.

4 Describe the role of work study in motivation of the construction worker. Discuss the reasons why it may be necessary to pay agreed standard rates of bonus for delays and describe how that money would be made available.

5 Assuming that the bricks stack on a 200 unit housing estate are placed as shown on *Fig 7.6* and that:
the labourer's pay is £2.50 per hour
he wheels the barrow at 2 metres per second
and each ramp costs £5 to erect

submit proposals for a more economic system of distributing the same number of bricks to the same level of scaffold.

8 Planning and programming

8.1 INTRODUCTION

The terms planning and programming are quite often used to refer to the same activity, but it should be fully understood that they are quite different processes. **Planning** is an attempt to forecast happenings taking into account trends, markets, finances, resource availability and many other factors. **Programming** is the use of techniques to time schedule those forecasts in a coordinated and economical whole.

Planning will require a certain number of predictions to be made as to the method of work to be employed, the resources to be used and the necessary finance required to fund those resources. These items may appear the most simple to forecast accurately until it is realised that they are affected by matters over which the firm has no control. These factors are the risks involved and are manifest in the economic climate, industrial relations and the actual site environmental conditions. There will obviously be a need to predict interest rates, price of materials, plant hire rates and the affects of such things on availability, delivery and quality.

The industrial relations situation may lead to disputes and stoppages followed by increases in wages. These occurrences not only apply in the construction industry but to those industries which supply the goods and services the contractor needs to purchase. The site environmental conditions will depend on the time of year, the actual weather encountered and the precautions which may be necessary to overcome them.

Programming uses the planning forecasts to schedule a multitude of predictions into a sequential chart of related activity. The relationship between each activity is based on forecast starts and completion, but not all these activities start once the preceding activity finishes some activities may start after the preceding activity is only partially complete. However, it is rarely essential for that start to take place at a particular time, therefore, there is an almost unlimited amount of flexibility in the relationship of one activity to another.

The other aspect of programming is the duration of the activities, this often depends on the resources applied to the activity. There is rarely a maximum amount of resources which will become unworkable. The extended nature of the construction site and the ability of the operatives to perform a wide variety of tasks means that flexibility with regard to duration is as large as that with relationship. Given this opportunity to manipulate resources a site manager may appear to have deviated completely from a programme and yet still be able to complete the whole project on time.

The opportunity to complete projects whilst not adhering to a programme does not detract from the benefits to be gained. Planning and programming produces the major benefit, similar to work study, of applying one's thought and actions to a singular task to the exclusion of others. Some people talk of crude programming techniques, but all the techniques are crude in that they are unable to simulate in detail that flexibility which is present on construction projects. What is often meant by this criticism is that the planning is crude.

The different programming techniques require inputs of varying detail to enable the programme to be drawn. Therefore, that technique requiring the simplest input is often termed crude, but the input may be more detailed than that for other more respected techniques. The whole point of this discourse is to demonstrate that it is the planning that is important and what is derived from the programme is directly related to the effort and detail put into the planning. There can really be no alternative, at whatever stage, to the most detailed planning possible. However, it must be remembered that the detail achieved in a programme is tempered by the time available and the cost.

8.2 PLANNING

There are two aspects of planning which must be undertaken for a project, these are staff organisation and layout planning, and the works planning. They will generally proceed together because decisions made on construction methods will affect the layout. The sequence to be followed in planning and programming the work is shown in *Fig 8.1*.

There are a number of appointments which must be made at the pre-tender stage. Firstly the contract must be allocated to an estimator who, either alone or with a team, will produce the forecasted cost in the form of a priced Bill of Quantities. There normally would also be one of the production staff assigned to the project to devise the methods of work and a planning engineer to produce the programme. To produce an accurate estimate and eliminate as much risk as possible from the tender a great deal of work is involved.

Once again time and cost are restraints on the detail which may be obtained. However, the more detailed the work the more likely the tender can be won because of the confidence that is present when judging risk. Whether such teams are used depends on the organisation of the firm. The work involved is often wasted but, if the contract is awarded, those who prepare the tender are the most well informed as to the content of the project. This fact may be used as an argument for an appointment of a site manager designate at the pre-tender stage.

The first appointments at the pre-tender stage should, where possible, be continued to the pre-contract stage. At this time, the contract having been awarded, it is necessary to consider the site organisation. Such organisations vary depending on the size and complexity of the project and the proximity of head office and the services it will provide. Therefore, there can never be one ideal organisation structure for a £1M contract, it will vary according to the factors. The most effective method of devising an organisation structure is to consider the duties and responsibilities that are required of all staff. Allocate them to job positions and decide from that list which will be carried out on site and which by head office. Such organisations can be changed so that they meet the circumstances of the contract. The site layout will also be considered in detail and has been explained in Chapter 2. These processes enable costs to be established for these continuing services.

The first step in planning is to analyse the project and define the tasks to be executed. This involves turning the drawings and bill of quantities into a number

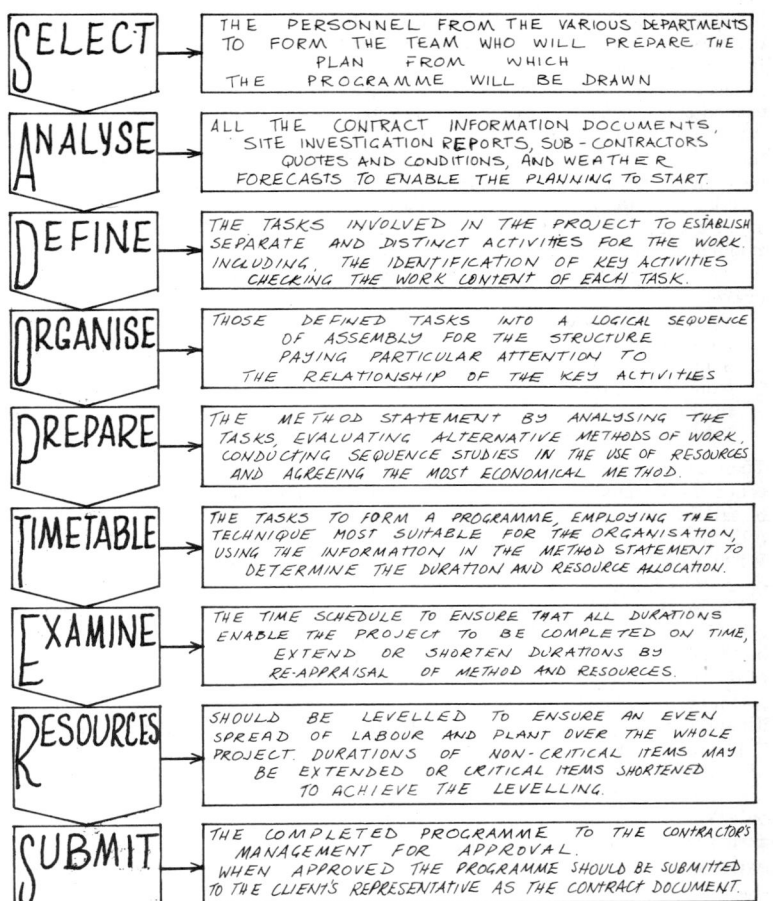

Fig. 8.1 Sequence of planning and programming the work

of operation based tasks which form the basis of the method statement and the activities to be incorporated into the programme. These tasks should be defined with regard to the practicality of separating and completing the programme to the exclusion of other tasks. It would be difficult to separate trench excavation and trench support when they would both be completed together. Similarly one might separate reinforcement from concrete in a complex retaining wall but not on a concrete slab where a simple mesh is placed just prior to the wet concrete.

There are no hard and fast rules other than the use of knowledge as to how the task should be performed. This may differ from firm to firm or between individuals but should never be taken for granted. Task definition is one of those details which, when not given adequate consideration, leads to poor results in the final programme.

The next step to be developed is the general sequence in which the tasks can be carried out. This is to enable the method statement to be written in a manner which mimics the actual erection of the building. Some sequences will differ due to the preference of site management, established practice in a firm or because of technological differences. First floor joists on a house can be built in or placed in joist hangars, therefore, the sequence will differ depending on the method used. There are many cases similar to this and they should receive the necessary explanation in the method statement. As a general guide the tasks to be incorporated in the programme should follow under the work categories given below:

Preparatory work;
Sub-structure;
Super-structure;
Non-load bearing structure and first fix;
Internal finishings and second fix;
External works.

These categories are used to produce the method statement. The sequence of tasks is not easily prepared because there are usually a number of operations which must be carried out at the same time. Reference should be made to these parallel operations in the method statement so that each is cross referenced to the other. When drawing up the sequence of tasks, it is always preferable to list 'key' operations and insert the others between them to suit the overall method.

The purposes for which a method statement is made are two-fold. Firstly it is to coordinate the effort of the contractors project team in operating to produce the building using an agreed method. Secondly it provides each section or department of the firm with detailed information. This is particularly true in the case of the personnel and plant departments. The method statement is much more than a task list and therefore it should fully describe the method of carrying out the work.

The format of a method statement may vary in different organisations. Quite often it includes output and duration for each task. Some organisations prefer to draw up a separate activities list giving this information but it is, however, still based on the method contained in the statement. The method statement must always contain the task name, quantity of work, method of construction, plant required and labour to be employed. An example of discrete items of a method statement is given in *Fig 8.2*.

In order to prepare a method statement as shown, the work sequences must be considered in detail. This process may be illustrated by considering the formwork for the casting of the superstructure of a multi-storey building. The sequence must be worked out as to how many column forms and how much slab formwork is required, the number of uses, its movement pattern from floor to floor, the time required before striking and so forth. These detailed sequence studies may require a small programme in themselves in order to determine the optimum solution.

8.3 PROGRAMMING

The programming of work is carried out by detailed planning to produce an overall programme of operations. This is later refined in stage and weekly

METHOD STATEMENT

Item No	Description of Operation	Quantity	Construction Method	Plant & Equipment	Labour	Duration	Remarks
1 1/1	Preparatory Work Site boundary Fencing	1040 linear metres	Excavate post holes at 2440 centres using post hole auger attachment. Erect 100 x 100 fence posts to a height of 2250 above ground level with 3 No. triangular rails. Set old plywood formwork 2440 by 1220 sheets 150 in the ground and secure to rails.	Wheeled backacter with post hole auger attachment. Hammers 2 Saws 2	3 labs		Ensure the exact boundary line as established is used.
2 2/1	Sub-Structure Strip top soil	1500 m²	Top soil to be removed to a depth of 200 mm and 60 m³ to be stored in stockpiles on the N.E. corner of the site - 25 metres away as shown on drawing 7984/1/SL/21. The excavation will be by crawler tractor fitted with a 1 m³ 4 in 1 bucket. The remainder of the soil is to be loaded into vehicles and deposited on the southland site for reuse. The vehicles will remove soil throughout the site strip process and when absent the tractor will continue to stockpile in the N.E. corner. Liaison on levels, area and direction of vehicles to be carried out by the Site Engineer.	Tracked crawler tractor with 4 in 1 bucket 1m³ capacity. 3 No. removal vehicles side height to suit tractor dump height. Level, theodolite, pegs and tapes.	Site Eng. 1 lab 1 op.		See item 6/8 for the use of stockpiled soil.

Fig 8.2 Example of method statement items

3	Superstructure					
3/1	Concrete Form-work	Columns To be 19 mm plywood, stiffened by 50 mm x 35 mm softwood at sides and fixed together with steel crate bands at 300 x 400 mm centres. Upstands of 100 mm to be formed after floor slab casting. Vertical stability to be provided by 2 No. push pull props fixed to battens on formwork and floor. One third of floor area columns cast at each pour.	33 Columns per floor 432 total	12 sets of column forms. Banding machine and 500 linear metres of steel band with 3500 joint clips 50 push-pull props	Erect 4 Jnrs 2 Labs	
		Slabs To be proprietory formwork system using steel framed panels 1200 x 600 mm and make up sections. Support from variable span steel beams supported on adjustable steel props. Floor slab to be cast in areas one-fifth length by full width utilising one full floor set of formwork and two extra bays of propping.	5 bays 10 m x 12 m 7 bays of propping Total area 8400 m²	675 m² of formwork with support beams props. Two extra bays of propping for 240 m²	Strip 2 Jnrs 1 Lab	
		General Formwork to be transported by crane. Cleaned and mould oiled by labourer. Repairs to be made in workshop located on site and transported at GL by dumper.		Tower crane with box cradle for slinging. 0.5 m³ dumper.	Crane Operator 2 Slingers 1 driver	see item 1/7 for crane see item 1/9 for workshop
3/18	Brickwork infill panels	The brickwork is to be constructed from an externally placed scaffold. All bricks to be transported by forklift to the materials hoist and raised to the required level. They will be moved by a manually operated hydraulic lifting trolley of 1 tonne capacity from the hoist into the building and broken down and distributed to the bricklayers by the labourers. Mortar to be supplied from central mixing plant.	300,000 bricks 21,500 per floor	Hoist to take a maximum load of 1 tonne with space to be loaded by fork-lift with a pallet. 1 hydraulic lifting trolley 1 tonne capacity 3 barrows to distribute bricks mixer (see 1/2)	2 No. 4/2 gangs 1 labourer to unload hoist 1 operator	See items 4/2 for blockwork see items 6/5 for external brickwork see item 3/16 for scaffold see item 1/12 for mortar mixing

Fig 8.2 (continued)

4		Non-load Bearing Structure and First Fix				
4/2	Blockwork	5,180 m²	This operation to commence on the ground floor and continue upwards. Blocks to be laid in gauged mortar off a tower scaffold 1.3 m high. Mortar to be supplied from central mixing plant. Door frames to be positioned by joiners and braced to floor, block layers are to fix a frame clamp at every second course. 12 mm margins are to be left on each side for plastering. Blocks to lower floor supplied by forklift, for upper floors by materials hoist with removal and distribution by manually operated hydraulic lift.	Hoist (see 3/18) Trolley (see 3/18) Mixer (see 1/2) 2 No. barrows	2 Jnrs 4 Blyrs 2 Labs.	See item 3/18 and 6/5 for brickwork See item 1/12 for mortar mixing
4/13	Services Carcassing	250 lin metres chase	All conduit and pipe runs must be set out ready for chasing at least 3 days before required. Chasing to be carried out by electric powered chase cutting machine. Position of holes in structure are to be provided at the pretender stage. All conduit and pipework must be fixed before the following finishes commence. (All sub-contractors to be informed of conditions).	Sub-contractor 1 chase cutting machine	Attendance 1 Lab.	Holes in structure if **not** shown drawing to be approved by structural engineer. See 1/4 for power provision
5		Internal Finishings and Second Fix				
5/4	Plastering	10,758 m²	To follow all carcassing and fixing.small tower scaffolds 1.3 m high to be provided (one per plasterer). 50 gallon water drum plus a hose water supply to be laid to the building. Mixing to be at the workplace by hand for backing and final coat. All tasks on one floor to be completed before the next floor commences. Delivery of materials to be by materials hoist.	2 No. 50 gallon drums Hoist (see 3/18)	4 Plastrs or sub contrs	see 1/15·for water supply

Fig 8.2 (continued)

5/10	Floor Tiling	8,400 m²	Floor tiling to follow the completion of decoration (item 5/20). Screeds to be cleaned and if necessary dried prior to the arrival of sub-contractors. Each room should be kept clear of workmen whilst the sub-contractor proceeds. Hoist required to deliver materials.	Space heaters if required.	Sub-Contrs Attendance 1 Lab
6	External Works				
6/3	Access Ways	4890 m²	Excavation to be carried out by tracked excavator with 1 m³ 4 in 1 bucket. The formation to be compacted by Tandem vibrating roller, 1000 mm hardcore blinded by 12 mm max size all in aggregate rolled to a smooth surface. Concrete edging to be placed at each side and backed with concrete. One tack coat to be applied using hand operated emulsion sprayer. Fine cold asphalt to be spread by hand and rolled with smooth wheel roller. Dumper to transport material.	Tracked excavator 1 m³ 4 in 1 bucket 1 Tandem vibrating roller 1.5 tonnes. 1 2½ tonne smooth wheel roller. 1 Dumper. 0.5 m. 3 rakes and spreader boards. Hand operated emulsion sprayer.	3 ops 1 dvr 3 labs

Fig 8.2 (continued)

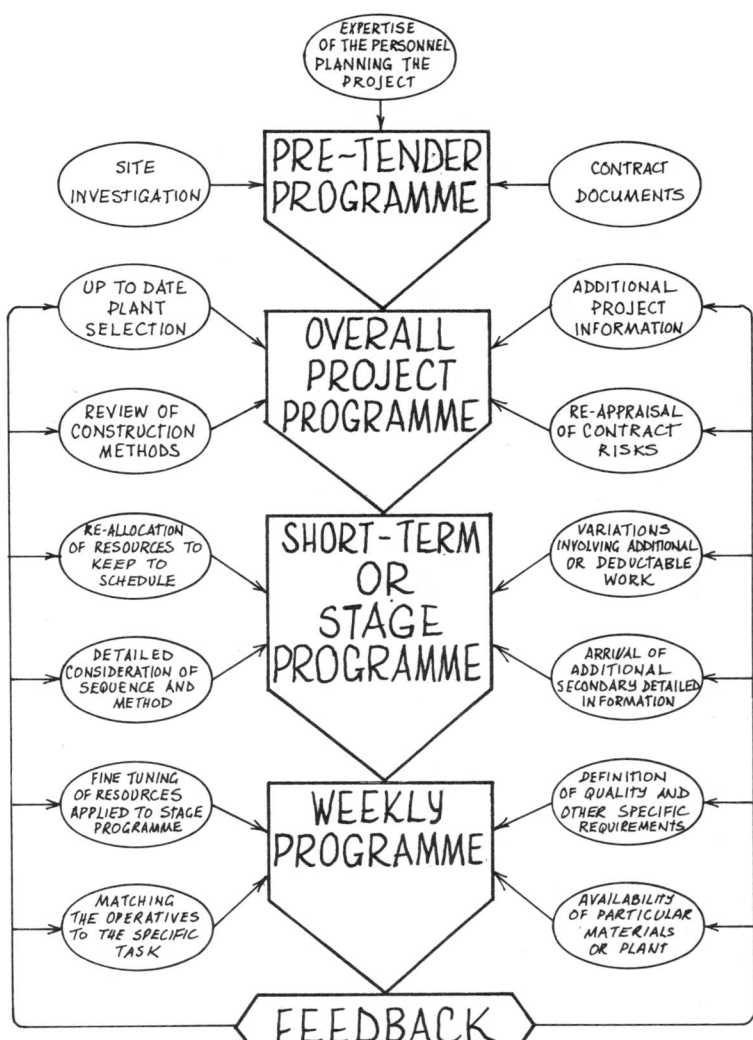

Fig 8.3 Evaluation of the programmes

programmes in order to finely tune the resources to take account of unforeseen difficulties. The evolution of the programmes from basic pre-tender to the weekly employment sheet is shown in *Fig 8.3*.

In the short time available between receipt of the invitation and submission of tender a programme has to be produced. It may involve quite detailed consideration of work methods, site conditions and sub-contract works, but the actual programme will consist of broad categories of work covering key operations. The objective of the pretender programme is to coordinate the schedule of work for the different departments. It indicates to the estimator the time required on site to complete operations, and to personnel the amount and type of labour required. The programme also enables provisional timings to be given to sub-contractors. A pre-tender programme brings together the different departments to form a team which has a common plan for the costing of the project. Once a tender is accepted and the contract awarded the pretender programme can be reconsidered.

The overall constructon programme is prepared using all the detailed planning which was done at the pre-tender stage. It would take account of any additional information received and be subjected to a detailed reappraisal by the designated production team. This programme is to be provided to the architect and is used to measure progress at monthly intervals. It is generally drawn up using broad categories of work and if drawn without computer assistance should be limited to between 50 and 100 activities. The less activities the easier to produce but the effectiveness is somewhat reduced.

This programme should indicate the earliest start dates and the latest finish dates for each activity giving some flexibility as to actual performance duration. The overall programme should also indicate the latest dates for the ordering and delivery of materials and the latest date that the secondary detailed information is required from the architect. The attention of the architect should be drawn to these dates by a letter accompanying the programme. The method of signposting these dates is shown in *Fig 8.4*.

The stage or short term programme is used to provide more detail for the production team on site. The short term programme is drawn up for a period of between 5 and 8 weeks; being redrawn after 4 or 6 weeks so as to provide a link with the previous programme. Stage programmes differ in that they may cover shorter or longer periods and are based on a stage of the project. Therefore, a stage programme for a multi-storey building could be for 16 weeks covering the sub-structure another for 20 weeks for the superstructure but a stage finishing programme for each floor could be 3 or 4 weeks. These stage programmes can be used concurrently so that a number of programmes can be in use at one time.

The link between these stage programmes is the overall programme. The details required in this programme will take account of the detail in the method statement and any changed circumstances. If some activities are behind schedule, the stage or short term programme allows for a reallocation of resources to the activities where they are most needed. The detailed difference between the overall and short term programme can be seen by using concrete as an example. An activity on the overall programme may be briefly concrete slab and foundations to basement; this would become a number of activities in the stage or short term programme. They may be concrete to pier foundations, formwork to Section 1 of slab, reinforcement to Section 1, concrete Section 1, formwork to Section 2 and so on, so that the programme is a week by week indication of the work to be completed.

The weekly programme is the device used to allocate tasks to individual operatives or gangs and is usually prepared on a Thursday or Friday on site. The Site Manager plans the work based on the amount completed in the previous four days. The detail for the floor slab may now be down to bays 1, 3, 5 and 7 in Section 1 on certain days. This programming can be given on the labour

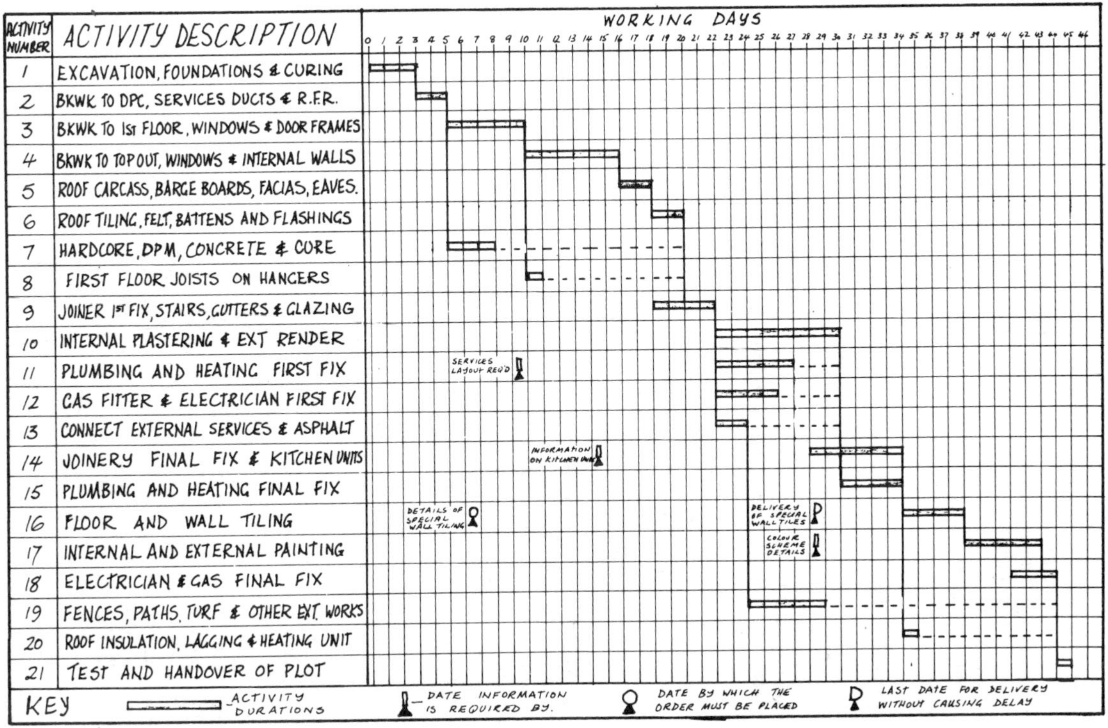
ACTIVITY NUMBER
ACTIVITY DESCRIPTION
WORKING DAYS
0 1 2 3 4 5 6 7 8 9 10 11 12 13 14 15 16 17 18 19 20 21 22 23 24 25 26 27 28 29 30 31 32 33 34 35 36 37 38 39 40 41 42 43 44 45 46
1 EXCAVATION, FOUNDATIONS & CURING
2 BKWK TO DPC, SERVICES DUCTS & R.F.R.
3 BKWK TO 1ST FLOOR, WINDOWS & DOOR FRAMES
4 BKWK TO TOP OUT, WINDOWS & INTERNAL WALLS
5 ROOF CARCASS, BARGE BOARDS, FACIAS, EAVES.
6 ROOF TILING, FELT, BATTENS AND FLASHINGS
7 HARDCORE, DPM, CONCRETE & CORE
8 FIRST FLOOR JOISTS ON HANGERS
9 JOINER 1ST FIX, STAIRS, GUTTERS & GLAZING
10 INTERNAL PLASTERING & EXT RENDER
11 PLUMBING AND HEATING FIRST FIX
12 GAS FITTER & ELECTRICIAN FIRST FIX
13 CONNECT EXTERNAL SERVICES & ASPHALT
14 JOINERY FINAL FIX & KITCHEN UNITS
15 PLUMBING AND HEATING FINAL FIX
16 FLOOR AND WALL TILING
17 INTERNAL AND EXTERNAL PAINTING
18 ELECTRICIAN & GAS FINAL FIX
19 FENCES, PATHS, TURF & OTHER EXT. WORKS
20 ROOF INSULATION, LAGGING & HEATING UNIT
21 TEST AND HANDOVER OF PLOT
SERVICES LAYOUT REQ'D
INFORMATION ON KITCHEN UNITS
DETAILS OF SPECIAL WALL TILING
DELIVERY OF SPECIAL WALL TILES
COLOUR SCHEME DETAILS
KEY
ACTIVITY DURATIONS
DATE INFORMATION IS REQUIRED BY.
DATE BY WHICH THE ORDER MUST BE PLACED
LAST DATE FOR DELIVERY WITHOUT CAUSING DELAY

Fig 8.4 Bar chart programme for two house plot

employment sheet shown in *Fig 5.10*. However, on simple projects where a small number of operatives are involved a discussion with the chargehand followed by an oral directive may be sufficient.

The other method which may be used is the blackboard. The plan of the building is drawn and the tasks are allocated using coloured chalk. This board then remains as a programme which can be consulted by all the supervisors as required. Whichever method is employed it is of paramount importance that the site manager checks that all the resources are available for the work to start and that arrangements are made for distribution to the workplace.

8.4 PROGRAMMING TECHNIQUES

The techniques used to place all the activities in a logical sequence to a time scale is a matter of choice for the planning engineer or the firm's organisation. The technique selected may in any case finally result in a bar chart. It should be remembered that the objective of a programme is to communicate the plan and therefore should be easily understood by all the users.

The bar chart or as it is sometimes called the 'Gantt' chart, is simply a number of bars drawn on a time scale to show the duration of each activity. The charts can be used to portray much more information than just the activities and these are included in the bar chart shown in *Fig 8.4*. The duration of each activity will depend on the construction method adopted and the gang size or plant employed.

However, there is a more intangible element which may be termed risk. This risk element takes account of inclement weather, plant breakdown, material and labour delays and other factors which may affect performance. When plotting the activities it is usually prudent to plan a target completion at about 10% before actual contract completion is due. This final period is used to clean up and remedy any minor discrepancies and if necessary to provide a buffer. The amount of buffer will depend on the risk element included in the durations.

The use of the critical path method (CPM) is reputed to provide more information with regard to key activities and the inter-relationship between these and other activities. This method of network analysis produces an arrow diagram consisting of events depicted by circles or nodes and arrows which represent the activities. The different types of nodes and the configuration to indicate different relationships are shown in *Fig 8.5*. The durations are placed below the arrows and the activity descriptions above the arrow.

For the purpose of effective communication, activity descriptions rather than a code should always be used. Once the durations have been allocated the earliest and latest event times can be established. This is done by adding the durations from the beginning to establish the earliest time an event can occur. Any node having two paths should have one followed until a node is reached having two activities entering. The other path should be numbered and the greatest sum of durations for either path entered as the earliest event time (EET).

To establish the latest event times (LET) the last event is numbered with its EET as the LET and then all durations are deducted along the paths to the beginning. When more than one arrow is meeting a node the smallest remaining sum is used as the LET. This numbering is shown on the critical path network shown in *Fig 8.6* which depicts the same activities as the bar chart example. The use of dummies and real time dummies are shown in both *Figs 8.5* and *8.6*. Details of event slack, activity float and critical path will be given later in section 8.5.

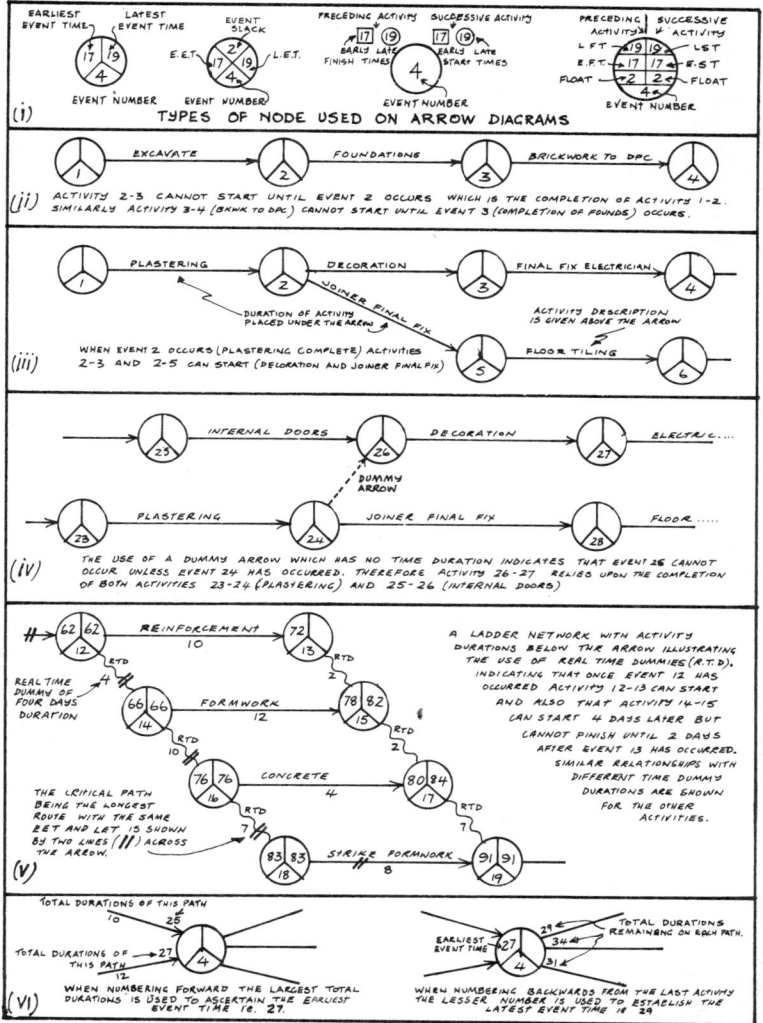

Fig 8.5 Basics of CPM network analysis

The other form of network analysis is precedence diagramming. This technique has one basic difference in that the activities are depicted by boxes; and arrows are used to indicate flow. Different boxes are used depending on the information required, the method used for all examples will be that known as cascade planning

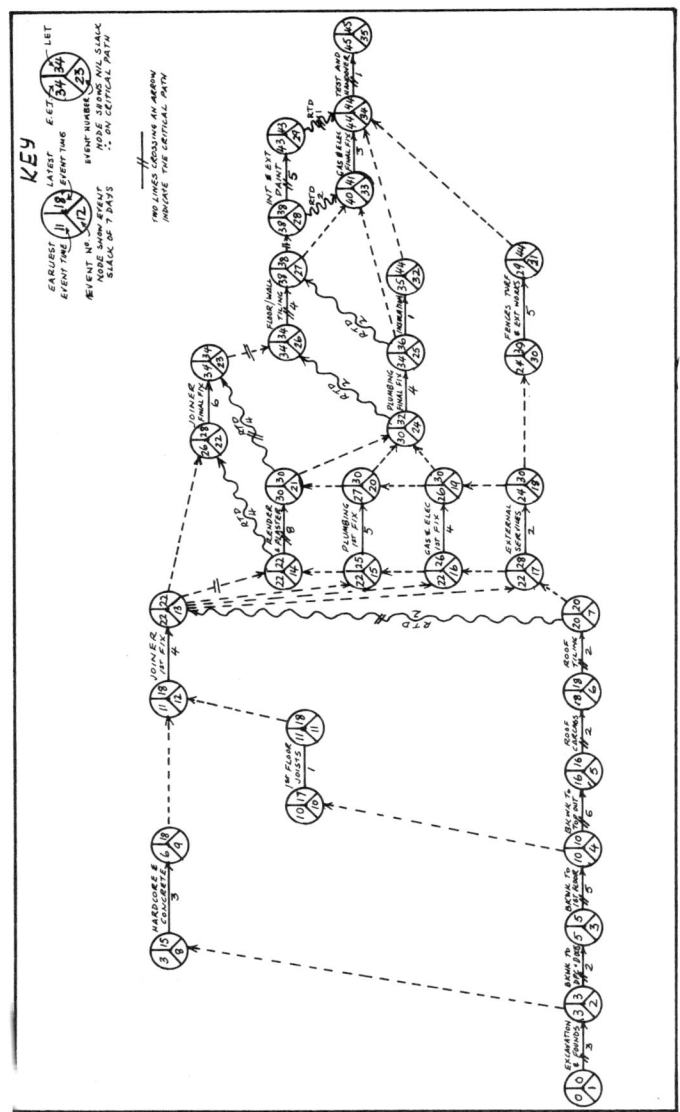

Fig 8.6 Critical path network for a two house plot

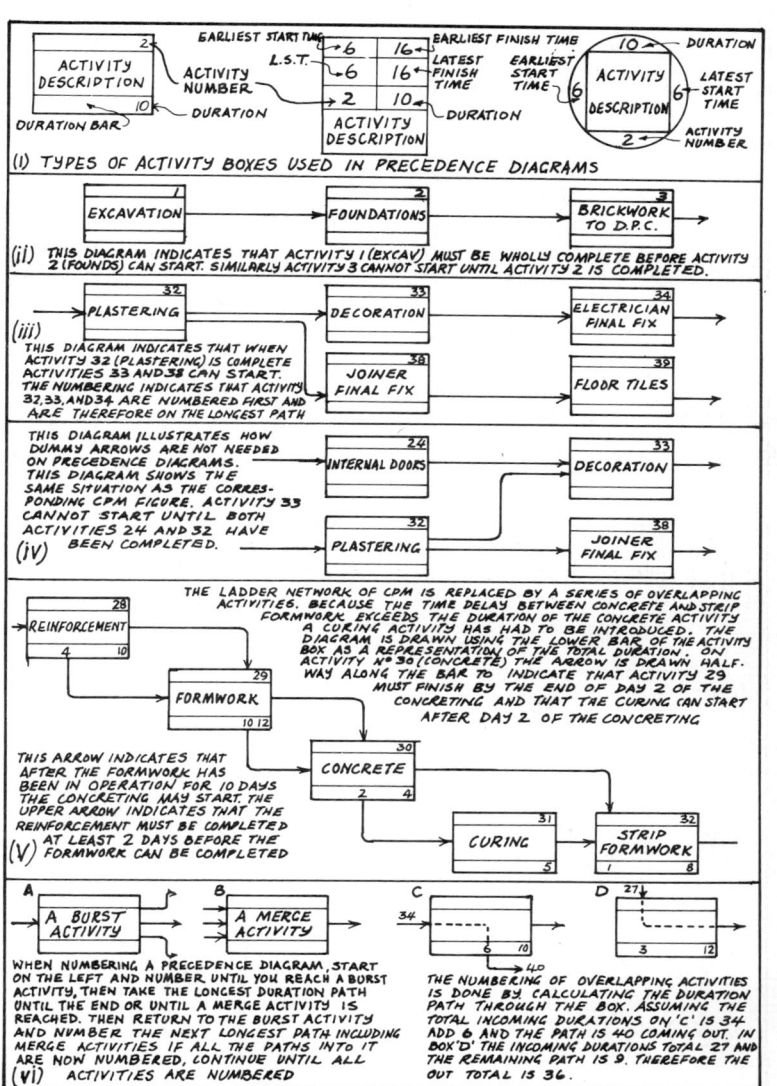

Fig 8.7 The basics of precedence diagram network analysis

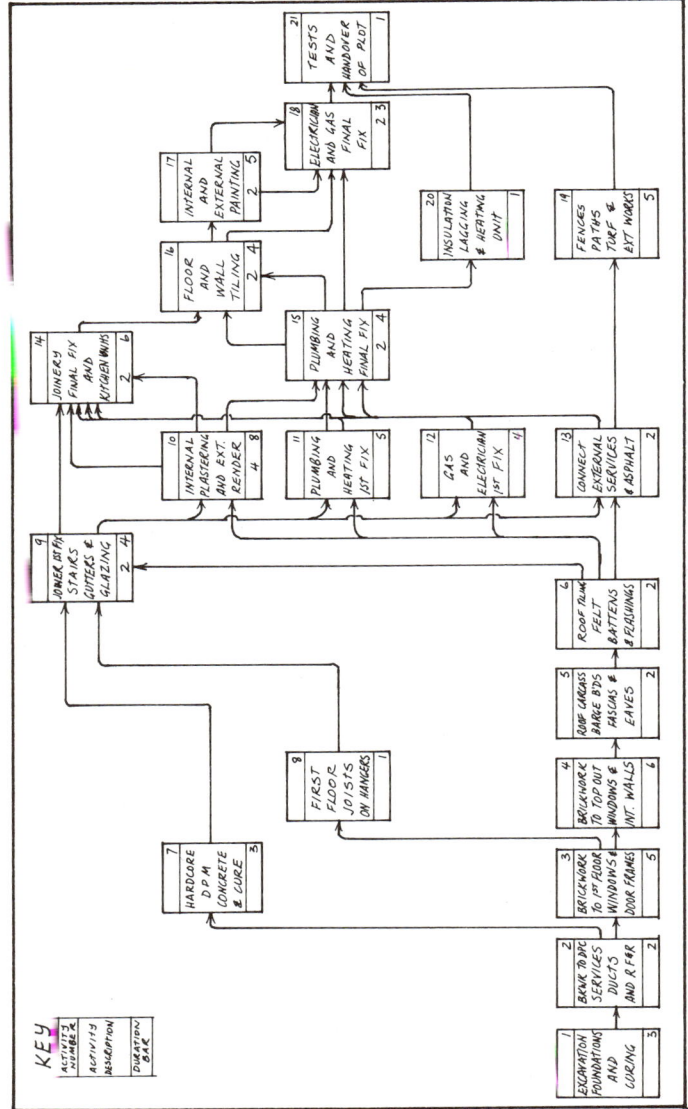

Fig 8.8 Precedence diagram for a two house plot

which produces a bar chart as the end product. The method of depicting the relationships between activities is shown in *Fig 8.7*.

When using overlap activities it is preferable to use the duration bar as representing the duration and arrows leaving and entering should be placed at the proportionately correct point. The numbering is carried out by starting at the beginning and numbering along the longest path of any burst activity until either a merge activity or the last activity box is reached. Before a merge can be numbered all arrows leading into it must be numbered.

In determining the longest path the durations may have to be added and the method of adding the overlapping activities is shown in *Fig 8.7* (vi). The numbering is sequential and is used as the order to draw the bar chart. An example of the drawing and numbering of the precedence diagram is shown in *Fig 8.8*. The activities and the activity numbers are those which relate directly to the bar chart shown in *Fig 8.4*.

The advantages and disadvantages are not clearly defined as bar charts produced from network analysis are often more advantageous than the original network. The bar chart itself is easily prepared, understood and amended. It has good presentation, is flexible and easily re-drawn. Unless drawn from a network the bar chart will not identify critical operations or the non-critical activities. The relationships between activities are not usually well depicted and there may be a lack of detail for cost and progress control. The critical path method separates the sequencing from the time scheduling and clearly shows interrelationships. The effects of delays and alternative decisions can be forecast.

The technique highlights key operations and allows detailed control mechanisms to be used. The disadvantages are that the even more complex inter-relationships on site cannot be truly reflected in the arrow diagrams and it is difficult to up-date. The networks are not easily understood and the flexibility is restricted without further programming work. The precedence diagram method produces a network which is more easily understood than the arrow diagram, but has all the disadvantages of the critical path method unless the presentation is done by producing a bar chart.

8.5 RESOURCE OPTIMISATION

The scheduling and levelling of resources can be achieved by three methods. The first is to use the available spare time to space the activities out, second to extend activities by reducing the resources allocated or third to shorten or crash activities by increasing the resources.

On any construction project there will be operations which may be started and completed over a period of time which greatly exceeds its duration. There are also certain activities which must be completed or they will delay the project completion. The critical path analysis shown in *Fig 8.6* indicates the critical path and event slack in each node. Where the EET and the LET are the same there is no slack and the activities with these nodes at the start and finish are usually critical. When the EET and LET are dissimilar the amount of slack is the difference between them. The term slack is applied to events and these can be converted into activity float.

As an example take the plumbing first fix activity in *Fig 8.6*. Event number 15

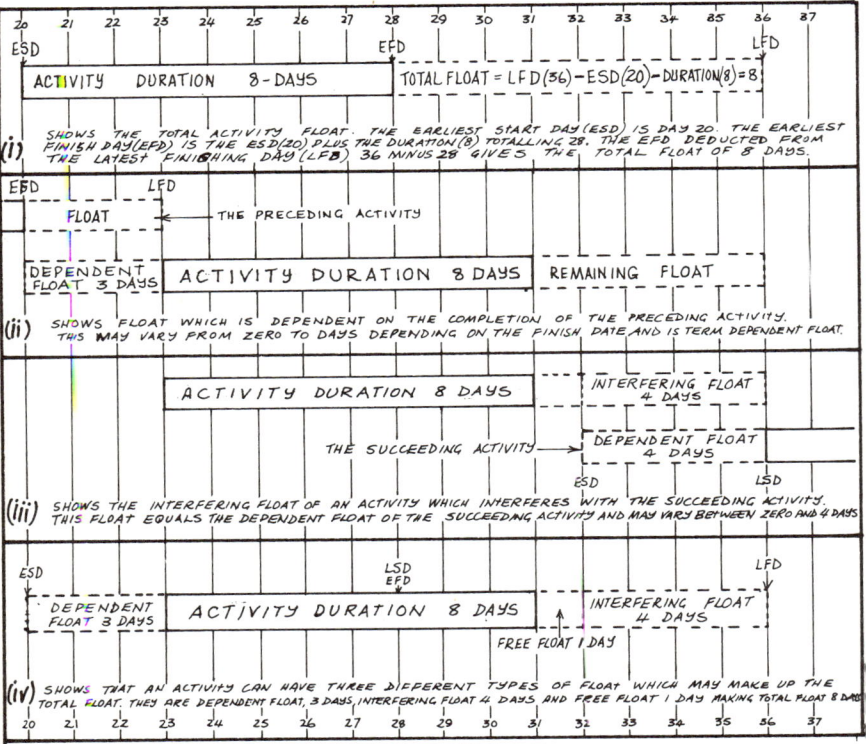

Fig 8.9 Types of float

indicates an EET of 22 which becomes the earliest start day (ESD) of the activity. Event number 20 indicates an LET of 30 which becomes the latest finishing day (LFD) for plumbing first fix. The activity has a duration of 5 days and can be started on day 22 and finished on day 30, therefore 5 days working has to be completed in 8 days. This provides float by LFD (30) minus the ESD (22) minus the duration (5) equalling 3 days. This float is total float and much will depend on the float available on preceding and succeeding activities.

The types of float available are shown in *Fig 8.9.* This can be demonstrated by Activity 13 and Activity 19 on the bar chart. Activity 13 is shown to have 6 days float up to the critical path between events 10 and 14. Activity 19 is dependent upon it and it will only have 9 days float, therefore the float is interfering in the case of Activity 13 and in the case of Activity 19 it has 6 days dependent float among its 15 days total float. This 6 days float may not be used and therefore at the completion of Activity 13 the free float available on Activity 19 can be calculated.

The advantages of the cascade method of programming can be seen by this additional information. The cascade down the uppermost steps of the bar chart is the critical path as all the items forming it have no float. This float is used to level the resources as shown in *Fig 8.10*. The first programme shows the labour resource unlevelled, the programme below shows the resources levelled by using float. Although the float is shown on the second programme it is no longer available unless the resources are increased above the 4 bricklayers and 2 labourers shown.

In *Fig 8.10* the programme could be levelled by allocating resources of just 2 bricklayers and 1 labourer. This will effectively double the time available and providing the overall float available allows this, it may be the best method. Similarly if the activities are critical they could be levelled by doubling the workforce to 8 bricklayers and 4 labourers, allowing each activity to be completed in an end-on situation. Within the total time of 66 days there are 32 days with a 2 and 1 gang and 46 days with a 4 and 2 gang. If an 8 and 4 gang were employed, theoretically the 2 and 1 gang days could be reduced to 8 days and the 4 and 2 gang days reduced to 23 days, making a total of 31 days which would easily fit into the programme.

However, this sort of increase in resources brings problems and increased costs. Firstly, the most economic gang size should always be used for planning and therefore to crash the activities would normally increase costs. The increase in production involves the use of more materials and other resources over a time period. This indicates that the site management has to plan more work, more materials delivery and therefore the workload is increased. Therefore, a doubling of the resources above the optimum does not always means a doubling of output and may require increased supervision.

The levelling of plant resources is usually an easier proposition as machines are available on short term hire and therefore a minor increase over a short period may be acceptable. The levelling is carried out in the same way as for labour by levelling all the plant required along the bottom of the programme. Once this has been completed and all the available float is used, the employment of the plant on each task should be considered.

Quite often plant of a certain capacity is selected and used for the largest task but it also performs all the other related tasks. Consider the hire of the larger machine for a short period and the use of a smaller machine on the related tasks. Similarly, when concrete mixers may have demands beyond their capacity do not increase the size, simply order ready mixed concrete to supplement for the peak period.

8.6 PROGRESS REPORTING

The programme represents a predicted work flow which, if adhered to, will result in the successful completion of the project. In order to measure the progress on a project comparisons need to be made against the predicted output.

The comparisons are made for the purpose of exercising control. This does not mean that the chastisement of staff should take place if progress fails to meet the predicted standards. The purpose of control is to indicate to the firm's management that action is required if the programme is to be followed. Such action is usually the outcome of an enquiry as to the reasons for insufficient progress. This enquiry will lead to a re-allocation of existing resources or the input of increased resources.

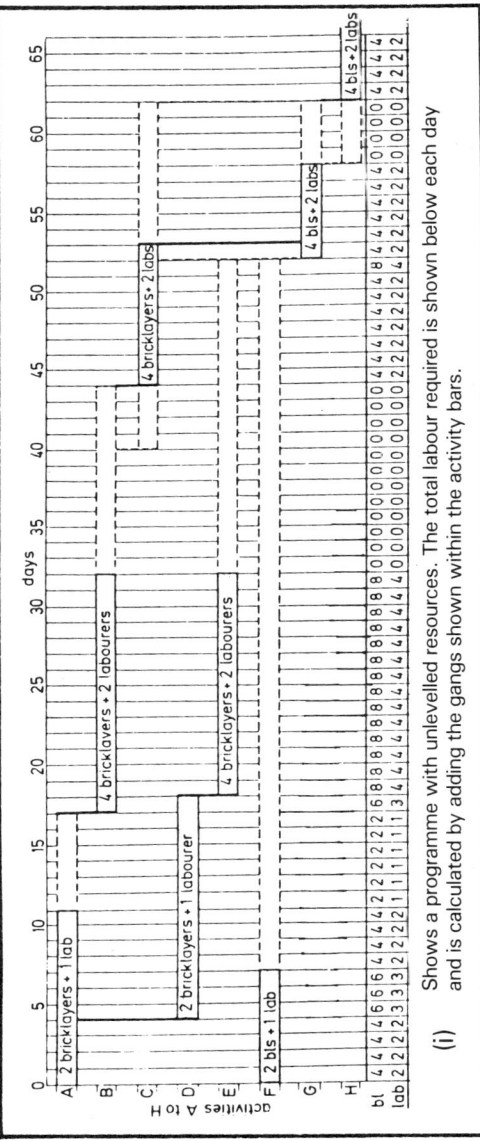

Fig 8.10 Levelling of the labour resource

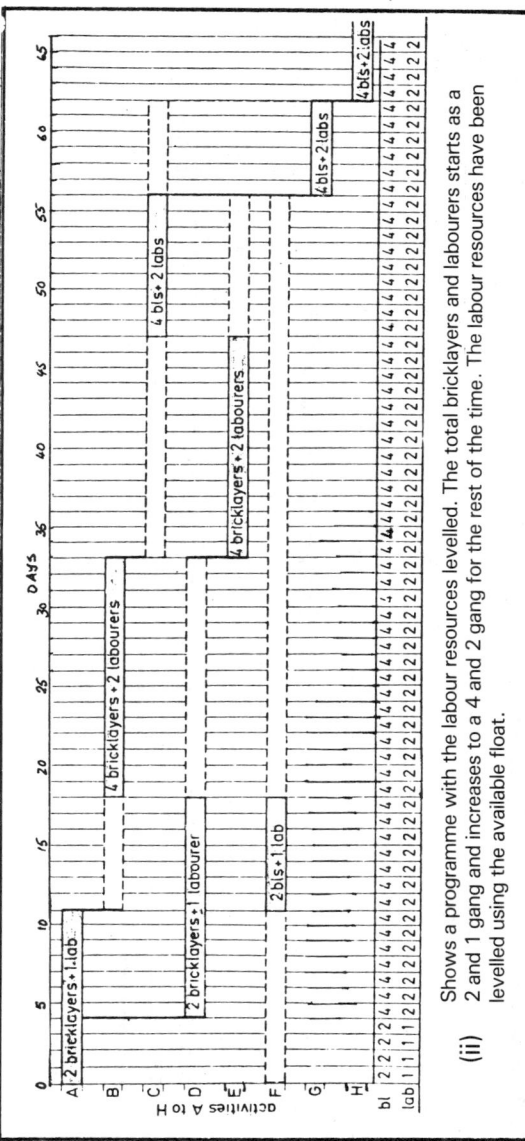

Fig 8.10 *(continued)*

THIS TWO LINE METHOD USE A SHADING CODE FOR EACH WEEK. THE UPPER BAR INDICATES THE PLANNED ACTIVITY START AND FINISH. THE LOWER BAR INDICATES THE WORK COMPLETED PROPORTIONATELY USING THE SHADE CODE TO INDICATE THE PERCENTAGE PROGRESS IN THE FIRST WEEK. ACTIVITY 1 WAS COMPLETED BUT ACTIVITY 2 WAS ONLY HALF COMPLETED. IN WEEK 3 WORK ON ACTIVITY 3 WAS COMPLETED, BEHIND SCHEDULE BUT ACTIVITY 4 WAS COMPLETED AHEAD OF SCHEDULE AND A TWENTY FIVE PER CENT PROGRESS WAS REPORTED ON ACTIVITY FIVE. WEEK 4 WAS A POOR WEEK WORK ONCE AGAIN FALLING BEHIND.

(i) TWO-BAR SYSTEM FOR RECORDING PROGRESS IN EACH WEEK

Fig 8.11 Recording progress on a bar chart

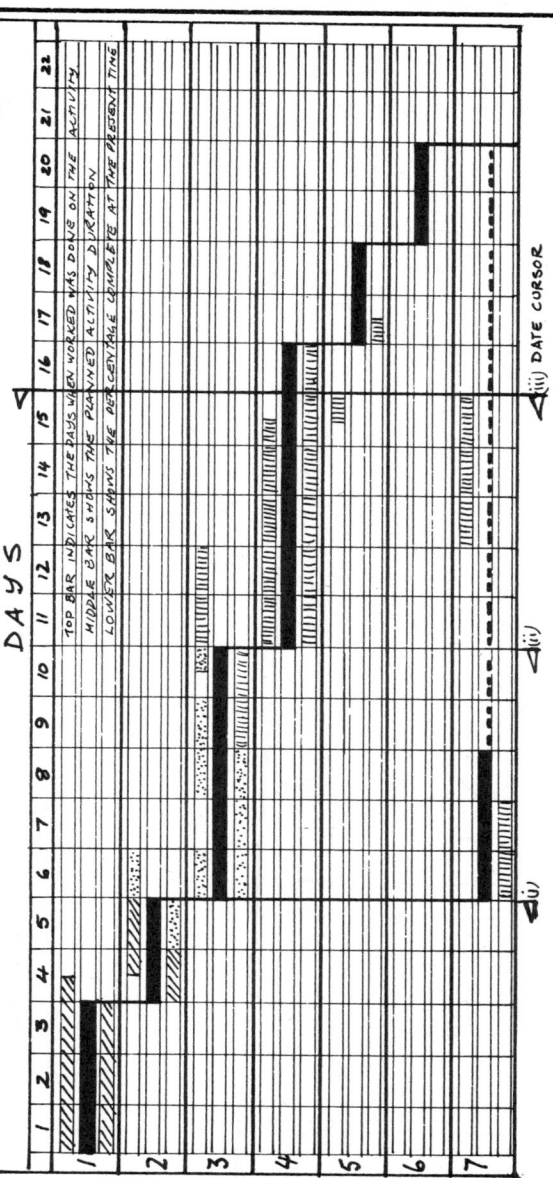

THIS THREE LINE METHOD DOES NOT NEED A SHADING CODE BUT IT IS USED HERE TO SHOW THE POSITION AS IT WOULD BE AT THE END OF EACH DATE CURSOR LOCATION. AT THE END OF DAY 5, THE FIRST DATE CURSOR LOCATION, SHOWS ON THE TOP BAR THE DAYS WORKED ON ACTIVITY 1, i.e. 3½ DAYS WHICH IS A HALF DAY LONGER TO COMPLETE THAN PREDICTED. THE 1½ DAYS SPENT ON ACTIVITY 2 HAS PRODUCED A 50% COMPLETION SHOWN ON THE LOWER OF THE THREE BARS. THIS ACTIVITY IS NOW ONE DAY BEHIND SCHEDULE. AT THE END OF DAY 10 THE 2ND CURSOR POSITION SHOWS THAT ACTIVITY 2 WAS COMPLETED ON DAY 6, ON ACTIVITY 3 THERE WAS NO WORK ON DAY 7 OR, ON THE MORNING OF DAY 10 BUT PROGRESS WAS 60%. AT THE THIRD CURSOR POSITION ACTIVITY 3 IS COMPLETED ON THE FIRST TWO DAYS, ACTIVITY 4 IS COMPLETED IN ONLY 4½ DAYS WHILST ACTIVITY 5 IS STARTED AHEAD OF SCHEDULE AND 3 DAYS WORK IS DONE ON ACTIVITY 7. THIS LAST CURSOR POSITION SHOWS A GOOD FINAL WEEK ON WHICH WORK HAS BEEN SEIZED AND IS NOW JUST AHEAD OF SCHEDULE.

(ii) THREE-BAR SYSTEM FOR RECORDING DAYS WORKED AND PROGRESS.

Fig 8.11 (continued)

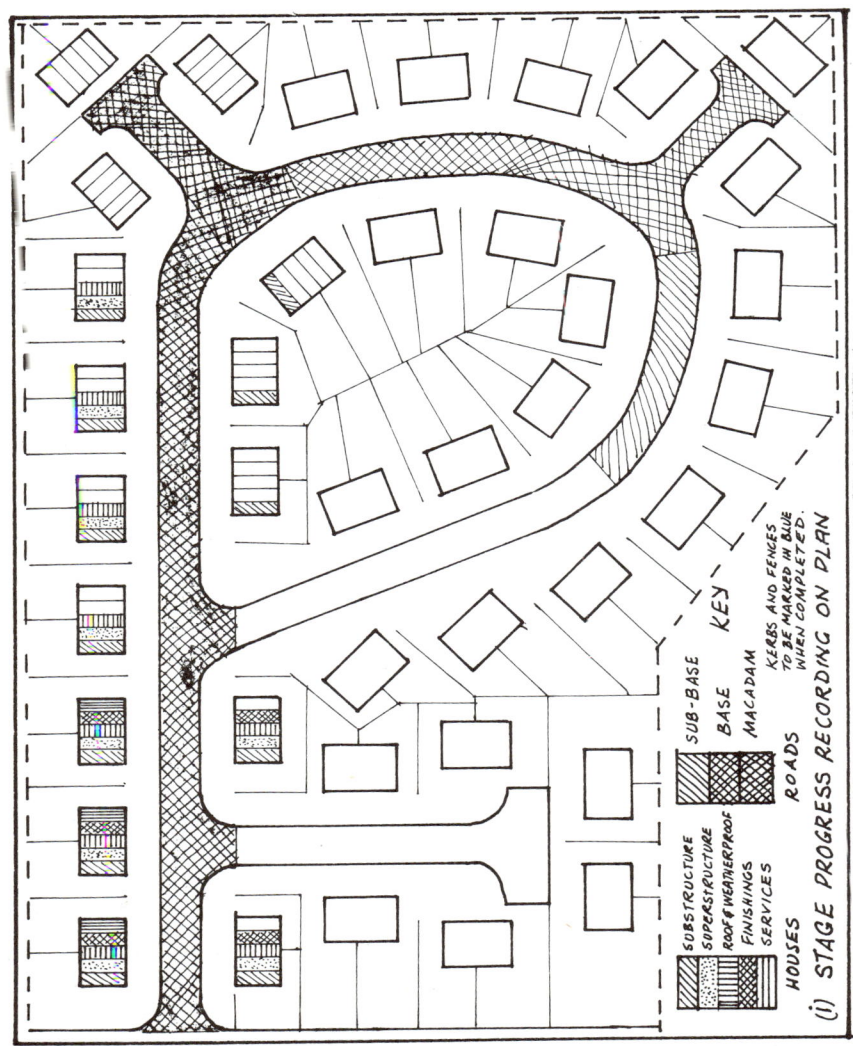

ACTIVITIES	\	1	2	3	4	5	6	7	8	9	10	11	12	...	43

PLOT NUMBER

Activity	1	2	3	4	5	6	7	8	9
1	1/2	2/2	3/2	1/2	1/2	18/2	19/2	20/2	21/2
2	3/2	4/2	5/2	1/2	1/2	10/2	11/2	12/2	13/2
3	10/2	11/2	12/2	18/2	21/2	22/2	8/2	9/3	4/3
4	18/2	19/2	21/2	27/2	1/3	7/2	8/3	10/3	11/3
5	19/2	21/2	24/2	25/2	4/3	1/3	2/3	11/3	13/3
6	22/2	24/2	3/3	25/3	6/3	8/3	11/3		
7	8/2	10/2	12/2	1/3	13/2	14/3			
8	1/2	19/2	17/2	18/2	15/3	17/3	19/2		
9	2/6	3/3	22/2	7/3	8/3				
10	8/3	19/3	19/3	14/3	24/3				
11	7/3	9/3	19/3	1/3	15/3				
12	7/3	9/3	10/3	11/3	14/3				
13	4/3	7/3	9/3	11/3	14/3				
14	14/3	16/3	16/3	17/3	19/3				
15	14/3	17/3	18/3	19/3					
16	27/3	23/3	24/3						
17	27/3	28/3	30/3	1/4					
18	30/3	24/3	4/4						
19	27/3	28/3	2/4						
20	22/3	24/3	3/3						
21	1/4	4/4	5/4						
DEPOSIT									
SOLD									
HANDOVER									

INSERT DATE OF COMPLETION OF EACH ACTIVITY FOR EACH PLOT

(ii) NUMERICAL RECORDING OF TOTAL COMPLETIONS BY DATES

Fig 8.12 (continued)

It is most unlikely that any construction project will run entirely in accordance with the programme. Some activities will be ahead and some behind schedule. The moment of progress recording should always show on the document. In the case of bar charts a date cursor should be placed on the actual day. This is usually a red tape or string fixed with drawing pins from the top to bottom of the programme. On other types a date should be inserted in pencil and changed as required.

The method of recording progress should be a reflection of the detail involved in planning. Crude planning requires only a crude form of progress reporting; detailed planning requires detailed reporting. The most used form of programme is the bar chart and it involves either a two or three bar system as shown in *Fig 8.11*. The two bar system can become complex because of the need to use different shade codes or colours for each week.

A simpler method is the three bar system which records more information and does not require different colours. The top bar indicates the days when work was undertaken on the activity. The lower bar is used to indicate the percentage complete using the planned duration on the middle bar as representing 100%.

Other means of recording progress are shown in *Fig 8.12*. These are particularly suitable for housebuilding but can be used on other sites if the system is developed. The use of the plan as the basis of recording progress allows only a five-stage report to be made. This may be suitable for the speculative builder who may develop a plot in accordance with market demands rather than a specific programme. It is, however, an excellent form of communication and it is possible to see at a glance the progress on any particular site.

The other system is a numercial rather than a pictorial system. The plot numbers or house designations are listed along the top and the activity numbers down the side; the completion dates are inserted when each activity is completed. This provides more detail but is difficult to read and provides no comparison between planned and actual. This system can also be developed into diagonally divided squares giving planned and actual dates. Its main advantage is that a large amount of information can be presented on a relatively small piece of paper.

Most progress reports are made weekly although easily measured projects like tunnel excavation or roads are often reported in linear metres per day or even per shift. The method of reporting the progress to head office is done by one of four methods. Firstly, a person can measure and record progress on site and then travel to head office and record the progress again at that location. Secondly, it can be compiled into a schedule stating that each activity is a certain percentage complete and that schedule sent to head office. Thirdly, a 'shuttle' programme is used where progress is recorded on the site copy and the 'shuttle' copy. The 'shuttle copy is sent to head office, progress recorded on their copy and the 'shuttle' returned for the next report. Finally, progress can be reported by telephone using the activity numbers, percentages and other information. This latter system requires a set procedure and terminology, to prevent misunderstanding.

The use of progress reports will depend on the accuracy of the information provided. Reports which result in unjust chastisement will only lead to the falsification of reports. It is therefore necessary for each report to be investigated to establish the true cause and effect before action is taken.

Progress reports are also open to criticism if they are not related to expenditure as it is easy to report progress 50% ahead of schedule until one discovers that expenditure is 75% above planned levels. Similarly an activity 10% complete but with 5% expenditure indicates a chance to capitalise on a particularly efficient operation. The combined reporting of progress and expenditure will be dealt with in Chapter 10.

8.7 QUESTIONS ON PLANNING AND PROGRAMMING

MULTI-CHOICE QUESTIONS

1. Planning is the process which requires the
   (a) Presentation of a programme for the architect;
   (b) Prediction of the method of work and the resources to be used;
   (c) Calculation of the duration of activities;
   (d) Selection of plant and labour.

2. Programming is the process which involves
   (a) The drawing of a critical path network;
   (b) Settling the start and completion date of a project;
   (c) Scheduling a multitude of predictions on a chart;
   (d) Writing a method statement.

3. The allocation of tasks to particular operatives can be combined with
   (a) The overall project programme;
   (b) The short term programme;
   (c) The weekly programme;
   (d) The stage programme.

4. The float which is always available on a particular non-critical activity is termed
   (a) Interfering float;
   (b) Total float;
   (c) Dependent float;
   (d) Free float.

5. Progress recording and reporting is necessary to
   (a) Indicate the need for corrective action;
   (b) Check the site managers performance;
   (c) Ascertain the accuracy of the programme;
   (d) Provide the supervising officer with information.

SHORT-ANSWER QUESTIONS (15-20 minutes)

1. Explain the need to define tasks prior to commencing the planning and programming of a construction project. Illustrate your answer with examples.

2. Describe the sections and layout to be used in a method statement. Give an example of a method statement for an operation which involves excavating a trench 300 m long with a width of 600 m and an average depth of 1.65 m.

3. Explain the procedure to be followed, using diagrams to illustrate your answer, when preparing a programme using critical path analysis.

4. Describe the use of overall, short term and weekly programmes on a construction site.

5. Describe a method of recording progress on a local authority housing contract of 300 dwellings. Describe how the reports would be made to head office.

QUESTIONS REQUIRING LONGER ANSWERS (30-45 minutes)

1. Discuss the premise that all construction projects are unpredictable and therefore planning and programming is of limited utility to the contractor.

2. (a) Explain the purpose for which a method statement is prepared.
   (b) Prepare a method statement for the work on the substructure shown on Drawing Number . . . .

3. Describe a programming technique suitable for the project shown on Drawing Number . . . . Give reasons for using the particular technique selected.

4. Describe how the resources of a project may be optimised.

5. Planning, programming and the reporting of progress are interrelated processes. Discuss this relationship and the benefits which may be gained by a contractor carrying out these processes.

9 Quality control

9.1 QUALITY DEFINITION

As in all management processes, objectives must be set and the organisation provided to achieve them. Management, therefore, carries the responsibility for quality even though its participation in production is only indirect.

Perfection may be a word closely related to quality but there must be a distinction between the two. Perfection, in practical terms, is like a carrot to a donkey, always out of reach. If this is the objective which is always out in front and the organisation can strive for, then it will serve a useful purpose. As progress is made in achieving quality the perfection objective also advances and is, therefore not attainable. The idea that a gap exists between perfection and practical achievable quality, when accepted, enables the gap to be measured and compared. For example if verticality is perfection in a wall then the gap may be expressed as ±5 mm in 5 m. Once quality is rated in this way then it can be controlled.

The quality of a whole building may not be so easily expressed but it is a result of many quality ratings for all types of products. The main problem is to ascertain who is to be satisfied with the quality. The designer and contractor are responsible to the client for the product and the quality of a structure may be defined as:

'The composite product characteristics of the manufactured materials and their on-site assembly that determine the degree to which the completed structure, in use, will meet the expectations of the client.'

Such a definition brings to the attention other factors than mere appearance and workmanship. The more difficult problems of reliability, durability, maintainability, adaptability and servicability have to be considered. The quality of a structure becomes much more widely based than the on-site production when this definition is used; it will include the quality of design and material selection as well as the actual production.

The ultimate quality of a structure depends on two major aspects, the quality of design and the quality of conformance as shown in *Fig 9.1*. The designer must take account of assembly problems, constructability and the need to coordinate the whole design of the structure, services, finishes and furniture into a single product. Major problems often arise because services and structure are not fully related and the provision of adequate details throughout the production process is essential. Failure to provide adequate information will lead to the contractor acting independently which could affect quality and cost.

The contractor must conform as near as possible to the design and the failure to do so will lead to a diminished quality of product. There must be adequate skills, care and technological knowledge among the operatives to ensure conformance. Equally management must plan and programme the storage and application of resources.

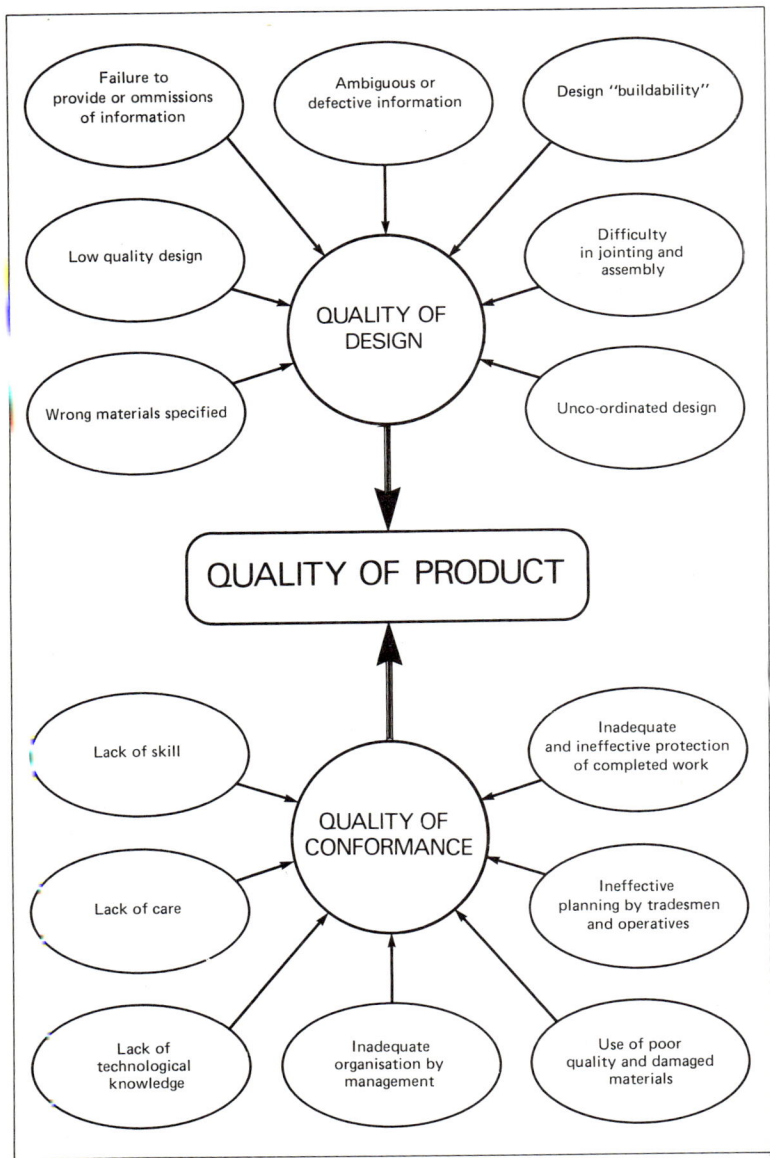

Fig 9.1 Causes of diminished quality

High quality costs money and therefore someone must pay for the better product, this will normally be the client. The contract tender system of allocating work in the construction industry often leads to the acceptance of the lowest tender. The conditions prevailing with regard to quality are such that each contractor who submits a tender perceives the required quality in his own way from the same information. The most important point is that the contractor should perceive a similar quality of product as the client.

Fig 9.2 illustrates the costs of inspection and prevention of low quality production plotted against the costs of remedying defective work. If there is disagreement over the quality standard required then the contractor may be involved in extra expense which diminishes his profit. Similarly, if defects are not remedied the contractor's profit will increase. It is important to stress the concept of the building team and the relationship between the professions. Team spirit and mutual trust is needed to help prevent this type of conflict and encourage the speedy resolution of problems.

9.2 RESPONSIBLITIES OF THE PARTIES

Each party involved in the construction process has responsibilities for quality. Those responsibilities are statutory, contractual and moral. Quality standards are laid down in various publications and documents, including BS 5606 which deals with accuracy in construction. The number of publications change frequently as new ones are published and amendments are issued to others.

The members of the design team have a responsibility to ensure that design aspects of the project are of acceptable quality as measured by the definition given earlier. The designer has a number of statutory regulations with which to comply; these include the Health and Safety at Work Act, Factories Act and the Public Health Act of which the Building Regulations form a major part. The regulations are formulated by central government and passed by Parliament.

The enforcement of building regulations is carried out by the local authority. They provide quality standards for fire resistance, structural stability and thermal insulation among other aspects. The designer also has a moral responsibility to meet the client's brief with regard to durability, appearance and fitness for use. The structure consultant is also bound by regulations regarding foundation and structural design.

The quantity surveyor who is mainly concerned with cost also has a responsibility to ensure that any cost reduction proposed will lead to a lessening of the client's expectations with regard to the quality of the product. The responsibility for cost should be related to the life cycle of the building, taking into account the future repair, replacement and running costs. The quantity surveyor also is responsible for the drafting of quality standards in the form of the specification for the approval of the architect. This contract document attempts to set out the quality of work required.

The main contractor has a statutory duty to comply with regulations, a contractual duty to carry out the work in accordance with the specification and a moral responsibility to provide the best quality for the price the client is paying. This responsibility also covers the performance of sub-contractors and it is in this area that problems arise. The contractor is responsible for his production and therefore has a duty to inspect and maintain standards of work. Site production management is not always capable of inspecting sub-contractor's work due to a

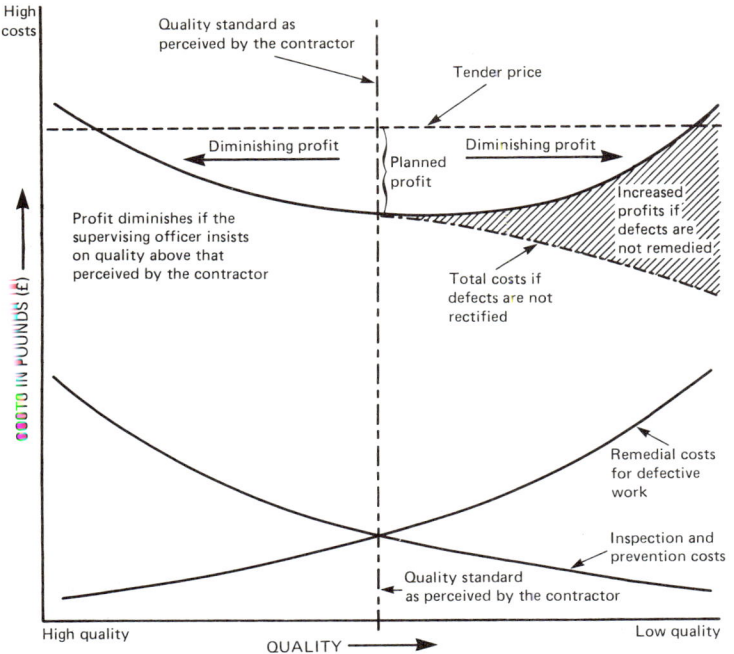

Fig 9.2 The relationship between quality costs and price

lack of technical knowledge. Specialist supervisors or inspectors may have to be employed to ensure compliance with quality standards.

The regular inspection of work and material is essential and there are advocates of a separate section of an organisation to carry out the inspection function. One of the major responsibilities of a contractor is to ensure that his management staff and operatives are properly trained so as to eliminate those causes leading to diminished quality conformance illustrated in *Fig 9.1*. A basic inspection procedure is shown in *Fig 9.3*.

The only appointed inspector on site for the client is the Clerk of Works and a contractor may often rely on his judgement as to the quality of the work. His main duty is to ensure compliance with the contract with regard to the quality of materials, goods and workmanship expended in the construction process. The contractor is obliged to carry out the works in accordance with the quality and standard specified in the contract. There is also a provision that where the quality and standards are not specified, they shall be to the reasonable satisfaction of the architect or supervising officer.

This is the aspect of perception, of what is reasonable, that leads to the conflict previously mentioned. The Clerk of Works is solely an inspector of works who reports defects to the supervising officer. The supervising officer may consider work defective which the Clerk of Works has not condemned and therefore liability for quality extends beyond the approval of this inspector.

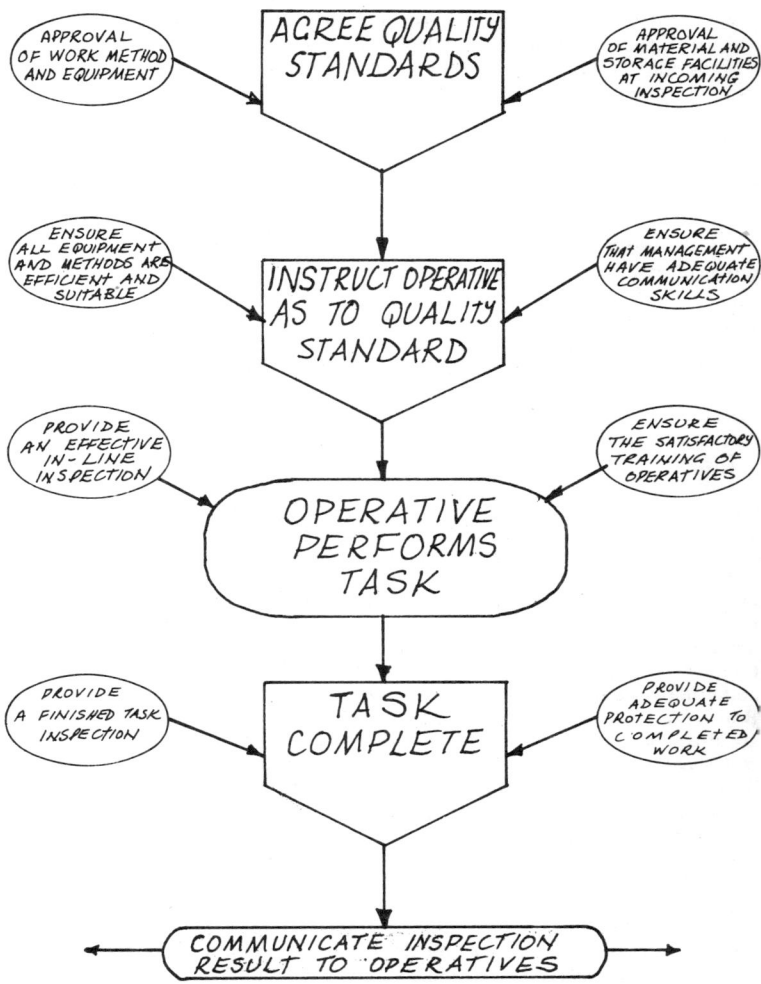

Fig 9.3 The procedure for quality conformance by operatives

The statutory inspectors are those appointed by the local authority in the form of the building control officer and those inspectors employed by the statutory authorities such as the gas and electricity boards. The building control officer has a limited role in quality inspection, in that he only approves the work at certain structural stages to ensure compliance with the building regulations.

The electricity board and other authorities inspect to ensure the installation is safe and in accordance with the relevant regulations before connecting the supply.

Their approval of installations does not alter the responsibility for defective work which may become apparent later. This will remain with the contractor.

Some other bodies have been set up as inspection units to provide guarantees of minimum quality, this is particularly true in the speculative housing market. In this case, the builders pay a fee to the organisation in return for which they get an inspection service and are allowed to advertise as approved by the organisation. Any persistent defective performance is met by the withdrawal of approval and removal from their register.

9.3 QUALITY STANDARDS

Quality control should be based on the concept that variance is a natural occurrence. There will always be some difference in the material being used, in the skill of the operative and in the quality of design. The standards which should be set are those which will enable the majority of the products to be within the specified limits but clustered around the centre. The variables should be such that the limits are approached in few instances. This is the attribute of consistency.

The purpose of setting the standard is to produce a practical, factual and measureable limit as an objective. The defined quality standards are of little use in the specification or bill of quantities, the place for them to be publicised is at the workplace, pinned to the wall or bench, in the operative's pocket or demonstrated by a sample.

The terms in which the bill of quantities and specification are written must be objective rather than subjective. Whilst high quality may be permissible as a general reference to the standard of a building it is quite inappropriate, for specific items. Other subjective terms like 'good' or 'the best possible standard' are also totally inadequate if they are to be used as an instrument of quality, even though authoritative definitions are sometimes given. Such statements as 'compliance with British Standards' or 'all goods should comply with the relevant British Standard' are also inadequate. Firstly British Standards sometimes conflict with each other as with such items as galvanising, where there are three different standards. Secondly British Standards have requirements, which must be met for the use of the Kite Mark, and recommendations which are discretionary. Unless full details of the British Standard and those recommendations are specifically mentioned in the document then no contractual obligations are placed on the contractor to comply.

British Standard Codes of Practice are mainly concerned with workmanship, they are discretionary and are couched in terms like 'neat' and 'clean'. They sometimes conflict with other codes, in that dimensional accuracy for the structure is not compatible with the dimensional accuracy of the finish. Such discrepancies, however, are continually being eliminated by revision of the documents. The site production manager should consult all the standards and codes so that the exact contractual obligation with regard to quality is known.

There is a tendency to ensure quality of fit by dimensional limits. This is a practical way of measuring how close the product should get to perfection. Dimensional exactness cannot be achieved on site with the same accuracy as machine-ground factory-producing components. The tolerances will depend on a number of factors, the first being the nature of the material and the properties that enable the operative to shape it. Timber can be manufactured to closer tolerances than concrete on site. Secondly the size and weight influence the ability to assemble it to 'tight fit' openings. Thirdly, the jointing techniques, particularly the jointing material, which is in turn affected by expansion and contraction characteristics.

The dimensional tolerances should be applied with care to components which fit into a space between frame members. Tolerances are given on a component, also for the space or alternatively for the frame member, this, unless carefully considered, can result in too large a joint gap or a too large component for the space. There is also a danger, when using components fixed to each other, of having an accumulated tolerance which leaves the total either under or over length.

Levels and trueness to slopes or verticality can be specified by referring to permissible limits of the gap allowed under a straight edge of a certain length. In these cases it is necessary to specify the type of straight edge so that there is no doubt as to the tests to be applied. The straight edge could be described as a metal bar 10 mm thick and 75 mm wide and 5 m long with both edges machined to a straight line. The specification should then read that there should not be a gap of more than 3 mm under the approved straight edge when it is placed in any position or direction on the surface. The specification of verticality can be given by stating an acceptable distance away from plumb over a certain height. This may be 6 mm over a height of 5 metres. Similarly the level of bed joints on brickwork can be specified.

Other methods of specifying quality are by performance of a material to be incorporated or by the performance of the completed structure. Thermal insulation standards are expressed in different ways using, thermal conductivity (k) in W/m°C, thermal resistance (R) in m^2°C/W and thermal transmittance (u) W/m^2°C, but the actual construction is also given. Building Regulations also specify the minimum quality in this area. Sound insulation is also expressed in a similar way using a permitted noise level in a room, stated in decibels (dB) as a specification. Walls can be measured by the reduction in decibels but it must be over a specified range of frequencies.

Moisture content of timber is another of the methods used and such items as the joinery timber should not exceed 9-12% moisture content. This is easily tested by on-site equipment so that a fair indication is given. More stringent and exact tests can then follow.

The most common of all performance specifications is concrete which is usually done in accordance with BS 5328 with due regard given to CP 110. Generally the concrete will be required to attain a compressive strength expressed in terms of N/mm^2 MN/m^2 or Mpa (1 newton = 1 pascal). Such tests are carried out at 7 and 28 days after the task is completed and therefore it is often necessary to view non-compliance in the manner shown in *Fig 9.4.*

Appearance is the most elusive of qualities to rate. Quite often the appearance will not alter the structural performance of the building and may be considered to be of minor importance. In fact, appearance is often considered to give greater satisfaction to the client than many other attributes and the aesthetic quality is of primary concern to the Architect.

The terms with which appearance can be described are usually subjective but attempts can be made to express requirements in more objective terms. Chips to facing bricks, splashes of mud or mortar can be specifically excluded. However, it would be better to rate the quality, particularly of chipping on facing bricks, as not to exceed 10% of the face area of any brick that at least gives a definite indication of the amount of picking needed by the bricklayers and should attract the appropriate price for such work. Colour changes in brickwork and knots in timber should be quantitatively stated if possible. Finally the use of samples and the construction of samples should be a practice which is allied to price and carried out before a final tender figure is accepted.

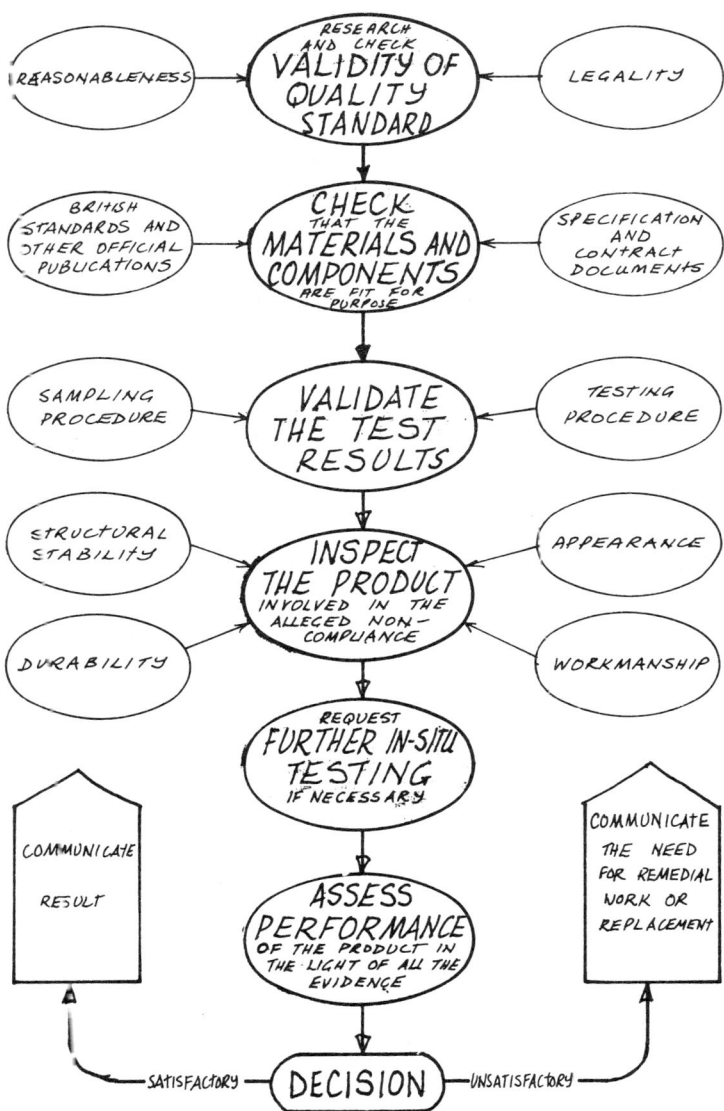

Fig 9.4 Action in the event of alleged non-compliance

9.4 TESTING

There are three main classes of testing — suitability tests, performance tests and functional tests. It is important that the tests are valid for the quality assurance which is sought. British Standards specify exactly how tests should be conducted and how the results should be expressed. Materials having a one hour fire resistance classification does not indicate that it will not catch fire in less than one hour, but indicates that under the standard test conditions it rated a one hour fire resistance classification for stability and integrity.

Suitability tests are those which are carried out on materials and components to ensure that they are fit for the purpose for which they are intended. These tests may be carried out on site or in the laboratory. The materials usually fall into two categories, firstly those that have been tested in accordance with an agreed procedure and granted some form of approval and secondly, those raw materials which need to be tested prior to incorporation in the work because the variations are likely to be such that no seal of approval or guarantee can be provided. The first group usually carries a BS kitemark or has been awarded an Agrément Certificate. The products are tested on a sample basis and then approved as

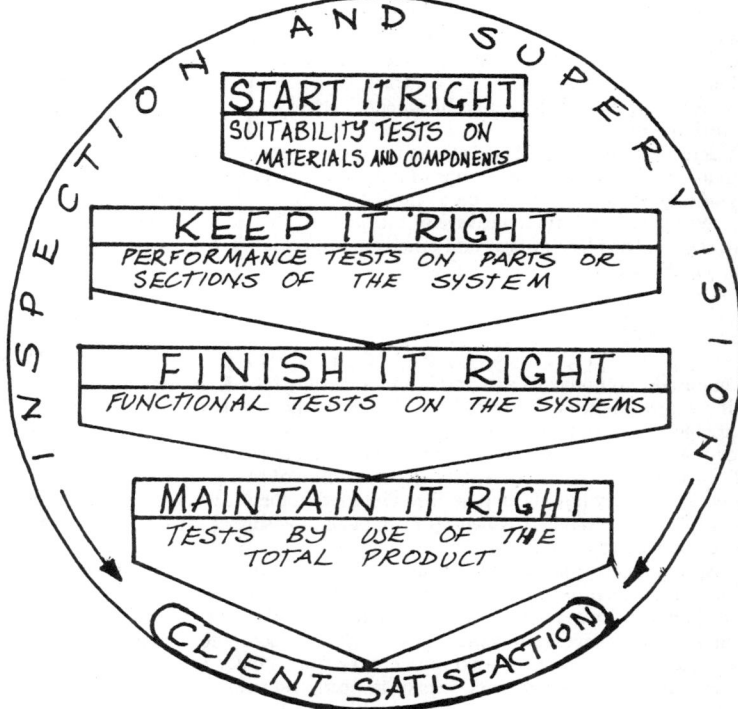

Fig 9.5 The place of tests in the production process

conforming to that test as was indicated in the fire resistance example. The latest type of test for timber is the stress grading scheme which expresses a fitness of timber for structural purpose.

The second type of material is exemplified by the tests which may be carried out on concrete materials. These tests may include sieve analysis or more appropriately moisture content tests on aggregates. These are followed by consistency tests such as slump and compacting factor tests. The test procedures are described in BS 1881. Suitability tests can be carried out on other materials quite often using a visual inspection against a descriptive standard such as is used in the amount of rust on reinforcing bars, although more exact measures are available.

Performance tests can be laboratory or site based and are meant to provide a safeguard against defects in quality which may be missed by suitability tests. The most common example is the cube compression test caried out on the mature concrete. Performance tests may also be conducted on assembled materials to test insulation qualities, on pipe joints to ensure no leaks, on drains and manholes to ensure performance. These tests are not conducted on whole systems but on separate parts to ensure that the completed section is capable of performing to the required quality.

Functional or final tests are those tests which are employed to ensure that both the full system and the product functions in accord with the original design objectives. These tests will involve, for example, running the heating system to ensure that the building reaches the required temperature, that the thermostats function and the main heat source responds. They are always performed on site and are sometimes required by the contract. Quite often these tests are part of the commissioning process because adjustments to the system cannot be finalised until all work is complete.

A defects liability period also allows for further remedial work which results from an inspection performed prior to the end of the period. These tests are followed by what may be considered the ultimate test — i.e. one of occupation. This test by use is the final measure of the quality of the structure and client satisfaction. The place of tests and other procedures in the construction process is shown in *Fig 9.5*.

9.5 SAMPLING

All materials, components and parts cannot be fully tested, so some method of testing a portion of the whole which will indicate the quality of the whole must be attempted. This is the principle of sampling which can be based on statistical theory, so that the results can be viewed with some degree of confidence.

The formulae to be used to establish the number of samples required and the degree of accuracy have been described and used in the activity sampling section of Chapter 7. However, the frequency of sampling to ensure adequate quality control is essentially an economic decision. The more often samples are taken, the higher the inspection costs and usually the quality. The less often samples are taken then the less the inspection costs with the probability of higher remedial costs. If the defined limits of tolerance are made absolutely clear then the system will work within those tolerances until variances indicate an unacceptable trend.

It is necessary to decide at what moment the system tends to drift away from the defined quality and then provide tests or inspections to control that drift. If a normal frequency distribution is representative of all the work units (population) then the intervals between the drift will depend on the tolerances. The percentage of production within each standard deviation indicates that the further away from the mean the tolerances are set the less the number of defectives and therefore the less frequent the sampling required as shown in *Fig 9.6*. The wider and flatter the bell shaped curve the greater the variability in the product. Numerous sets of sampling tables are available based on different distribution curves which will give the number of samples which need to be taken.

The overall quality of the product is made up of two distinct classes of characteristics — termed variables and attributes. The variables are usually characteristics which can be measured, i.e. length, breadth and height and also, the thermal, acoustic and fire properties. The attributes are those mainly concerned with appearance, such as the face must be free of chips or scratches, smooth with no trowel marks. These are much more difficult to define and to control by sampling.

All the attributes have a generally appreciated acceptance or rejection level but between the two is a zone of indecision. The width of this zone of indecision will usually be allied to the definition of the attribute in the specification as shown in *Fig 9.7*. The zone of indecision if applied to variables, can be narrowed if a larger sample is taken thus increasing the probability of acceptance because the probability of selecting good units increases as defective units are removed. The amount of work units in this zone is of borderline quality and it will not matter too much if the work is either accepted or rejected.

The control of variables is conducted by two main measures. The first is the average or mean which is the nominal control value about which the tolerances are set. The second is the standard deviation which measures the variability about the mean as has been shown in *Fig 9.6*. The control tolerances should be set within the limits which the machine or process can achieve. If tolerances are set within one standard deviation that means that 32% of production will be rejected. Therefore the tolerances are unrealistic if an economical price is to be paid.

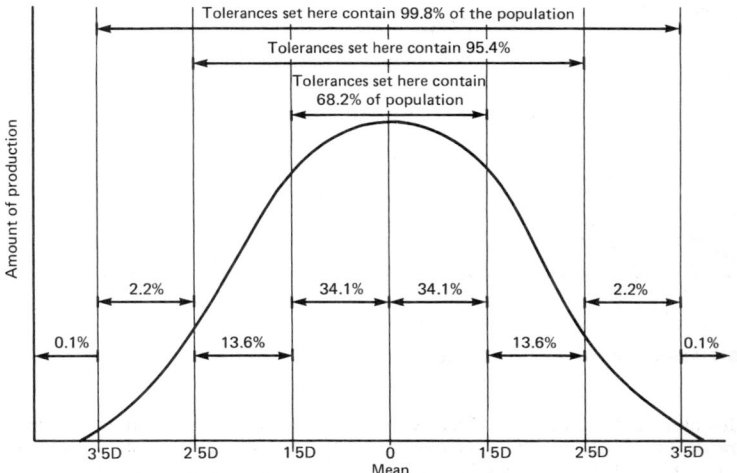

Fig 9.6 Normal frequency distribution curve

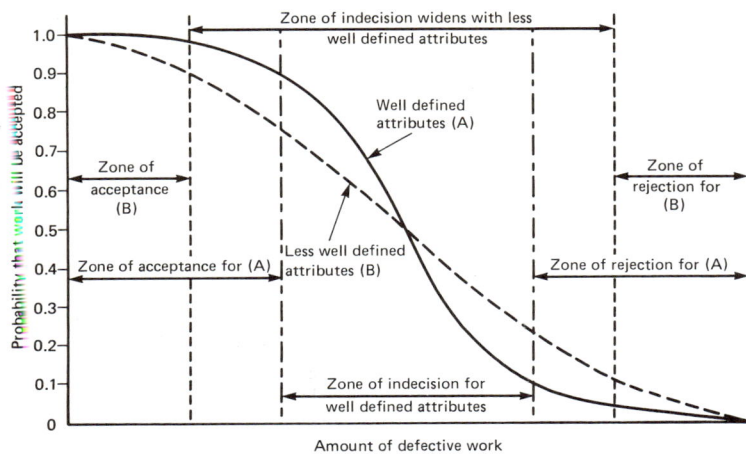

Fig 9.7 Zones of acceptance rejection and indecision for quality attributes

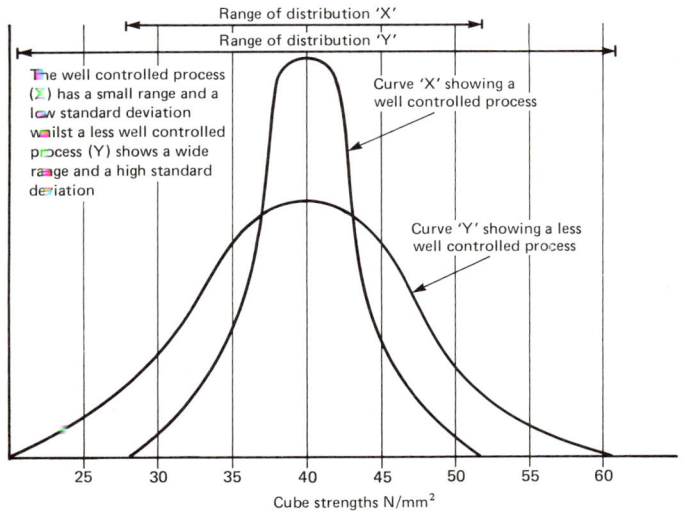

Fig 9.8 Curves indicating different degrees of control

However the variables and therefore the tolerances will alter depending on the shape of the normal distribution curve. In *Fig 9.8* two distributions are shown, the X curve shows that most cubes lie in a very narrow range, indicating that the concrete is of consistent strength. The Y curve is spread over a large range showing wide variations in results and therefore indicating a poorly controlled process.

The control of variables can be carried out by the use of control charts. These charts are based on the two main measures. The chart shown in *Fig 9.9* is for concrete compressive strengths as tested by a 28 day cube test. The nominal line and the upper and lower limits are fixed by the specification. It is necessary to set control or warning limits and they are a product of the range of results which can be expected according to the standard deviation of the predicted results. Usually a number of samples are made and the standard deviation (SD) is applied to the table shown in *Fig 9.10* by multiplying the SD by *K,* i.e. an SD of 5 N/mm² and an acceptable failure of 1 in 50 will set the control limit at $5 \times 2.05 = 10.25$. If the acceptable ratio is 1 in 10, then the control limits will be set as shown in *Fig 9.11*.

The number of samples, in the case of concrete it is cubes, that should be taken should never be less than ten and preferably twenty-five. This type of control can be adopted for any quantifiable tolerance be it cube strength, brick length or timber cross sectional area.

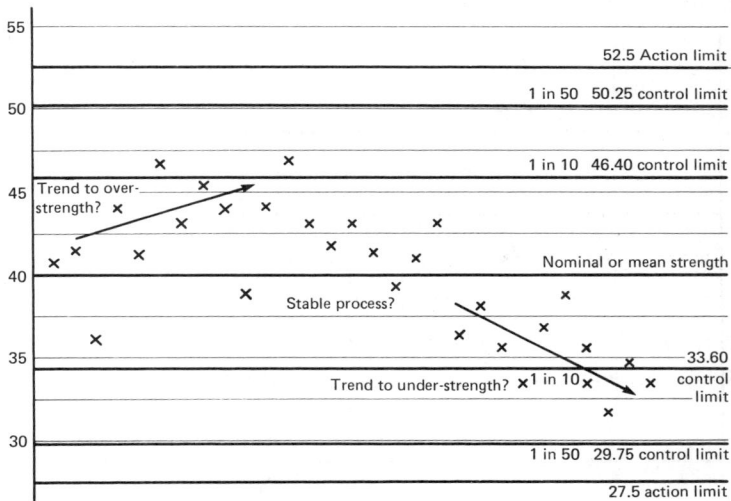

Fig 9.9 Control chart for concrete compressive strength—variable

The control of attributes is carried out by a chart which records the number of defectives allowed in each sample. The limits will be set at the levels

$$\text{Action } c + 3\sqrt{(c)}$$

$$\text{Warning } c + 2\sqrt{(c)}$$

where *c* is the acceptable number of defects per sample. If 3 units is the acceptable average the limits are:

$$\text{Action } 3 + 3\sqrt{3} = 8.19 \text{ say } 8$$

$$\text{Warning } 3 + 2\sqrt{3} = 6.46 \text{ say } 6$$

These limits are shown in the control chart in *Fig 9.12*.

PROPORTION FALLING BELOW THE LOWER CONTROL LIMIT		k
PERCENTAGE	RATIO	FACTOR
1	1 in 100	2·33
2	1 in 50	2·05
2·5	1 in 40	1·96
3	1 in 33	1·88
4	1 in 25	1·75
5	1 in 20	1·64
10	1 in 10	1·28
16	1 in 6	1·00

Fig 9.10 Factor determining control limits

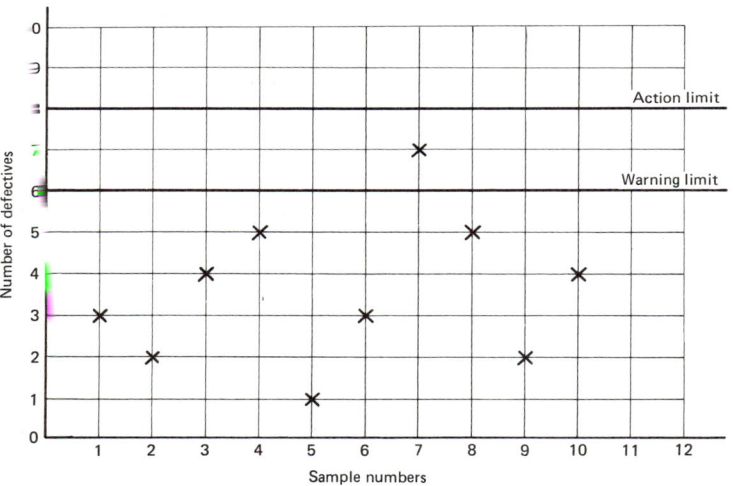

Fig 9.11 Control chart for attributes

The number of defectives found in each sample is plotted on the chart and, if the general trend is towards the warning limit, then the process which is producing the defects should be checked. It is only when the action limit is reached or exceeded that the sample should be rejected, but there is always a tendency to take further samples as the number of defectives reaches the warning limit.

The control chart is a running commentary on the process being monitored. If it was used to check the visual attributes of brickwork the inspector could determine trends which may enable the site manager to counter-act some aspect of the organisation which is demotivating the bricklayer. This example in a sense demonstrates that the use of charts does the monitoring but it is only the production man who can do the controlling. Quality control can be said to be up to 20% statistical analysis but the remainder is common sense and attitude of mind.

9.6 QUESTIONS ON QUALITY CONTROL

MULTI-CHOICE QUESTIONS

1 The quality of a building is measured by the satisfaction of the:
   (a) Architect;
   (b) Clerk of Works;
   (c) Contractor;
   (d) Client.

2 The quality of conformance is the responsibility of the:
   (a) Builder;
   (b) Local Authority;
   (c) Structural Engineer;
   (d) Architect

3 Deemed-to-satisfy construction details appear in the:
   (a) Construction Regulations;
   (b) Bills of Quantities;
   (c) Building Regulations;
   (d) Fire Protection Booklet.

4 Tests may be classified under three main headings, they are:
   (a) Suitability, performance and functional tests;
   (b) Stress, strain and compressive tests;
   (c) Dimensional, visual and sample tests;
   (d) Arrival, in-store and erection tests.

5 The percentage population falling within the range of two standard deviations either side of the mean in a normal distribution is:
   (a) 68.2;
   (b) 95.4;
   (c) 99.8;
   (d) 34.1.

SHORT-ANSWER QUESTIONS (15-20 minutes)

1 Define the quality of a building and explain the measures that are required from the designer and contractor to ensure an acceptable quality standard.

2 Describe the procedures which may be necessary to ensure effective quality control of concrete delivered to site in a ready-mixed condition.

3 Prepare a check list which may be used by a site operative to carry out an inspection of a load of 20 000 facing bricks on delivery to site.

4 Describe how statistical analysis could be used for quality monitoring on site.

5 Describe the action you would take, as Site Manager, if a test carried out by an outside agency showed that the material being used was of insufficient quality to meet the specification

QUESTIONS REQUIRING LONGER ANSWERS (30-45 minutes)

1. The building team, in total, is responsible for the quality of a building. Discuss how the interaction between the team members may assist or detract from the quality of the completed product.
2. Discuss the meaning of quality in building and its relationship with costs and price.
3. Discuss the purpose of tests and the relevance of testing to the quality of a building.
4. Define the purpose of building regulations and discuss their influence on the quality of a building.
5. "When objective terms are not available then a specification written in subjective terms is better than nothing." Discuss this statement giving examples from the building industry to illustrate your answer.

10 Site cost control

10.1 ELEMENTS OF COST

In order to ensure the adequate control of costs it is essential to understand how those costs arise. In the construction industry costs are not so easily determined as they are in a manufacturing industry. The problems of identification are the most difficult. The elements of cost are shown in *Fig 10.1*.

The total cost is the total of all the firms costs to carry out the work. These may be historical costs for work completed or predicted costs for work to be completed. They comprise two main elements — variable costs and fixed costs. These terms are ideals and most fixed costs are variable in the longer term and those which are variable in the medium term are referred to as semi-variable. Variable costs are usually closely related to direct costs in that they are those which are directly related to the work and vary with the amount of production. Direct costs are sometimes referred to as prime costs. Fixed costs are related to the indirect costs in that the majority do not vary with the amount of production.

All indirect costs are not fixed, some do vary with production but they are usually small and inseperable from the major costs. Head Office costs are fixed and the site must contribute towards them. Such costs include all the administration tasks, buyers, planners and senior managers. The other fixed costs in the construction industry are those contained in the preliminaries bill of

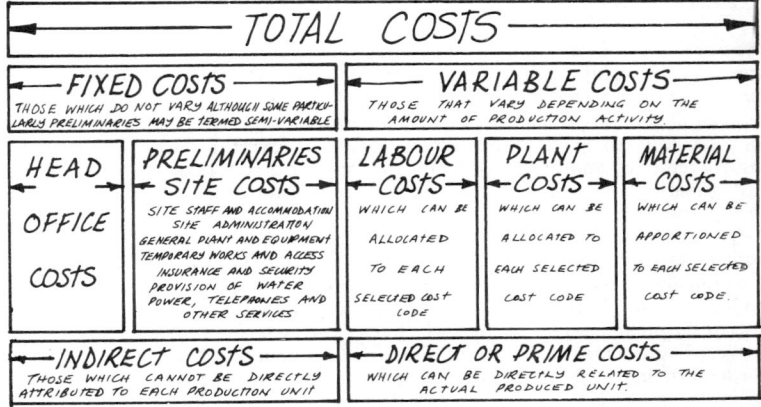

Fig 10.1 Elements of costs

quantities. These costs include such items as site staff, insurance, site accommodation, site administration, water, electricity, telephones, general plant, temporary works and many other items depending on the work.

As an example of varying fixed costs, a tower crane on site is a fixed weekly charge but the amount of electric power it uses will depend on performance. However it is unlikely that the power consumption can be separated from other electrically-powered plant or that it can be allocated directly to a task. A construction firm must then make a decision as to what type of cost it is and from that decision flows the degree of control to which it will be subjected.

The direct or variable costs on site are the labour, plant and material costs. It is usually easy to allocate labour costs, but consider the odd job employee. There is always likely to be one of these employed on a site who will make tea, clean offices, assist in production crises and tidy up the site. If he is not included in the preliminaries to what is the cost charged? Similarly if he works on production for half a day to what section are the costs charged.

Plant when working on specific tasks is charged to that task but when employed for general use it is usually a fixed cost in preliminaries. Similar problems as to those of labour sometimes occur with plant. Materials are a problem in that bulk items such as the raw materials for concrete are very difficult to apportion. This often leads to a historic apportionment depending on the amount of completed work. However, this often excludes small items of concrete and therefore distorts the cost of other items.

The identification of costs and their allocation to each element is the first step in deciding what type of cost control system is to be used. It is of little importance as to what system is employed, the major factor is that the system is consistent throughout the firm. The system selected will depend on the control required over each major item of cost and will vary from firm to firm. Any changes introduced should be such that continued comparisons should be made even though the new method may be more detailed. There are a number of systems of costing which overlap and intertwine but most construction firms use a form of standard costing.

10.2 COST SYSTEMS

There are numerous designations for different costs and cost systems. *Fig 10.2* attempts to rationalise them for the construction industry. The main objective must not be what name shall be given to the cost system but does it help to give early warning of an inadequate production performance. The system itself does not produce anything but may be expensive to run. It must therefore show a positive return by improved production and estimating performance.

Marginal cost is that cost which is added for each additional unit of production. The units may be batches depending on the actual size of the unit. However, the marginal cost is intended to show any increase in variable costs and marginal costing was a system developed to produce the necessary information. This system of costing involves the identification of all variable costs and their allocation to the production tasks. In the construction industry this will mean all the semi-variable costs in the preliminaries and some which may also be included in head office charges. This is a mammoth task for the variable products and conditions under which a firm may work in the construction industry. It is a sophisticated system which is most useful when it is necessary to select a method of work, as the 'true' cost of alternatives will be available.

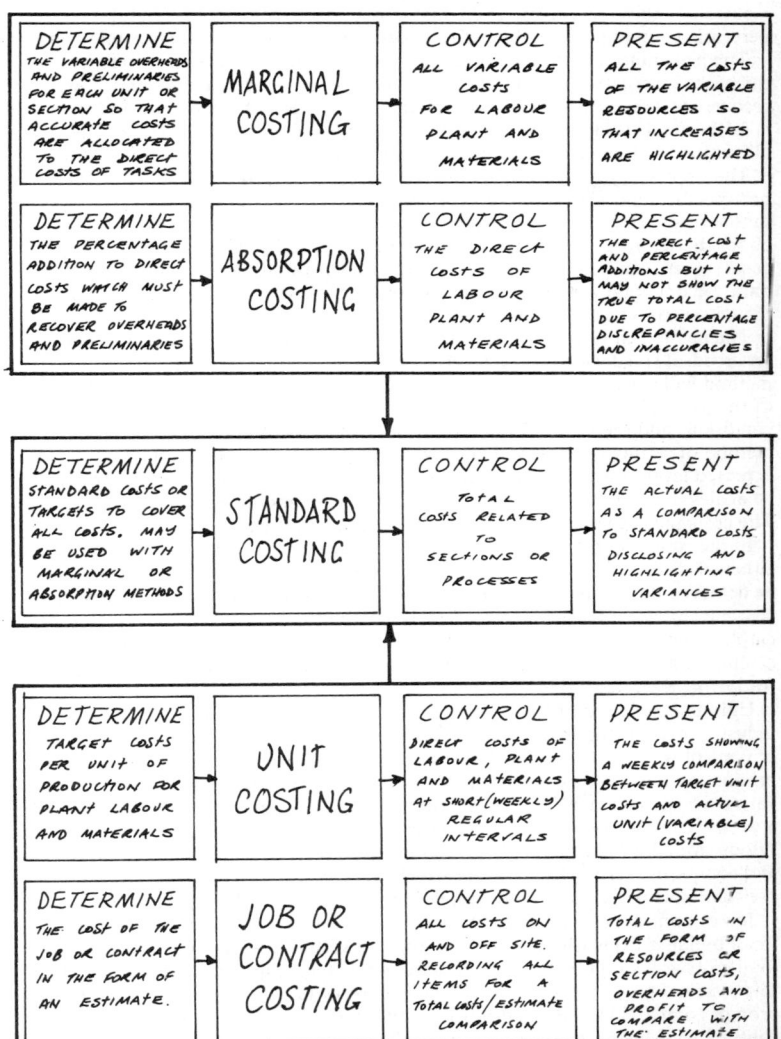

Fig 10.2 Cost systems for construction

Absorption costing approaches the problem in a different way, by assuming that fixed costs are contributed to by all the production sections. They are charged on a percentage basis. This may involve a percentage added to labour plant and materials depending on the proportion of fixed costs considered to be fairly

incurred by these resources. There may also be a further charge, again by a
percentage, on the whole of the direct costs plus their individual absorption costs.

The percentage additions will be related to the anticipated level of activity and
therefore if activity does not reach this level than all the fixed costs may not be
recovered. It is however related to expenditure and the time spent on an activity. It
is fairly simple to apply, but decisions taken may be based on the erroneous
allocation of fixed costs in a disproportionate amount.

The previous two methods are used to arrive at the costs of production but are
not specifically designed for control. Standard costing is designed for cost control
in that it is necessary to set pre-determined targets. There are two main points
about the setting of target costs. Firstly they must reflect management's intended
costs rather than be based on past records which contain inadequate performance
data. Secondly they must be achievable or otherwise site management will ignore
them and cost control rendered useless.

The method of setting standard costs is based on different views. They may be
set as **'ideal standard costs'** reflecting a 100% efficiency and ideal conditions, this
method will always entail some degree of failure due to the conditions and nature
of the work. The **'basic standard cost'** assumes an expected output in ideal
conditions and then some allowance must be made for poor conditions. The third
method of setting is by **'expected standard costs'** these take account of the
expected level of performance and the actual conditions. This latter method may
be achievable but may also include allowances for conditions which do not occur.
The costs may then become a contributory factor to waste.

In the construction industry, expected standard costs are used in the estimate but
either of the other two types of standard costs may be used in quoting standards to
be achieved by site management. Standard costs do cover all costs including fixed
cost but this makes it difficult for actual day to day site control. It is necessary to
employ unit or job costing for this purpose but these are systems of standard
costing. Standard costing can also use absorption or marginal costing as the basis
for setting the target costs.

Unit and job or contract costing when adopted for use in the construction
industry involves the setting of standard costs or targets which can be the subject
of control within the construction firm. Unit costs are usually those costs per
production unit such as per m^2 or m^3. They are most easily recorded as only the
variable costs such as labour, plant and materials are used. The result will provide
a weekly comparison of production costs for site management. The unit cost
system does not indicate major losses without some means of adding total costs
and comparing them with the standard. It follows that any construction firm will
use some sort of hybrid costing system for it to match the firms requirements.

Job or contract costing is a once and for all costing which is most suitable for
small building firms who have jobs lasting between one week and a month. The
total costs are computed at the end of the work and compared with the estimate.
The essential task here is to ensure adequate recording during the work to ensure a
prompt comparison at the end. Larger firms will adopt this approach to each
contract when all costs are compared to the estimate.

10.3 GRAPHS AND CHARTS IN COSTING

When cost information has to be presented to busy managers, it is better to use a
form which attracts their attention to the salient points. The detailed study of

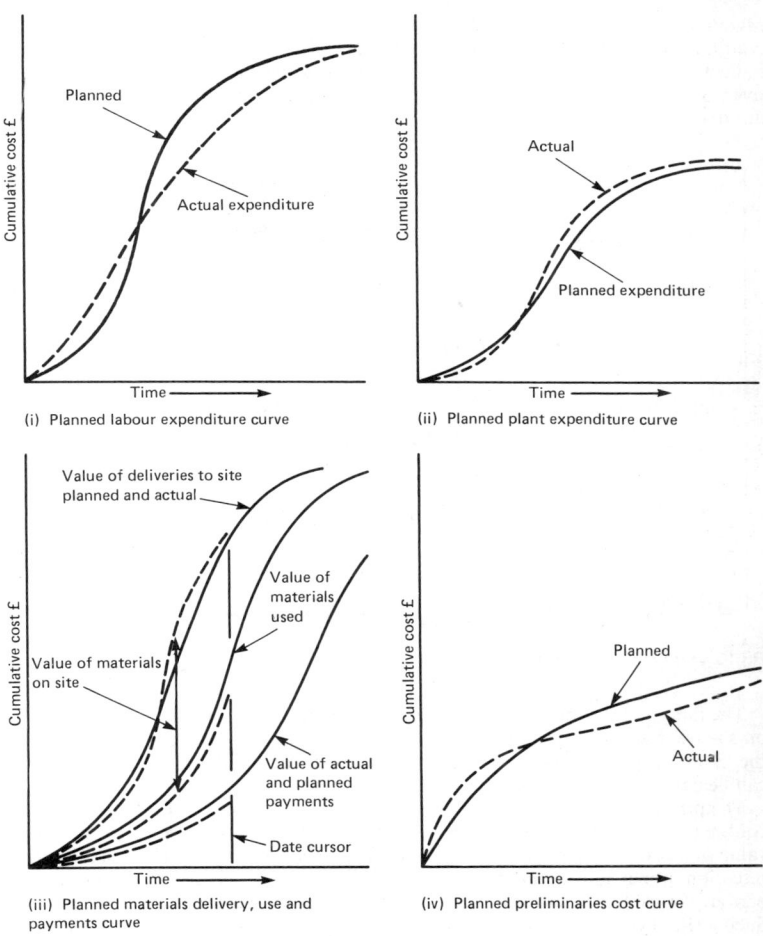

(i) Planned labour expenditure curve
(ii) Planned plant expenditure curve
(iii) Planned materials delivery, use and payments curve
(iv) Planned preliminaries cost curve

Fig 10.3 Cumulative individual resource cost curves

numerical data should be avoided where possible. The use of graphs or charts is ideal for such communication and they should be easily interpreted and drawn.

The most simple of all cost curves is the 'S' curve for cumulative expenditure on individual resources. *Fig 10.3* depicts four typical graphs which plot cost against time. This information should only be considered in conjunction with physical progress. The labour (i) and plant (ii) graphs are straight forward single curves. The materials (iii) shows three curves. The first shows the value of materials delivered, the second curve shows the value of materials used and the gap between should indicate the value of stocks on site. The last curve indicates expenditure on materials in the form of payment of invoices. The curves in this instance may continue beyond the duration of the contract. Preliminaries (iv) are shown to indicate that all items can be treated in much the same way. Sub-contractors and overheads can have graphs drawn to indicate expenditure as can the cost of accidents.

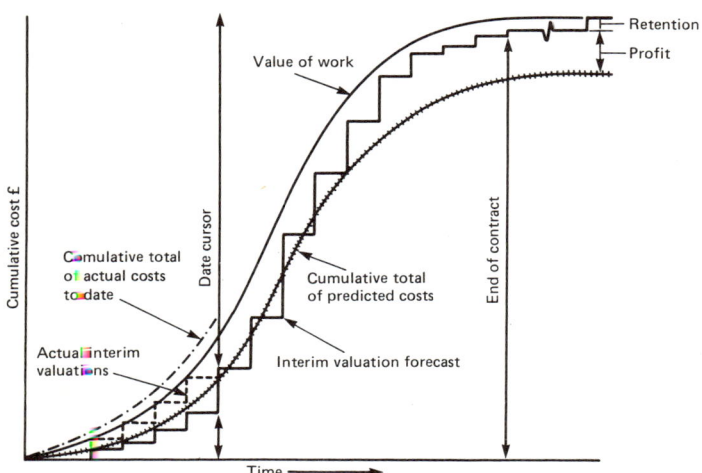

Fig 10.4 Contract cost curve

The labour chart can be supported by histograms indicating the number of men on site by trade and by total. This provides additional information when reading the 'S' curve graph. In all cases where expenditure can be forecast then the actual can be compared with the planned costs.

The production of individual cost curves leads to the eventual development of a contract cost curve as shown in *Fig 10.4*. This curve shows the predicted costs and value of work together with a forecast of interim valuation payments. Profit and retention money is shown at the top of the curves, past the end of the contract period. Where the interim valuations fall below costs a negative cash flow exists. Such a situation usually occurs at the start of a contract and funding is carried out from existing cash assets or borrowing.

The graph also shows the actual interim valuation income and the actual costs to provide an instant comparison. The date cursor shown is to indicate the point in time to which the actual costs refer. The information on this chart can be separated into two charts, one for valuations and another for costs. If the same scale is used a simple overlay will again combine the information.

The separation of the income chart from the cost charts leads to a single contract chart (i) as shown in *Fig 10.5*. If the contract continues beyond a year then an annual moving income curve can be drawn. The separation enables the actual income to be more clearly recorded and absorbed. They also provide the basis of the firm's 'Z' chart (ii) in *Fig 10.5*. The chart clearly shows a rise in the moving income curve over a year but a recession and a failure to win contracts will

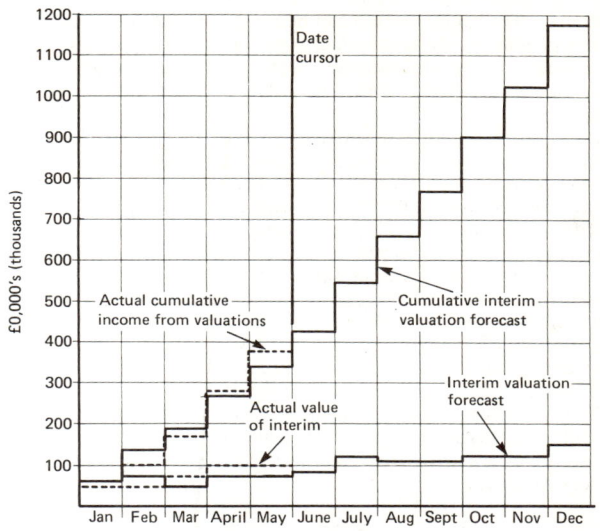

(i) Planned annual income from a single contract

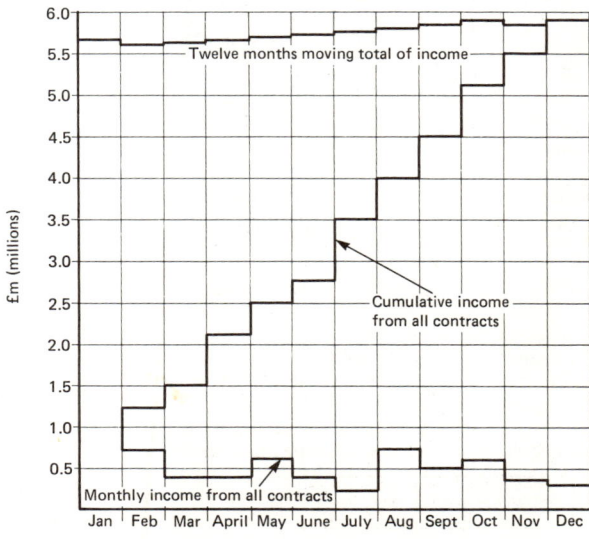

(ii) Planned annual income from all contracts in 'Z' chart form

Fig 10.5 Income and Z charts for contracts and firms

lead to a fall in the curve. The forecasted fall can be used to ensure that the right contracts are won at the right time to ensure that production activity is maintained at the level which the firm considers its optimum. Optimum levels of production can be found by the use of other charts using the costing systems which have been previously mentioned.

A break-even chart portrays a number of different concepts which enable decisions to be made on levels of activity and prices. As with all charts the resultant information is only as accurate as the input. The construction industry faces particular difficulties when attempting to determine accurate costs of operations. These difficulties should not deter management from attempting to identify, allocate and control costs. The break-even chart will show likely profits or losses at different levels of output. Output in the case of a construction firm may have to be measured as cost of work completed in a month or year, whilst sales is the value of work over the same time period.

Typical examples of break-even charts are shown in *Fig 10.6*. These charts show the relationship between marginal and fixed costs and indicate the level of output when the operation moves from loss into profit. This intersection is known as the break-even point. The rate of growth of profit earning for a suitable volume of work can also be determined from these charts. The chart will also indicate the firms margin of safety which is the difference between the break-even point and the total value of work produced.

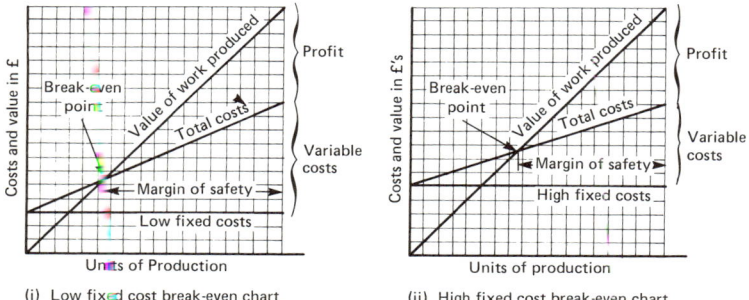

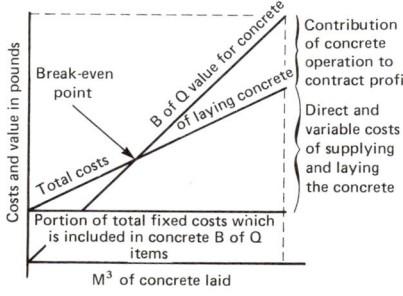

(iii) Break-even chart for a concrete operation

Fig 10.6 Break-even charts

The margin of safety is demonstrated in *Fig 10.6* (i) and (ii). The size of the margin of safety is a guide to the stability and strength of a business. If the margin is large there can be a considerable reduction in the value of production and profits can still be made. If the margin is small a reduction in the value of work produced could be a very serious problem. The margin of safety is increased when low fixed costs are present.

Other factors such as high variable costs or low value of work produced also contribute to a smaller margin of safety, however, the most important influence on the margin is fixed costs. Firms operating in a speculative market where demand and production activity are likely to vary considerably would need to have very low fixed costs in order to survive. The predominance of smaller firms or the use of sub-contractors by large firms in the speculative housing markets is an indication that fixed costs are kept as low as possible.

Break-even charts can be used to indicate the contribution that a particular activity is making to profits. A break-even chart is shown in *Fig 10.6* (iii) for concrete production. Once again the accurate identification of the fixed cost contribution of the operation is essential if the chart is to provide information which can be useful.

When variations are issued in a contract, break-even charts for an operation can show how the profit of a contractor has been reduced by the reduction in the volume of work. Should such reductions be large enough to be deemed to alter the scope of the contract some analysis must be conducted to settle the amount of compensation.

The time taken to complete a contract can be determined by a break-even chart. The charts which have been shown have all been based on straight lines, although in practice fixed costs, variable costs and the value of work produced are unlikely

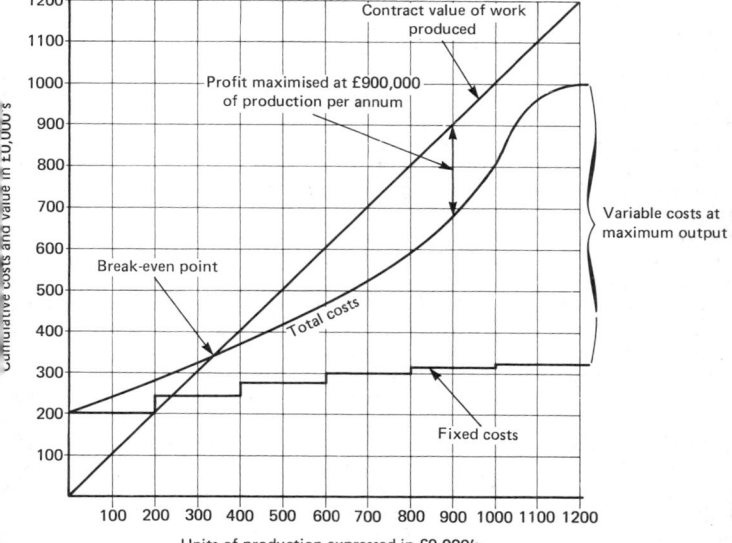

Fig 10.7 Break-even chart for a construction firm

to have smooth increments or remain static. Costs do not always vary in direct proportion to production, therefore, the maximum profits may not be earned at the maximum level of production. This point is illustrated in *Fig 10.7*. The units of production are expressed in the value of production per annum.

In the construction industry the fixed costs are also likely to rise with increased turnover, this is shown by the stepped rise of the curve. The rise in variable costs only increases when they approach the £1 M mark. If a firm's output was to settle at the optimum, assuming all the curves are a true reflection of the costs, then it would be at about £900 000 per annum. Therefore the ideal contract time for a £1.2m contract would be 16 months. It would not be profitable to perform this contract if activity was reduced below a production cost of about £360 000 per annum. However, break-even graphs should always be viewed with caution taking account of other happenings.

10.4 THE RECORDING OF COSTS

If decisions are to be based on the information contained in cost records then that data must be accurate and allocated to its correct coding or heading.

The first factor to be considered is the need to define what costs are allocated to each type of cost. Whether a marginal, absorption, standard or hybrid costing system is used, items of expenditure must be identified and allocated. One major item includes such costs as transport allowances to operatives and staff, non-productive overtime payments, holiday money and other costs. All these could be charged to overheads as they are not true costs of production. As an example, a six-month contract in close proximity to a labour centre will attract far less travel allowance than one 20 km away. Some firms use an all-in rate for costs which includes all these items; very similar to absorption costing. Secondly, do the contracts pay directly for major servicing on plant? If plant has a major servicing every six months, a contract which employs the items for four months pays no servicing whilst one having the item for eight months pays for two servicings. Such problems can be overcome by an hourly rate, again all-in.

The contracts must obviously contribute to Head Office costs, so what are Head Office costs and how are they allocated? If they include plant administration and the buying organisation does a maintenance contract using little or no plant and small quantities of locally purchased material pay as much in proportion as a major contract? Finally the question of preliminaries has to be dealt with, under marginal costing such items as tower cranes should have the actual time spent on activities allocated to each cost code.

However, accommodation and staff may have to have a percentage addition to all activity costs. Consider the basis of the original estimate, if all the preliminaries are costed separately they should be controlled separately, therefore they should be allocated to a preliminaries coding.

Finally, there are problems with the differences between the estimate and tender. The estimate is the cost of carrying out the job as predicted by the contractor. This should be under ideal conditions as was identified under standard costing. At the adjudication of the estimate there is an addition of costs for risks and overheads with the final addition of the required profit. Cost control on site is concerned with the actual costs contained in the estimate and therefore attempts must be made to record the costs of production separately from overheads and those charges which are attributable to the risk element.

In order to record these costs certain spending or production centres need to be identified. These are usually termed cost centres, and in the construction industry each site is a cost centre, and when combined with the buying, plant, contract, surveying and other departments will make up the total expenditure of the firm. Each cost centre must have its rules for recording costs to enable an analysis of expenditure to be easily conducted.

The site cost centre will allocate its costs to certain cost codes, these codes should be related to the original cost source which is the bill of quantities. Therefore the best coding system begins with each bill heading, for example:

01 Preliminaries
02 Excavation
03 Concretor
04 Bricklayer
05 Drainlayer
06 Plasterer
07 Roofer
08 External works

This list provides an indication of the basic coding which may be used. The second item in the code may be using a letter but could equally be another number. As an example of the secondary coding the following lists may be used.

01 Preliminaries
A Staff
B Accommodation
C Administration
D Plant
E Services

02 Excavation
A Oversite
B Reduced level ne 1.5 m deep
C Trenches
D Small pits
E Basements ex 1.5 m deep

These secondary lists are not exhaustive but give an indication of the type of information that should be recorded. The third group of figures should give further details as follows:

01 Preliminaries
D *Plant*
01 Cranes
02 Excavators
03 Dumpers
04 Transport
05 Fork lifts
06 Concrete mixers

02 Excavation
C *Trenches*
01 Ordinary ground
02 Sandy/gravel

03 Sand/loam
04 Clay/loam
05 Clay
06 Rock

Both items can now be developed to infinite detail providing that the largest items are dealt with first. The person using the cost code needs very little information other than the bill of quantities items.

Using the code 01/D/01 is a crane on preliminaries and the next set of figures or letters could indicate the material being moved or the section of the bill of quantities being assisted. In the latter example if the crane was moving or assisting drainlaying then 05 could be added to the code. The excavation codes could be 02/B/05 with further explanation by depth and width so that 600 mm wide may be '02' and up to 1 m deep 'A', so that excavating trenches in clay to these dimensions becomes 02/B/05/02/A.

Such coding needs to be related to a cost centre and the latter can be permanently identified by the use of two letters such as PL for plant and BU for buying. Contracts can be identified by similar related letters which can be easily associated with the contract.

Card filing or microprocessors can be used to record costs, the latter being the most appropriate because they will be able to produce graphs and charts of the information provided, almost instantly. The coding system must be allied to and suitable for the storage method and above all provide useful information for cost control and feedback for future estimating.

10.5 SITE COST CONTROL

Site cost control is concerned with the control of those variables on site which can be analysed and action taken to improve production or reduce costs. The semi-variable costs which have relationships, which are extremely difficult to identify, with the production activity, are recorded not for control but to provide a historic comparison and feedback. The site manager is responsible for the day to day running of a contract and is most concerned with labour plant and materials. The basis of such a control system is shown in *Fig 10.8*.

When the cost control of labour is undertaken as advocated in Chapter 5 the planning and allocation of work is integrated with the control. The labour employment sheet shown in *Fig 5.10* contains provision for the insertion of a cost code above every task description and for the target per hour. Comparisons can be made on this sheet but it is more likely that the information will be extracted and submitted in another form. This sheet can be used to enter labour employed in activities which are semi-variable such as on-site staff and other preliminaries.

The allocation of these resources can be as detailed as required because each task beyond the five spaces can be allocated on additional sheets. Any casual work which has not been planned such as emergencies, daywork or unloading unscheduled materials arrivals can be added to the sheets. It is expected that a well trained supervisory force would ensure that all the tasks the operatives performed under their direction, were recorded.

Plant cost recording is more difficult because it is usually a split responsibility. In such cases a clear definition of responsibilities with regard to the recording and allocating of cost must be made. Similarly, this is where there is likely to be some

Fig 10.8 The principles of site cost control

dilemma as to what constitutes overheads, direct variable and semi-variable costs. The forms shown in *Figs 5.7, 5.8* and *5.9* are an attempt to ensure that as many costs as possible are directly allocated. This will also enable the most accurate costs to be considered if a machine evaluation is conducted when considering a new purchase. The sheets contain provision for cost coding whilst all the additional costs can be proportioned in relationship to the hours spent on each task.

WEEKLY STATUS SHEET

	OPERATION				PROGRESS						COSTS			
REFERENCE NUMBER	DESCRIPTION INCLUDING REFERENCES AND COST CODING IF REQUIRED	ORIGINAL PLANNED QUANTITY	ADJUSTED QUANTITY	STATUS LAST WEEK PLUS OR MINUS PERCENT	TOTAL PLANNED UNITS	TOTAL ACTUAL UNITS	TOTAL PLANNED PERCENTAGE COMPLETE	TOTAL ACTUAL PERCENTAGE COMPLETE	STATUS THIS WEEK PLUS OR MINUS PERCENTAGE	PLANNED TOTAL EXPENDITURE	ACTUAL TOTAL EXPENDITURE	PLANNED COST PER UNIT	ACTUAL COST PER UNIT	TOTAL COSTS STATUS PLUS OR MINUS
1	Excavate trenches 02/13/05/02/A	2000 m		+1%	250 m	200 m	12.5	10	−2.5	2500	2100	10.00	10.50	+100
2	Concrete in founds 03/D/04/02	700 m^3		0	70 m^3	50 m^3	10	7	−3	840	590	12.00*	11.80	−10
3	Brickwork to DPC 04/A/02/01/88	2000 m^2		0	50 m^2	40.4 m^2	11.5	2	+0.5	450	650	15.00*	16.25	+50

LABOUR ONLY *

Fig 10.9 Weekly cost and progress comparison

The forms illustrated can be adapted to meet the particular costing requirements of the firm and whilst some calculation may be necessary the best systems enable a direct transfer of information to the subsequent status and cost reports.

The monthly materials statement shown in *Fig 5.5* and the weekly materials received report shown in *Fig 3.8* will enable the cost of materials to be computed and if necessary allocated to the different codes. Some difficulty may be experienced in assessing the quantity of materials incorporated and the stocks on site.

The accurate physical and cost control of materials is one of the main contributing factors to the prevention of waste. However, it must be repeated that the contributions to productivity made by the effectiveness of the system must exceed the cost of that system.

All the information recorded and gathered with regard to labour plant and materials is now brought together in a status sheet which is shown in *Fig 10.9*. The weekly status sheet is based on the physical progress report and related to the programme operations. These operations, in a fully integrated system, would reflect the main cost code areas. The whole purpose of the status sheet is to illustrate the comparisons between the planned and actual progress and cost.

The one problem is with variations in the quantity of work. Often work is commenced, for example, on an item which has a provisional quantity, and half-way through the amount is increased. The column headed 'adjusted quantity' allows for any alterations and the smaller percentage progress because of the change in the base amount. The percentage status of progress last week gives a link to the previous report and comparison with this week is easier. The total costs status gives a chance to compare the costs and they should be highlighted by deficit amounts being indicated in red or by the use of brackets.

The status sheet provides a weekly report but it may be far more important to submit a full monthly report to assist in the compilation of the interim valuation. This cost report should be submitted under cost code headings giving the total expenditure under each sub-code, and split into plant, labour and materials. The final totals are compared with planned expenditure and physical progress. The information gathered by the site weather records, daywork sheets, 'Q' sheets, site diary and all the other records are brought together to provide a full picture of the past months activity. This cost report should accurately reflect the profitability of the contract and review the problems and delays which have occurred.

10.6 QUESTIONS ON SITE COST CONTROL

MULTI-CHOICE QUESTIONS

1   Variable costs are those which:
    (a) vary over a period of time;
    (b) vary directly with production activity;
    (c) change between one accounting period and another;
    (d) do not vary with production but with other factors.

2   Standard costing is based on the:
    (a) allocation of overheads by percentage;
    (b) determination of targets to cover all costs;
    (c) job or contract estimates;
    (d) direct costs of production only.

3 The margin of safety in a break-even chart lies between:
   (a) maximum total value and total costs;
   (b) the fixed costs total and maximum variable costs;
   (c) the break-even point and the total value of work produced;
   (d) high and low fixed costs.

4 Cost codes should be based on categories of work which are:
   (a) easily recognised and direct;
   (b) broad by key operations;
   (c) matched to programme activities;
   (d) most useful in meeting the objective.

5 Site cost control should:
   (a) ensure that site management is controlled;
   (b) provide adequate information for bonus payments;
   (c) indicate lack of progress;
   (d) assist in improving productivity.

SHORT-ANSWER QUESTIONS (15-20 minutes)

1 Describe break-even charts and how they may be used in the construction industry.

2 Describe the elements which make up total costs in the construction industry.

3 Explain one of the following costing methods:
   (a) marginal; (b) absorption; (c) standard.

4 Describe a suitable system of cost coding for a construction firm, giving an example.

5 Explain the objectives and principles of on-site cost control.

QUESTIONS REQUIRING LONGER ANSWERS (30-45 minutes)

1 Discuss the methods of costing which may be used by a construction firm indicating the most appropriate method for a firm with a £5 m annual turnover.

2 Discuss the identification and allocation of expenditure on a construction site. Explain how any problems may be overcome.

3 Describe how the direct variable costs may be controlled on site. Illustrate the answer with specimen forms.

4 Using any example within your experience prepare a cost report covering two trades or work sections.

5 Describe the relationship between physical progress, delays, construction problems and cost and explain how they could be reported to head office.

Index

Absences, 31
Absorption costing, 171
Accounts, petty cash, 30, 31
Accuracy in recording, 81
Activity float, 136
Activity numbers, 141
Activity sampling, 111
Adaptability, 153
Administration, questions, 47, 48
Administrative provision, 17
Agendas, 54, 55
Allocation of labour, 31
Allowances, 109
Appearance, 153, 159
Appointments, 126
Architect's Instructions, 37, 40, 45
'As built' drawings, 37
ASME symbols, 100
Aspects of communication, 3
Aspects of planning, 126
Aspects of safety, 14
Attendance, 87, 88
Attributes, 163, 165, 166
Authority, 83, 84

Bar-chart, 135
Bar-chart progress, 146, 147
Barriers to communication, 5
Basic time, 106
Basic time abstract, 109
Benefits of communication, 6
Bonus targets, 120
Bonus-target abstract, 120
Bonus-target procedure, 121
Break-even charts, 176, 177
Break-even point, 176
British Standards, 66, 155, 158
BS Codes of Practice, 158
Building Regulations, 155

Cascade method, 143
Chairmanship, 53, 57, 58
Checklists, 8, 12
Cleanliness of sites, 71
Clerk of Works, 39, 156

Communication barriers, 5
  benefits, 6
  characteristics, 26, 28
  decay, 1
  definition, 3
  external links, 26, 27
  internal links, 28
  process, 4
  questions, 6, 7
Comparison of payment methods, 122
Confirmation in writing, 27
Construction Regulations, 9
Consultation meetings, 52
Contract information flow, 2
Contractual disputes, 46
Control charts, 165, 166
  limits, 166
  of plant, 75
  of Pollution Act, 10
  of labour, 79
Coordination
  factors affecting, 92
  of sub contractors, 93
  principles, 92
Correspondence, 27
Costs
  centres, 179
  codes, 178, 179
  curves, 172, 174
  elements, 169
  fixed, 169
  Head Office, 169
  identification, 170
  indirect, 169
  labour, 170
  materials, 170
  plant, 170
  questions, 183, 184
  reports, 182, 183
  system, 170, 171
  total, 169
Cranes, task definition, 72
Critical path method, 137

Date cursor, 150, 174
Dayworks, 45

Layworks record sheet, 46
Decision making meetings, 52
Defects liability, 162
Definition
  of planning, 125
  of programming, 125
  of quality, 153
  of sub-contractors, 83
  of tasks, 71, 72, 126
Degree of accuracy, 111
Degree of control, 164
Delays, 43
  causes, 119
  notification of, 43
  records, 43
Delivery inspection, 66
Delivery notes, 31
Demolition safety, 14
Diary, daily site, 29, 43
Dimensional limits, 158
Dismissal, 31
Distribution curve, 163
Domestic sub-contractors, 83
Drawings
  administrative procedure, 38
  amendments, 37
  'as-built', 37
  register card, 39
  storage, 37
Drying rooms, 17
Durability, 153
Durations, 125

Earliest event times, 136
Effective communication, 3
Employment sheet
  labour, 79, 136
  plant, 77, 78
Engagement of labour, 31
Erection of structure, 16
Event slack, 136
Excavation safety, 15
Excavation tasks, 71
External communication links, 26

Factors
  plant efficiency, 74
  plant time, 75
  productivity, 117
Feedback, 3, 79, 81, 180
Field count sheet, 112
Filing systems, 27

Financial incentives, 117, 121
Fire prevention, 9
Fixed costs, 177, 178
Flexibity, 125
Float-types, 142
Flow diagram, 100, 103
Flow process chart 100, 102
Food Hygiene Regulations, 9
Foundation work-safety, 16

Gang activity sample, 113
General attendance, 87
Goods received report, 35

Highways Act, 10
Human factor, 98

Incentives
  financial, 117
  non-financial, 117
  objectives, 117
  procedure, 121
  questions, 124
  reasons for, 119
  rewards, 118
Information,
  booklet materials, 67
  flow, 1, 2
  meetings, 51
  needs, 62
  quality, 62
  receipt record, 45
  resources, 63
  suitability, 62
Inspectors, 156, 157
Instructions,
  architects, 37, 40
  sheet, 41
  urgent, 40
Internal communication links, 28

Job costing, 172

Labour allocation sheet, 32
Labour employment sheet, 80, 136
Labour only sub-contractors, 83, 90
Labour utilisation, 80
Latest event time, 136
Letters, 27
Levelling of resources, 141
Local Government Act, 10
Lockers for operatives, 17

Maintainability, 153
Marginal costing, 170, 171
Margin of safety, 177
Materials
  administrative procedure, 36
  calculating quantity, 64
  categories of, 65
  control, 64
  handling plant, 66
  information booklet, 67
  monthly statement, 68
  reconciliation, 66
  responsibilities, 70
  return sheet, 35
  schedule, 33, 34, 64
  storage, 18
Matrix analysis, 84, 85
Meetings
  agendas, 54, 55
  arrangements, 56
  attendance, 53
  chairmanship, 53, 57, 58
  contract administration, 51
  internal control, 49
  management/employees, 51
  minutes, 57–60
  objectives, 53
  planning, 53
  purpose of, 51
  questions, 60, 61
  sub-contractor, 49, 89, 90
  types of site, 49, 50
Memoranda, 28
Methods of communication, 3, 4, 28
Method statement, 128–132
Method study, 97, 100, 101
Models, 105, 106
Motivation, 118
Moving income, 174
Multiple activity chart, 115, 116

Network analysis, 137
Network example, 138
Nominated sub-contractors, 43, 84, 92
Nominated suppliers, 43
Nominated by architects, 83

Observed time, 106, 107
Occupiers Liability Act, 10
Offices Shops and Railway Premises Act, 9
Overall programme, 134

Overheads, 181
Overlapping activities, 141

Payments to sub-contractors, 95
Persuasion meetings, 52
Planning, 125, 127
Planning and programming questions, 151, 152
Planning a site layout, 19
Planning of meetings, 53
Plant
  attributes, 73
  choice of, 72
  efficiency, 74
  employment sheet 77, 78
  materials handling, 66
  mobile, parking, 18
  procurement, 73
  selection of, 73
  service sheet, 76
  static, siting, 18
  task definition, 71
Precedence diagram example, 140
Precedence diagrams, 137, 139
Pre-tender programmes, 134
Procedure
  drawings, 38
  materials, 36
Process of communication, 4
Programming, 125, 127, 133
Progress recording, 150
Progress reports, 143–149

'Q' sheet, 41
Quality,
  costs and price, 156
  definition of, 153
  diminished, 154
  non-compliance, 160
  of conformance, 153, 154, 157
  of design, 153, 154
  questions, 167, 168
  responsibilities for, 155
  specification, 159
  standards, 155, 158
Quantity surveyor, 155
Query sheet, 42
Questionnaire for sub-contractor, 85, 86

Rating, 106, 107
Register of drawings, 37

Reports,
  categories of, 25
  on sub-contractors, 94
  standard format, 25, 28
Resources
  allocation, 143
  information, 63
  levelling, 144, 145
  of production, 1
  questions, 81, 82
  utilisation, 79

'S' curves, 173
Safety in production, 14
Sampling, 162
Sanitary conveniences, 17
Scheduling, 141
Schedule, materials, 33, 34
Sequences, 125, 128
Serviceability, 153
Services coordination, 92
Services location, 13
Setting up site, 19
Short term programme, 134
Site administration questions, 47, 48
Site boundaries, 13
Site cost control, 181
Site investigation, 11
Site investigation, check list, 12
Site layout
  contract requirements, 9
  example, 20
  factors, 8
  need for, 8
  objectives, 19
  office detail, 21
  planning, 19
  questions, 23, 24
  siting of plant, 18
  subcontractor, requirements, 11
Site relationships, 39
SREDIM, 100, 101
Stage programme, 134
Standard costs, 172
Standard deviation, 163
Standard time, 110
Statutory notices, 10
Statutory registers, 11
Storage area programme, 22
Storage, types of, 18
String diagram, 104, 105

188

Subcontractors
  areas for storage, 23
  coordination, 93
  meetings, 49
  nominated, 43
  payments, 95
  performance, 94
  progress report, 91
  questionnaire, 85, 86
  questions, 95, 96
  safety, 87
  selection, 84
Systematic sampling, 114

Targets
  bonus, 120, 121
  financial, 120, 122
  time, 120, 122
Tasks
  definition of, 71, 72
  work content, 99
Telephone, 28
Temporary works, 14
Testing
  classes of, 161
  place of, 161
Three dimensional modes, 105, 106
Time sheets, 31
Time study, 106
  abstract 108, 109
  allowances, 109–111
  example, 108
  procedure, 107
  standard time, 110
Two dimensional models, 106

Unit costing, 172
Utilisation of labour, 79
Utilisation of plant, 79

Variable costs, 181
Variables, 163
Verticality, 159

Wastage, 69
Waste, 69
  causes of, 69
  direct, 69
  indirect, 69
Weather record charts, 43, 44
Weekly cost and progress, 182
Weekly programme, 134

Welfare facilities, 17
Work content of tasks, 99
Workmanship, 153
Work measurement, 97
Work study
  application, 98
  factors, 97
  questions, 123, 124

'Z' charts, 175
Zone of acceptance, 164
Zone of indecision, 163
Zone of rejection, 164

Butterworths Technician Series

Mathematics

Mathematics for Technicians 1
F Tabberer

1978 192 pages 246 × 189 mm
0 408 00326 X Limp Illustrated

Mathematics for Technicians 2
F Tabberer

1978 156 pages 246 × 189 mm
0 408 00371 5 Limp Illustrated

Science

Physical Science for Technicians 1
R McMullan

1978 96 pages 246 × 189 mm
0 408 00332 4 Limp Illustrated

Building Construction, Civil Engineering, Surveying and Architecture

Building Technology 1
J T Bowyer

1978 96 pages 246 × 189 mm
0 408 00298 0 Limp Illustrated

Building Technology 2
J T Bowyer

1978 96 pages 246 × 189 mm
0 408 00299 9 Limp Illustrated

Building Technology 3
J T Bowyer

1980 104 pages 246 × 189 mm
0 408 00411 8 Limp Illustrated

Civil Engineering Technology 3
B J Fletcher and S A Lavan

1980 96 pages 246 × 189 mm
0 408 00426 6 Limp Illustrated

•Construction Science and Materials 2
D Watkins and J Fincham

1981 192 pages approx 246 × 189 mm
0 408 00488 6 Limp Illustrated

•Site Surveying and Levelling 2
W S Whyte and R E Paul

1981 160 pages approx 246 × 189 mm
0 408 00532 7 Limp Illustrated

Heating and Hot Water Services for Technicians
K Moss

1978 168 pages 246 × 189 mm
0 408 00300 6 Limp Illustrated

Electrical, Electronic and Telecommunications Engineering

Electrical Drawing for Technicians 1
F Linsley

1979 96 pages 246 × 189 mm
0 408 00417 7 Limp Illustrated

Telecommunications Systems for Technicians 1
G L Danielson and R S Walker

1979 112 pages 246 × 189 mm
0 408 00352 9 Limp Illustrated

•Transmission Systems for Technicians 2
G L Danielson and R S Walker

1981 72 pages approx 246 × 189 mm
0 408 00562 9 Limp Illustrated

•Radio Systems for Technicians 2
G L Danielson and R S Walker

1981 96 pages approx 246 × 189 mm
0 408 00561 0 Limp Illustrated

•Radio Systems for Technicians 3
G L Danielson and R S Walker

1982 112 pages approx 246 × 189 mm
0 408 00588 2 Limp Illustrated

Electrical and Electronic Principles 2
I R Sinclair

1979 96 pages 246 × 189 mm
0 408 00433 9 Limp Illustrated

Electrical and Electronic Applications 2
D W Tyler

1980 204 pages 246 × 189 mm
0 408 00412 6 Limp Illustrated

Electronics for Technicians 2
S A Knight

1978 112 pages 246 × 189 mm
0 408 00324 3 Limp Illustrated

Electronics for Technicians 3
S A Knight

1980 160 pages 246 × 189 mm
0 408 00458 4 Limp Illustrated

Electrical Principles for Technicians 2
S A Knight

1978 144 pages 246 × 189 mm
0 408 00325 1 Limp Illustrated

Electrical and Electronic Principles 3
S A Knight

1980 160 pages 246 × 189 mm
0 408 00456 8 Limp Illustrated

•Electrical and Electronic Principles 4/5
S A Knight

1982 176 pages approx 246 × 189 mm
0 408 01109 2 Limp Illustrated

Mechanical, Production, Marine and Motor Vehicle Engineering

Vehicle Technology 1
M J Nunney

1980 112 pages 246 × 189 mm
0 408 00461 4 Limp Illustrated

•Vehicle Technology 2
M J Nunney

1981 96 pages approx 246 × 189 mm
0 408 00594 7 Limp Illustrated

•Engine Technology 1
M J Nunney

1981 120 pages approx 246 × 189 mm
0 408 00511 4 Limp Illustrated

Manufacturing Technology 2
P J Harris

1979 96 pages 246 × 189 mm
0 408 00410 X Limp Illustrated

•Manufacturing Technology 3
P J Harris

1981 104 pages approx 246 × 189 mm
0 408 00493 2 Limp Illustrated

•Fabrication, Welding and Metal Joining Processes — A textbook for Technicians and Craftsmen
C Flood

1981 160 pages approx 246 × 189 mm
0 408 00448 7 Limp Illustrated

•Materials Technology for Technicians 2
W Bolton

1981 128 pages approx 246 × 189 mm
0 408 01117 3 Limp Illustrated

•Materials Technology for Technicians 3
W Bolton

1982 128 pages approx 246 × 189 mm
0 408 01116 5 Limp Illustrated

•Materials Technology 4
W Bolton

1981 128 pages approx 246 × 189 mm
0 408 00584 X Limp Illustrated

Mechanical Science for Technicians 3
W Bolton

1980 128 pages 246 × 189 mm
0 408 00486 X Limp Illustrated

•Mechanical Science for Higher Technicians 4/5
D H Bacon and R C Stephens

1981 256 pages approx 234 × 156 mm
0 408 00570 X Limp Illustrated

•Thermodynamics for Technicians 3/4
D H Bacon and R C Stephens

1982 96 pages approx 234 × 156 mm
0 408 01114 9 Limp Illustrated

Engineering Instrumentation and Control
W Bolton

1980 144 pages 246 × 189 mm
0 408 00462 2 Limp Illustrated

To. Michael J
with best ~
Bridget Hole

TWO THOUSAND YEARS
AT MIDDLE WHARF

TWO THOUSAND YEARS AT MIDDLE WHARF

A History of Maidenhead in Verse
By Bridget Hole

Published By Acorn Forum

First Published in Great Britain 1996

Published By:
Acorn Forum
5 Kings Grove
Maidenhead SL6 4DA
Berkshire

© Copyright Bridget Hole

Printed by:
ProPrint
Riverside Cottage
Great North Road
Stibbington
Peterborough PE8 6LR

ISBN: 0 9527947 0 5
All Rights Reserved

ABOUT THE AUTHOR

Bridget Hole was born in Yorkshire but grew up in Maidenhead. The fourth of five children, she was educated at All Saints C of E School, the County School and secretarial college and went on to study for a diploma in youth work. Married, with a son and a granddaughter, she still lives in Maidenhead.

Other titles by the author:-

A LETTER FROM HOME
DRIFTS OF BLUEBELLS
UBI CARITAS

This book is dedicated to my sister
ELIZABETH PEAKE DIXON 1928-1991
Who taught me to read and introduced me to the magic of books.

Throughout her teaching career, 'Libby' enriched the lives of hundreds of children with her love and commitment to her profession.

My thanks to my nephew
JOHN J TOMLINSON, B.A.
For the illustrations

INTRODUCTION

Two thousand years' ago, Maidenhead, in Berkshire, was just a small clearing by the River Thames in Windsor Forest, about twenty miles from London, where a wharf had been built to process and transport the wood brought down from Bisham Woods en route for Windsor.

The name Maidenhead has had many varied and interesting explanations but the most likely is that it is a derivation of Midden Hythe, the Anglo-Saxon spelling of Middle Wharf.

Henry VI gave Maidenhead a royal charter, which was withdrawn by Henry VIII and restored by Queen Elizabeth I. Further charters were granted by King James I, King Charles II and King James II.

Maidenhead, now a part of The Royal Borough of Windsor and Maidenhead, has taken part in the evolution of England and her history mirrors that of the rest of the country.

CONTENTS

The Romans	1
The Anglo-Saxons	7
The Middle Ages	12
The Reformation 1534-1559	20
The Seventeenth Century	26
The Coaching Era	30
The Victorians	41
The River	51
Worship and Education	63
The Twentieth Century	74

1. THE ROMANS

Julius Caesar was fascinated by England, which he called 'The tin Island', and he brought his army from Rome to conquer it in 55 B.C. The Roman soldiers crossed the sea and travelled up the River Thames where some of them settled at the place which we now know as Maidenhead, where the fertile Thames Valley was ideal for arable farming. They built settlements high above the flood plain, at Cox Green and Castle Hill; their villas were constructed of brick and thatch and had underfloor heating and bathrooms. They also built a comprehensive network of roads across the country. But the Romans were not acclimatised to the damp atmosphere of the Thames Valley and many of them died of 'English' diseases such as pneumonia, asthma, rheumatism and arthritis and were buried in a graveyard by the river at Bray.

The stylish, expensive clothes and jewellery which the Romans wore were a marked contrast to the drab apparel of the natives who existed by trying to scratch a living from the land or the river and their lifestyle must have been a source of envy, especially to the young Angles. The Romans left after nearly five hundred years leaving behind a thriving agricultural economy.

1 VENI VIDI VICI
2 CASTLE HILL VILLA
3 FATHERLY ADVICE
4 MORE FATHERLY ADVICE
5 A LONELY GRAVE

VENI VIDI VICI

The woodland folk took refuge behind an upturned raft
The boats which sailed into Middle Wharf were not of local craft
The strangers in their bright array
Had obviously gone astray
From where?

As the ornate boats docked at the wharf the Romans jumped ashore
The woodland folk were startled by the strange, bright clothes they wore
The peasants sensed a danger
From these a-plumaged strangers
From where?

The timid wharfmen peered out from the safety of their hide
At the colourful armoured soldiers gathered by the riverside
The centurions at Middle Wharf
Fell into ranks and then marched off
To where?

CASTLE HILL VILLA

The natives were allowed to live in their clearing by the Thames
The Romans found some higher ground to build their settlements.

They dug the footings for a villa high up within the woods
Where they would not be troubled by recurring winter floods.

Bricks were shaped and baked in kilns and rafters hewn from wood
And soon a settlement appeared where only trees had stood.

The natives watched in awe as the men from over the sea
Built houses with windows and chimneys, a wondrous sight to see.

The Romans dug up the old cart tracks where oxen had dragged their loads
And used gravel and stone and flint to construct a network of roads.

The source of water had hereto been drawn from river or stream
The Romans tapped the underground springs for water sparkling and clean.

They built a tank on Castle Hill to use as a water store
They heated it in metal pipes concealed beneath the floor.

The residents of Middle Wharf were filled with admiration
For the Romans who enriched their lives, who imported civilisation.

FATHERLY ADVICE

No, my son, you may not go to the bath house on Castle Hill
I've never agreed with such goings on, and I never will
Men, as many as twenty, all in the bath together,
Besporting themselves in nakedness, with no shame whatsoever
Washing themselves with fancy oils in front of total strangers
No thought for common decency, no regard for moral dangers.

Since time began we have kept ourselves scrupulously clean
By washing on the river bank by the ever-flowing stream
To wash in moving water is the only sensible way
To attend to your ablutions at the end of every day
Listen to your father, Son, I'll never tell you lies
It is my bounden duty to give you good advice.

Get yourself down to the wharf, where the clear, cold water rushes
And wash yourself in private, well hidden by the bushes
Make sure no women or girls are about before you start to strip
And watch out for the water rats, they'll give you a nasty nip
Mark my words, Son, no good will come of the Romans' lack of modesty
Their lewd behaviour will be the downfall of the Holy Roman Dynasty.

MORE FATHERLY ADVICE

No, my girl, you may not go out with the soldier from up on the hill
I've never agreed with such goings on, and I never will
We know nothing of him except that he has travelled here from Rome
It is likely that he has a wife and children waiting for him at home
I've seen the girls with the soldiers, hussies one and all
They bring shame upon our their families, camp-followers they are called.

You'll marry Cedric, son of Jon, just as I have planned
He has a hut deep in the woods and sixteen acres of land
His hut is furnished comfortably with two chairs and a sturdy table
And he's presently carving a lump of oak to make you a baby's cradle
He'll make you a good husband, he's a strong, hardworking lad
So you can forget all that nonsense, all those fancy ideas that you had.

No arguments, the subject's closed, do not argue with me
No daughter of mine will bring disgrace upon this family
I'll not discuss it further, I've had my final say
If I catch that Roman sneaking around, be sure, he'll rue the day
Go help your mother with the washing, she's down beside the creek
And I will make arrangements with Jon for a wedding within the week.

A LONELY GRAVE

The Roman soldiers sailed up the Thames
To Maidenhead and set up camp
They were not prepared for the British climes
The Thames Valley was cold and damp.

On leaving Italy the weather was fine
But on arrival at Maidenhead
They succumbed to the lack of sunshine
By Spring a great number were dead.

They were not immune to British diseases
Like asthma and bronchitis
The Latin warriors from over the seas
Were soon crippled with arthritis.

The Romans built a graveyard
Down by the river at Bray
To bury the their fallen comrades
The numbers grew by the day.

How sad to sail across the sea
Leaving family and friends in Rome
To die so ignominiously
So very far from home.

7. THE ANGLO-SAXONS

When the Romans left in the sixth century A.D., England was plunged into the dark ages. The Saxons, from Europe, had made many raids on the country during the Roman occupation but had always been defeated; now, with the Romans gone, they sailed across the sea in their longboats and took over the country. The Saxons were warrior tribesmen under the leadership of a chieftain and they brought terror to the island with their acts of cruelty and barbarity. They were uncivilised and knew nothing of building with brick or of modern sanitation or of road building and they let the Roman villas fall into ruin after looting them of anything valuable; the roads were not maintained and soon reverted to cart tracks. These new Anglo-Saxons built themselves houses of wood and, when they were not fighting and pillaging, they farmed the land. Saxon graves, including that of Chieftain Taeppa, which have been excavated in Tapow, on the opposite bank of the river to Maidenhead, have yielded gold, bronze, fine glass and examples of their weaponry which are on show at the British Museum. Taplow is another derivation of Anglo-Saxon - Tap (Taeppa's) Low (Mound) - and Taeppa's Mound can still be seen in the grounds of Taplow House. Not many examples of Saxon dwellings have survived as they did not build with the same strength and thoroughness as the Romans.

The country gradually became more peaceful, most villages had a church and the monasteries were full of treasure, until even fiercer tribesmen came in 800 A.D. and terror ruled once more. At first, The Danes also called Norsemen or Vikings, attacked the monasteries nearest the coast, stole all the riches, killed the monks and escaped back across the North Sea, but eventually they steered inland, some of them coming up the Thames to Maidenhead where they stole horses and attacked the surrounding settlements. The Danes were heathens until they were converted to Christianity by King Alfred.

The Saxons and Danes co-existed until 980 A.D. when a new tribe of Danes came roaming the country, burning, killing and seizing land; but when their king, King Canute, was converted to Christianity he ruled well and wisely.

On the Thames at Cookham near Maidenhead, is Sashes Island where there are fortifications built in Saxon times and Viking burial grounds have been unearthed in nearby Sonning and Reading.

1. CHIEFTAIN TAEPPA
2. THE LONGBOATS HAVE BEEN SIGHTED
3. THE WOOD CARVERS

1. CHIEFTAIN TAEPPA

Wails of mourning rend the air
Cries of woe, abject despair
As warriors by the wharf declare
Chieftain Taeppa is dead.

Bury him in the marshy ground
Cover him with a grassy mound
For a thousand years he will not be found
Chieftain Taeppa is dead.

Put his jewels in the grave
Arm this Saxon warrior brave
With his axe, his bow, his stave
Chieftain Taeppa is dead.

2. THE LONGBOATS HAVE BEEN SIGHTED

Come, quickly, hide within this den, my sons and little daughter
I've dug it deep, well out of sight, to save you from the slaughter
The longboats have been sighted, Windsor has been ravaged
No man or woman or innocent child is safe from the heathen savage.

Mother, hush the children, keep the entrance covered
The invaders will show no mercy should we be discovered
The old, the frail and the very young will have a watery grave
The rest of us will spend our lives as the barbaric Saxon's slaves.

We laboured hard with pick and axe to quarry out the stones
To construct and maintain a network of sturdy Roman roads
We hewed the wood and baked the bricks with which to build the homes
Of Caesar's men who came to Middle Wharf and settled here from Rome.

We tilled our fields and grew the corn to make our daily bread
We laboured long from dawn t dusk to keep our families fed
Five hundred years we lived in peace with the Romans to protect us
Now they have left us on our own, the invaders will not respect us.

Come out, my friends and neighbours, the barbarians have sailed away
But a lookout must be posted down the river at Bray
The hordes are massing at the river mouth, and there can be no dispute
Within a month our lives will be shattered by the fiendish Saxon brutes.

3. THE WOOD CARVERS

We fell the trees to earn enough to keep ourselves alive
And send it down the river to be sorted at Middenhythe
Before it can be moved to Windsor to build the wooden fort
Those Saxons commandeer it and our work is all for nought.

I understand your anger, friend, but you really must agree
That the longboats of the Vikings do justice to any tree
The figureheads which grace the boats, standing proudly fore and aft
Reveal their natural talents as they shape their sailing craft.

You may be right, good neighbour, give praise where it is due
The skill of the savage mariners is a splendid sight to view
But I wish that they would move away and ply their trade elsewhere
If they continue to plunder trees, Bisham Woods will soon be bare.

21. MIDDLE AGES

In 1066 the Normans, from France, landed at Hastings and killed Harold of the Saxons and most of his men; William of Normandy (William the Conquerer) declared himself King of England.

King William wanted to know how much his new kingdom was worth so he commissioned a countrywide census of every town, village and hamlet; completed in 1086, this is known as the Domesday Book. Names from one thousand years' ago still survive in Maidenhead - Ghilo de Pinkney (Pinkneys Green), Knight Ellington (Ellington Park and Ellington Road), and De Spencer, a Norman Knight (Spencers Farm Estate). The King gave manors (areas of land) to his Knights, Barons and Abbots in return for their loyalty to the crown, and these men leased land to villeins (serfs) in return for working for their master, without pay, for three days a week and providing him with produce. This was called the Feudal System. The area known as Ellington (Elentone) was held from Ghilo de Pinkney by two villeins and comprised six people, four cottages, one plough, sixteen acres of woodland and ten pigs; it was valued at sixty shillings.

In 1215, King John signed the Magna Carta at Runnymede, a short way down the Thames near Windsor, which eased the lot of the peasants for a while, but the King's promises were soon broken.

In about 1280 a wooden bridge was built over the Thames at Maidenhead and the town expanded with shops and inns alongside the High Street (Bath Road) and a market. The wharf was now very busy with barges coming up from London.

In 1452 a charter was granted to Maidenhead by Henry VI, allowing a corporation to be formed to administer the spiritual and commercial affairs of Maidenhead; this was dissolved in 1547 by Henry VIII and restored again in 1582 by Queen Elizabeth I. Further charters were granted to the town by King James I in 1604, King Charles II in 1662 and King James II in 1685.

The manorial system continued throughout the Middle Ages and there were many manors in and around Maidenhead, some of them surviving to the present day.

N.B. 'Court of Pie Powder' is from the French description of peddlers - Pied Pouldreux (dusty footed).

1. THE SERF
2. THE MANORS
3. SHALLOW PROMISES
4. THE SIEGE OF MAYDENHETH BRIDGE
5. GOOD QUEEN BESS
6. THE GATECRASHER

1. THE SERF

Forgive me, Master, I am empty-handed for my hens have ceased to lay
They've all gone sick so I cannot bring the eggs for you today
Neither have I milk to bring, the cow has sadly died
And the heat has melted the butter I owe, it's completely rancified
We've all been ill, myself, the wife and our baby daughter
I beg you, Sir, please absolve me from my obligations this quarter.

You snivelling villein, you wastrel serf, don't come grovelling to me
It is all written down in the finest script, the terms of your tenancy
Twelve eggs a week, some pork and ham, two loaves of finest bread
How do you expect me to live, to keep my family fed
Where are the logs to heat my manor, where is the hay for my horse
Bring all my dues by the morning or I'll move you out by force.

At dead of night the wretched serf stole out into the night
His frightened wife and ailing child walked closely by his side
They reached the wharf where willing hands helped them to escape
Deep into Windsor Forest where, with friends, they would be safe
They lived as outlaws from that day, free and happy folk
No longer paying homage, no longer chained to the yolk.

2. THE MANORS

Brave knights who fought to maintain the crown with bow and lance and sword
And all who found favour with the monarch, were given a rich reward
A stretch of land to call their own, as far as the eye could see
With a manor house to live in, their's in perpetuity
A mile west of the river, a truly impressive manor
With land stretching to Braywick, was bequeathed to Adam Shoppenhanger
Another Adam, de Burnham, was granted Lillibrooke
Ricaldo de Norreys was given Ockwells, he was Henry III favourite cook
The Abbots of Cirencester held the Rectory of Cannon Hill
A fearless knight, Henry de Baggisiste, held Cruchfield at Hawthorn Hill
Robert de Shiplake earned his spurs and he was justly proud
When, in the fourteenth century, he was granted the manor of Stroud
King Henry VI wardrobe master inherited the manor of Ockwells
From his ancestor, Ricaldo, Henry III grandmaster of vittles
Why did the king bestow more favours on his servant Johnny Norreys
By giving him the manor of Hynden and also the manor of Mores?
The manor known as Bullocks changed hands in fifteen sixty-four
For services to Elizabeth I, it was awarded to Ralph More
Edward the Confessor did something rather silly
He bequeathed the throne of England to the Norman knight, King Billy
To repay Edward's beneficence the Conqueror undertook
To protect his widow, Queen Edith; he gave her Shottesbrooke
The mediaeval manor houses were fortified and built to last
And many proudly stand today as a tribute to our past.

3. SHALLOW PROMISES

Come all you good citizens who in Maidenhead abide
Please join us on the river for a celebration ride
We'll board the boats down by the wharf and gaily sail away
Stopping only to take on more passengers at Bray.

If you miss the boats there'll be a party down beside the ferry
We'll eat and drink 'til nightfall, we'll dance and we'll be merry
For this day, Anno Domini twelve hundred and fifteen
Such a novel event will happen, one which has never before been seen.

His Majesty, King John, has grudgingly agreed
To meet his barons and knights by the river at Runnymede
With great pomp and ceremony he will sign a legal charter
This document to be known henceforth as the Magna Carta.

Before his dissatisfied subjects the errant King John will kneel
And mark the historic scroll with the official royal seal
Rejoice and be happy, enjoy it while you may
The king will forget his promises by next mid-summers day.

4. THE SIEGE OF MAIDENHEAD BRIDGE

Richard the Second was most displeased when Henry seized his throne
He plotted to overthrow him and reclaim it as his own
The supporters of Richard hatched a plot that really was quite chilling
They invited Henry to a tournament where they could ambush and kill him
When the loyal Duke of York informed Henry of this he recoiled
And cancelled his engagement, once more the rebels were foiled
A spy in Richard's camp went to Henry and made it known
That they planned to take Windsor Castle and put Richard back on the throne
Then Richard's men laid siege to the bridge at Maydenheth
They held the country to ransom while plotting Henry's death.
In January fourteen hundred, for three consecutive days
The Bath Road came to a standstill, nothing travelled either way
Urged on by the Earl of Kent, the beleaguered people in town
Gave their support to Richard to bring King Henry down
Richard's men were overcome and free passage over the Thames was restored
When Henry's troops came to Maidenhead the traitors were put to the sword
The rebel leaders were beheaded and put on public view
The uprising against King Henry the Fourth was finally subdued.

5. GOOD QUEEN BESS

'Maydenheth has served me well and I have deemed it fit
To honour the worthy citizens by bestowing a charter on it'
It was the year of Our Lord fifteen eighty-two
When the queen gave credit to the town, which was long overdue
'Hooray for Good Queen Bess, long may she reign' they cried
And celebrations could be heard from Cox Green to the riverside
From that most auspicious day, the commonalty
Was given complete freedom to elect their own authority
A warden had first to be elected, a man of impeccable standing
Bob Davus was chosen for this high office, a man with credentials outstanding
Two bridgemasters were elected, to work as equal partners
Charles Pagett was chosen to serve with his friend the worthy John Hartnell
Eight burgesses were chosen to act as town recorders
To liaise with the warden and carry out his orders
Silvester Feckes, Geoffrey White, Edward Lockere, Robert Noke
William Orams, Thomas Lambden, Robert Wynche and Robert Rhodes
Permission was then given to raise further tolls on the bridge
A charge for every wagon and horse, a charge for every carriage
A court of Pie Powder was set up at all the markets and fairs
To insure the honesty of traders as they peddled their home-made wares
'Hooray for Good Queen Bess, long may she reign' they cried
As the celebrations continued from Cox Green to the riverside.

6. THE GATECRASHER

The hunters in Windsor Forest had a very successful day
But as dusk fell by the River Thames a hunter lost his way
His servant, who rode close to him, offered to ride on alone
To find a trail back through the forest which would lead them safely home.

No, I am too hungry to wait until we return to the castle
We'll follow the road into Maydenheth and find an eating hostel
They rode on into the High Street and unsaddled at The Beare
Come, Innkeeper, we're hungry men, bring us your bill of fare.

I beg you, Sir, to pardon me but you cannot eat here today
'Tis Lent and all the food is reserved for the guests of the Vicar of Bray
Good Parson, may we share your vittles, throughout the day we've fasted
Truly, Sir, there is more than enough, the surplus would only be wasted.

The trenchermen soon cleaned their plates, healthy appetites were sated
Brandy and fine wines were served as for the bill they waited
We left for a day in the hunting field, we took no money to spend
I will reimburse you later if you will pay our share, my friend.

Certainly not! said the vicar, we have never met before
You've imposed on my hospitality! and with that he swept out of the door
How different was this vicar from a previous one in that post
Father Simon would not have denied a man food, he was the perfect host.

The curate was a poor man, but his charity was quite fervent
He dug deep into his pockets and paid for the man and his servant
King James, for he the hunter was, rewarded the pious minister
By promoting him over the vicar's head, he installed him as Canon of Windsor.

20. THE REFORMATION 1534 - 1559

In 1534, Pope Paul III excommunicated Henry VIII for divorcing his first Wife, Katherine of Aragon, this being against the church's teaching on the indissolubility of marriage. Henry broke from the established Roman Catholic church and declared himself to be 'The Supreme Head of the English Church'. Henry VIII had six wives:- Katherine of Aragon (divorced), Anne Boleyn (beheaded), Jane Seymour (died in childbirth), Anne of Cleves (divorced), Catherine Howard (beheaded) and Katherine Parr; only Katherine Parr survived him.

King Henry VIII married his fourth wife, a German princess, Anne of Cleves, for political reasons as he was anxious to have the support of the Lutherans in Germany but he disliked her on sight. Nicknamed 'The Flanders Mare', it is said that she was dirty and coarse and so ugly that on sight of her, horses bolted in the street. After only six months, Henry divorced her and banished her from his sight, giving her the manor of St. Ive in Maidenhead. His chief advisor, Thomas Cromwell, who had arranged the marriage, was put to death.

Religious upheaval followed the reformation of the church, with swings between allegiance to the Catholics and the Protestants through the reigns of Henry VIII (1509-1547), Edward VI, (1547-1553) Mary (1553-1558), a staunch Catholic and Elizabeth (1558-1603), a staunch Protestant. The churches were in turmoil, bishops were burnt at the stake, monasteries were closed and their wealth confiscated.

Throughout this era, the Vicar of St Michael's church in Bray village, in the borough of Maidenhead, believed to be Simon Alleyn, remained in his living changing from Catholic priest to Protestant parson to suit the current monarch. This 16th century Vicar of Bray is lampooned as a turncoat in the famous song about him but it is possible that he considered his mission to preach the gospel to be more important than the squabbles of mere mortals and that there is only one Supreme Head of the Church - God.

The monasteries had been a sanctuary for the poor, the sick and the elderly who could not care for themselves and when Henry VIII closed them the most vulnerable of his subjects were left to perish.

Protestantism finally became the national religion of England in 1559 in the reign of Elizabeth I.

1. CHARITY
2. THE FLANDERS MARE
3. WHICH HAT TODAY

1. CHARITY

Much has been said of the lifestyle of monks, before the Reformation
That they were rich and often drunk and owned most of the wealth of the nation
But a fact that should be recorded before that era is forgotten
Is their unconditional charity toward the sick and the downtrodden
Puerperal Fever was a scourge and many poor mothers perished
Their helpless babes were taken in and by the good monks cherished
The terminally ill, who would otherwise die in loneliness and pain
Were nursed with love and gentle care until the grim reaper came
The old, the lame, the cripple, and the mentally distressed
Were welcomed into the monasteries and by the good monks blessed
No outcast or frail orphan was ever turned away
Food and ale was proffered and a comfortable place to lay
The traveller, weary on his journey, and the ever increasing poor
Were given money and sustenance at the almonry door
King Henry and the Pope became locked in a bitter quarrel
The Pope resolutely refusing to condone the King's lax morals
King Henry then renounced the Pope, Catholicism was suppressed
The refugees were abandoned when the monks were dispossessed
The stronger ones begged for alms on the streets of Maidenhead
The weaker froze in the cold night hours, by morning they were dead
The outcome of Henry the Eighth's matrimonial offences
Brought cruel hardship on his people, dire consequences
High on the list of heinous crimes over twenty centuries
Must rank the dissolution of the hospice monasteries.

2. THE FLANDERS MARE

The family of Ive held a manor in the town
The land and the manor house were a favour from the crown
It gained the prefix 'Saint' in a very curious way
When it was twinned with Bisham Priory, about three miles away
King Henry quarrelled with the Pope and denounced Catholicism
He dissolved all the monasteries, including the Priory at Bisham
Henry tired of his third wife and married Anne of Cleves
This union was tempestuous and mercifully very brief
He married her in January in the year of fifteen forty
Six months later she was just another royal divorcee
The King wished to be rid of the ugly Flanders Mare
Her looks were so repulsive that folk would stop and stare
He looked around to find a place to dump his vexatious wife
He chose an estate at Maidenhead, the manor of Saint Ive
In fifteen fifty-seven Anne died peacefully in her bed
More fortunate that the King's first Anne who completely lost her head
For another four hundred years the manor house graced the town
Until, in nineteen fifty nine, the council pulled it down
No trace is left of the manor house, the Town Hall now stands where
King Henry abandoned his fourth wife, the ugly Flanders Mare.

3. WHICH HAT TODAY?

Good Morrow, Father Simon, a blessing on your day
May I walk the causeway with you and talk with you a way?
I am confused as to your credence as the Vicar of Bray
Is your loyalty to Pope or King as in the church you pray?
Will your sermon on this Sunday please his Papal Eminence
Or is it to our noble King you'll bow in reverence?
Catholic or Protestant, which hat will you wear today
My faith is greatly tested, can you my fears allay?
The parson smiled upon the man and gave him this reply:
This church was built to honour God, to praise and glorify
Remember the first commandment, 'Thou shalt have no other God but Me'
Thou shalt not worship King nor Pope nor secular deity
I call upon the archangels, Michael, Gabriel, Raphael,
Chamuch, Jophiel, Zadkiel and the spirited Uriel,
To witness my fidelity to God in heaven above
A God who reigns eternal, a God who rules with love.
The rhythm of the psalmody as I lead my flock in prayer
Rises heavenward to Almighty God, and this I do declare
Saint Michael's church will ring with praise until infinity.
To Father, Son and Holy Ghost, the Blessed Trinity.

26. THE SEVENTEENTH CENTURY

1603. The trial of Sir Walter Raleigh, accused of conspiracy against King James I, was moved to The Greyhound Inn in Maidenhead High Street because the Black Death disease was rife in London; he was found not guilty. He was tried again in London 1618, found guilty and hanged. In 1625, James I was succeeded by Charles I and his autocratic rule caused a civil war. The historic period of the Cavaliers (led by Charles) and the Roundheads (led by Oliver Cromwell) comes down the centuries as romantic and swashbuckling, when, in fact, it was as brutal and dehumanising as all wars.

There is a famous picture showing King Charles meeting two of his children, Princess Elizabeth and the Duke of Gloucester, entitled 'When Did You Last See Your Father?' The children did not betray their father but today we know the answer to be the Greyhound Inn, at Maidenhead, where Raleigh was tried. The date was July 15 1647. Charles 1st was executed in London in 1649.

The site of the Greyhound Inn, which burnt down in 1735, is where the National Westminster Bank now stands and a plaque on the wall of the bank commemorates the historic meeting between King Charles and his children.

1. THE COURT NOW STANDS AT MAIDENHEAD
2. THE SECRET MEETING
3. BRAYWICK CAMP

1. THE COURT NOW STANDS AT MAIDENHEAD

The Black Death will not this trial postpone
Raleigh will for his treason atone
For his wicked plot against the throne
Bring the prisoner in!

In Maidenhead upon the Thames
We'll set up court and names the names
Of those who plot against King James
Bring the prisoner in!

The Greyhound Inn will be secure
With windows barred and bolted doors
We'll place a mounted guard before we
Bring the prisoner in!

NOT GUILTY! rings out loud and clear
The people of Maidenhead give a cheer
Now off on the high seas the sailor will steer
Let the prisoner out!

2. THE SECRET MEETING

Look at me boy, when I speak to you, and answer my questions direct
Where now is your father in hiding, and when was it last that you met?
Come answer me, Sir, I'll brook no deceit
The truth I will have if it takes me all week.

Don't cry, little Miss, you'll come to no harm if you tell me what I want to hear
Were you in Maidenhead town last week, speak up, you have nothing to fear
Which Inn did you visit along with your brother
Was it the Greyhound or was it another?

The children stood with hands at sides, heads held proudly high
Cromwell's men could not cow them as they stubbornly made no reply
King Charles was safe, they would not tell
They loved their father far too well.

3. BRAYWICK CAMP

From his vantage point upon Braywick, Oliver Cromwell could stand
And watch the stealthy Cavaliers as they crept across the land
And down by the river they could be seen rowing up from London
The cannons were primed, 'TAKE AIM, FIRE!' the battle had begun
The cannons stationed at Braywick Camp belched out 'til it was night
Most of the Cavaliers were captured and the others put to flight
Charles's men were no match for Cromwell, they laid their weapons down
And the Ironside standard was raised aloft, high over Maidenhead town
The frightened, captured horses were treated very well
But the Cavaliers were imprisoned in damp and draughty cells.

No Cavaliers disturbed the peace that night as Cromwell the river scanned
The boats which pulled in at the wharf were loaded with contraband
In the dark of night, to evade the watchmen, the crafty smugglers came
With perfumes and fine wines brought in from Portugal, France and Spain
From the cellars under Cannon Hill through to the river bank
A maze of underground tunnels joined the wharf to Braywick Camp
As the barrels of illicit liquor were carefully unloaded
The myth of the sober Ironsides was finally exploded.

30. THE COACHING ERA

There were many coaching inns in Maidenhead in the eighteenth century, including The Sun, at the bottom of Castle Hill, and The Bulle, The White Horse, The Saracens Head, The Beare, The White Harte and the famous Greyhound in the High Street. The poorer travellers used the numerous back-street taverns.

In 1772 George III gave permission for the re-building of Maidenhead Bridge to accommodate the heavy traffic of carriages and the new bridge was officially opened in 1777.

The first Royal Mail coach, bound for London, travelled down the Bath Road (A4) to Maidenhead on August 2nd 1784 stopping at the Sun; the Sun had facilities for stabling up to forty horses and was an ideal choice for a post course where the mail ws exchanged and the horses changed.

All the inns competed with each other to welcome the coaching trade. Less than welcoming were the highwaymen and footpads who lay in wait to hold up the coaches on the Thicket, an area of dense woodland, to rob the travellers. The legendary Dick Turpin (1705-1739) plied his nefarious trade there from 1736 to 1737 in partnership with Tom King, another highwayman. When Tom King died in 1737, Dick Turpin moved to Lincolnshire and then to Yorkshire. He was finally caught and hanged at The Mount, outside the walls of York in 1739, aged 34.

Another highwayman, believed to be an ostler from the Sun, robbed the travellers on the thicket and then gallloped back to the inn to comfort them, often being gratefully rewarded with trinkets which they had hidden from him earlier.

In the eighteenth century, coaches brought racegoers to Maidenhead to the race course which ran from the thicket to Cox Green; these wealthy travellers were rich pickings for the highwaymen. George III brought his family to the races in 1787. The race course closed in 1815.

George III and his wife, Charlotte, had fifteen children. The King suffered from a mental disorder and was certified mad in 1811; his son, afterwards George IV, became Prince Regent.

1. THE HIGHWAYMAN
2. THE OSTLER
3. FIRE!
4. THE NEW BRIDGE
5. THE GOLDEN AGE OF COACHING
6. TRAVELLERS REST
7. A DAY AT THE RACES

1. THE HIGHWAYMAN

Along the Bath Road ,clippety-clop
The stalwart coach horses kept up a fast trot
Their eyes set upon the next comfort stop
Clippety-clop, clippety-clop

Fast through the thicket, clippety-clop
Their nostrils were spuming their hooves were red hot
No time to be spared on clearing that spot
Clippety-clop, clippety-clop.

'Stand and deliver', clippety-clop
The highwayman discharged one warning shot
'Your money or your life or I'll spare you not'
Clippety-clop, clippety-clop.

Money and fine jewels, clippety-clop
The audacious thief stole the whole lot
Then swiftly sped off into the copse
Clippety-clop, clippety-clop.

2. THE OSTLER

The stage coach pulled in late at The Sun
It had been held up by a highwayman's gun
The passengers lost, the highwayman won
Welcome to The Sun!

Ned the ostler strove to win
The trust of visitors to the inn
He'd call aloud as they came in
Welcome to The Sun!

I will carry your luggage Ma'am
You're trembling, let me take your arm
Come inside you'll be safe from harm
Welcome to The Sun!

Oh Sir, you've been so kind to me
You helped me in my misery
I must repay you handsomely
Welcome to The Sun!

The lady then became quite bold
And from within a secret fold
In her skirt she gave him a brooch of gold
Welcome to The Sun!

The ostler whistled through his teeth
The lady would have died of grief
If she knew he was the hooded thief!
Welcome to The Sun!

The crafty ostler saddled his steed
And galloped off into the night at speed
But this time he did not succeed
Welcome to The Sun!

The watchmen who were waiting by
Hung him from the oak tree high
No more will travellers here him cry
Welcome to The Sun!

3. FIRE

The Greyhound Inn continued to thrive
'Til seventeen hundred and thirty-five.

'Twas dead of night at the coaching inn
When the buxom maid let her lover in.

Master and mistress were out of sight
Gone to London for the night.

The brazen girl re-locked the door
And led her beau to the very top floor.

They canoodled there by candlelight
Way into the small hours of the night.

FIRE! FIRE! the alarm cry went around
As the Greyhound Inn was burnt to the ground.

'Tis said the maid knocked the candle over
As she romped and frolicked with her lover.

Before indulging in illicit delights
The wench should have blown out the lights.

4. THE NEW BRIDGE

In bygone days the journey to the West was very, very slow
The traffic came to a sudden halt at the river by Taeppa's Low
The travellers had to queue and wait in turn for the ferry boat
To carry them to the further bank to continue along the Bath Road.

The King gave his permission for the warden to raise a pontage
To pay for repairs and maintenance on Maidenhead's wooden bridge
One penny for every coach and carriage and cart which travelled over
One penny for every boat which went under, sailing along the river.

A hermit lived beside the bridge, he spent his day in prayer
When not collecting the toll money and pocketing his share
The bridgemasters' dipped into the fund to pay for celebrations
Such as a success in the hunting field and other obscure occasions.

The original bridge stood by the wharf for nigh five hundred years
Until the eighteenth century when serious defects appeared
It groaned beneath the weight of heavy carriages and carts
And finally the wooden bridge split and fell apart.

The people cheered His Worship the Mayor when the foundation stone was laid
For the new bridge which was being built over the Thames at Maidenhead
In seventeen hundred and seventy-seven, with solemn pomp and ceremony
Maidenhead Bridge was officially opened by Mr Penyston Portlock Powney.

The tolls upon the Maidenhead Bridge were continually increased
Until the traveller said 'enough's enough, this highway robbery must cease'
A band of irate motorists, in nineteen hundred and three
Pitched the tollhouse into the river, now passage across the river is free.

The bridges are possibly the most important part of Maidenhead's history as they link London with the West.

1287	A wooden bridge was built.
1337	Edward III gave permission for a pontage (toll charge).
1582	Elizabeth I charter allowed for further pontage.
1772	Foundation stone laid for a brick bridge in the reign of George III.
1777	Brick bridge opened.
1839	Brunel railway bridge built parallel with brick bridge.
1903	Toll gates were removed.

5. THE GOLDEN AGE OF COACHING

'Ta-ra, Ta-ra' the sound of the post horn
Is heard from the Bath Road at six in the morn
This stirring sound signalled the imminent approach
Of the eagerly awaited ROYAL MAIL COACH.
Immaculate horses with long flowing manes
Were harnessed to coaches with flamboyant names
That stirred the imagination, like Lightening and Rocket
Greyhound, Express, Silver Bullet and Comet.
The lumbering STAGE WAGGONS were usually late
They catered mostly for the lower class trade
The passengers travelled with the merchandise
Thirty or more crammed like cattle inside.
The well-to-do travelled in the four-horse POST CHAISE
The doyen of carriages in Georgian days
The young men-about-town chose horses quite frisky
To pull their smart LANDAUS, their SULKEYS and WHISKEYS.
The hood of the PHAETON could be folded down
When the aristocrats were parading in town
And. lastly, the mini-coach, a utility rig
Two wheels and one horse, the multi-purpose GIG.
In the year of Our Lord eighteen thirty-nine
Brunel built a bridge for the Great Western line
The Royal Mail then came by train to Maidenhead
The golden age of coaching, alas, was pronounced dead.

6. TRAVELLERS REST

The wealthy stage coach passengers booked in at the Sun
Assured of a warm welcome when their tiring journey was done
For the price of a silver sixpence they could even hire a maid
Snowy white linen on the dining table was laid
Feather quilts and downy pillows to lay their weary heads
Brass warming pans were heated to take the chill off their beds.

The passengers on the stage waggons were not welcome at the Sun
The inns at which they rested were dreary and badly run
They ate off wooden trestles, no fancy napery
Their dirty straw-filled mattresses were over-run with fleas
No maids danced attendance on these second class clientele
But compared with the foot traveller they really fared quite well.

The dusty footed traveller who walked into an inn
Was rudely shown the door and told to walk right out again
A man with neither horse nor carriage was too low to be recognised
In the rigid social strata where the poor were much despised
If he had tuppence in his purse the traveller might find haven
In a miserable third class hostelry, a bawdy backstreet tavern.

7. A DAY AT THE RACES

Please take us for an outing, Papa, we have all been extremely good
We've studied our books and practised our music, done everything that we should
And you need a respite, Dear Papa, away from the cares of the state
An outing will surely benefit your health, you've been acting most strangely of late.

Very well my dear children, but we cannot go far, I need to be always on call
The unrest in France is reaching a crisis and the consequences will affect us all.
From Windsor 'tis a short way to Maidenhead, Papa, where the racecourse is open today
We can take a picnic and enjoy the horse racing, we'll all have a wonderful day.

What do you know of the people of Maidenhead, are they all loyal to me?
Not like those wicked colonials who threw all my tea in the sea?
Maidonians have long been noted, Papa, for their loyalty to the crown
The residents will be highly honoured to have you visit their town.

The royal party left Windsor Castle with bright and happy faces
As they set off in a fleet of carriages for a day at Maidenhead races
King George III was feted with the utmost dedication
Then hurried back to Windsor to take his medication.

41. THE VICTORIANS

Maidenhead grew at a great pace in the nineteenth century and her history has been comprehensively documented since 1869 when the Maidenhead Advertiser was first printed, broadcasting such news items as the vicar who was arrested for riding his bicycle on the pavement in 1876, the scarlet fever epidemic in 1896 and modern day hi-tech computer crime.

The stagecoaches had brought travellers to the town for over two hundred years and then the railway came as far as Taplow in 1838, crossing the river in 1839 via Brunel's Bridge, bringing more people and more prosperity. The railway bridge across the Thames at Maidenhead, designed by Isambard Kingdom Brunel (1806-1859), is the longest brick built single span bridge in Europe. This railway bridge and the road bridge which runs parallel with it, are the subject of a famous painting by Turner entitled 'RAIN, STEAM AND SPEED'.

The population of Maidenhead in 1801 was less than a thousand, a hundred years' later, in 1901, it was thirteen thousand.

Elegant houses were built for the rich merchants and tradesmen as Maidenhead prospered but there was a very wide gap between the rich and the poor. The old, the sick and the destitute were cared for in the Union Workhouse (the Poor Law Institution) in Courthouse Road where they had to work twelve hours a day at gruelling tasks to earn their keep, and husbands and wives, parents and children were segregated.

In 1833 a law was passed making it illegal to employ a child under nine and much later, in 1870, the Education Act was passed requiring all children to attend school up to the age of eleven, with exceptions made for children needed to work on the farms or help at home. Most of the schools which were founded in Maidenhead in the nineteenth and early twentieth century were church schools, carrying on the tradition of teaching the three R's and scripture.

An accident on the railway, when a badly injured workman died after being carried five miles on an improvised stretcher to the workhouse infirmary, showed the need for a hospital in the town. In 1879 St Luke's Cottage Hospital was built and run by public subscription.

Public utilities came to Maidenhead in the nineteenth century: gas 1835, street lighting (gas) 1836, county constabulary 1855, fire brigade (voluntary) 1866, telephone 1883 and electricity 1897 (officially switched on in 1902). The council resisted calls for main drainage and a public library, arguing that the provision of these two services would be a waste of the rate payers money.

1. THE UNION WORKHOUSE
2. THE BRUNEL BRIDGE
3. THE COTTAGE HOSPITAL
4. QUEEN ANNE HOUSE
5. THE CLOCK TOWER

1. THE UNION WORKHOUSE

Get out! you know you're not allowed within the women's section
Next time you'll be evicted, of that there is no question.

Sir, fifty years we have been wed and never a day apart
To separate us now would truly break our hearts.

The beadle showed no pity and pushed the old man so hard
He stumbled and fell right heavily out in the workhouse yard.

The icy wind blew cruelly as the rough hewn funeral biers
Were lowered into the paupers' graves, no-one shed a tear.

The ceremony was short and as the parson strode away
Frozen earth was thrown in where the tragic couple lay.

But the old folk were contented, their wish was satisfied
For all eternity to rest, together side by side.

2. THE BRUNEL BRIDGE

With a judder of brakes and a hissing of steam the Great Western train came to rest
Passengers and freight were transferred to a stagecoach to continue their route to the West.

The bridge on the river near Maidenhead town, where the Thames runs it's easterly course
Was not built for strength but just for the use of yeomen with wagon and horse.

To mark the occasion in suitable style, when Victoria R came to reign
The worthy town burghers commissioned a new bridge, to herald the age of the train.

The river officials decreed that the arch should be built to a meticulous plan
Made solely of brick with one central pillar, a single continuous span.

The Doubting Thomases threw up their hands, It will never stand!, they did shout
The design is too weak, it will crumble and fall, lives will be lost there's no doubt.

I will build you a bridge, said a young engineer, exactly as the plans state
It will bear the steam engines and carriages too, will withstand whatsoever the weight.

With a defiant whistle and a billow of steam the brave iron horse chugged along
From Bucks o'er to Berks and on to the West, proving the pessimists wrong.

A cheer for young Isambard Kingdom Brunel, lets give him a Hip Hip Hooray
Fifteen decades of safety, through five sceptred monarchs, and his bridge still stands proudly today.

3. THE COTTAGE HOSPITAL

Oh, woe is me, I did not see the two thirty-seven train
And now I am mortally injured and overwhelmed with pain
Have courage, mate, we'll get some help, we'll soon have you made better
Said his workmates as his broken body was lifted onto a makeshift stretcher
Where are we going? the workman cried, Which way are we heading?
We are going along the Bath Road to the hospital in Reading
That is fourteen miles away, I will not last that long
Please take me to the infirmary at the Workhouse Union
The workhouse matron did her best but she was not qualified
The injuries proved fatal and the wretched workman died.

Determined that such a tragedy must never happen again
The residents of Maidenhead held a meeting in Brock Lane
By generous public subscription the money was soon found
To build a cottage hospital in the centre of the town
As a direct result of the accident on the Great Western railway line
The first patient was admitted in eighteen seventy-nine
A paper sorter, a lad of fourteen, occupied the very first bed
He was hospitalised in November and treated for a scalded leg
It was intended that St LUKE'S COTTAGE HOSPITAL would permanently remain
As a worthy testimony to the workman who was hit by a train.

4. QUEEN ANNE HOUSE

The most attractive building that was locally to be seen
Was built of hand-made bricks and tiles from the kiln at Pinkneys Green
Each brick, each chimney pot, each individual ridge tile
Was crafted at the brickworks in their own distinctive style.

Charles Cooper founded the Brickworks in eighteen hundred and twenty
And soon his wares were in demand to build houses for the gentry
Cooper's products, each one fired and moulded with a craftsman's pride
Were much in demand locally, and exported far and wide.

QUEEN ANNE HOUSE was built at the bottom of Castle Hill
As a showplace for Cooper's products and to show his workmen's skills
The bricks, each one hand-fired, were an awesome sight to behold
The finials on the roof gables stood out proud and bold.

For ninety years the house stood there, the pride of Castle Hill
A tribute to the craftsmen who toiled at the brick kilns
Then Maidenhead needed a new road with which to by-pass the town
So the beauty that was QUEEN ANNE HOUSE was wantonly pulled down.

5. THE CLOCK TOWER

Come lasses and lads, your Mums and your Dads, your Gran and your Aunty Kate
Bring all your friends and relatives to help us celebrate
We'll dance and we will sing
We'll make all Maidenhead ring
Hip Hip Hooray this is the day of the official opening
This date in history
Is the Diamond Jubilee
The Queen has reigned for sixty years, God Bless her Majesty
The Queen has reigned for sixty years, God Bless her Majesty

Come neighbour and friend, a handshake extend to all who are gathered here
To mark our love and true respect for the one we hold so dear
The crowds will be regaled
The architects will be hailed
When the clock tower by the King Street bridge is finally unveiled
This date in history
Is the Diamond Jubilee
The Queen has reigned for sixty years, God Bless her Majesty.
The Queen has reigned for sixty years, God Bless Her Majesty.

From thirty-seven to ninety-seven Victoria has reigned supreme
Today we all pay homage to our great and gracious Queen
We are so proud of our
Magnificent clock tower
It reminds us of our heritage on every passing hour
This date in history
Is the Diamond Jubilee
The Queen has reigned for sixty years, God Bless her Majesty
The Queen has reigned for sixty years, God Bless her Majesty.

The clock tower, which stands in King Street at the entrance to Maidenhead railway station, was built to commemorate the diamond jubilee of Queen Victoria (1837-1897) and was officially opened in 1899. In 1995 the mechanism was taken away for servicing and the brickwork was cleaned and repaired.

51. THE RIVER

Old Father Thames has flowed through Maidenhead to London and the sea since pre-history. A wooden bridge was constructed over it in 1280 bringing traffic along the road from London to Bath (now the A4) and from that time, the town began to grow. The river was used for trade, goods being moved by barges pulled by horses, until the nineteenth century when it was mainly taken over for leisure. The origin of the lock at Maidenhead is obscure but in 1746 it was operated by a family named Ray who had a mill on the island beside it, and Richard Ray was appointed as the first official lock-keeper in 1773; the Ray family bought up most of the land around the lock and have eleven roads names after them in the area. The lock was last re-built in 1912. Another name for a miller is a boulter and the lock is now known as Boulters Lock and the mill is an hotel named the Boulters Inn.

Between the 1890's and the beginning of the 1914-1918 war, Maidenhead was the playground of the 'smart set' who motored up from London, and a row of houses between the two bridges was notorious for the gaiety girls who entertained men there, mostly officers from the Brigade of Guards. Skindles Hotel and the Brigade of Guards Club, on either side of the Maidenhead bridge were much frequented by Edwardian society including the guests of the Astors of Cliveden and the Grenfells (Lord and Lady Desborough) of Taplow House. This all came to an end in 1914 when the young men went off to the war, many of them being killed in action including a son of the mayor, Tom Stuchberry, and two of the three sons of Lord Desborough.

In 1940, during the 1939-1945 war, Geoffrey Messum, of Messum's Boatyard in Bray, sailed to France with a flotilla of volunteers to rescue soldiers stranded on the beach at Dunkirk; he safely evacuated 23 men.

In October 1974 Queen Elizabeth II made a river journey through the Royal Borough of Windsor and Maidenhead, the only monarch to do so.

The swans on the Thames belong to either the reigning monarch or the Dyers and Vintners Company. Since mediaeval times it has been the custom to round up the swans annually to check the marks on the older birds and mark the new cygnets; this is called Swan Upping and is carried out by Swan Uppers under the direction of the Queen's Swan Master. The Turk family, from Cookham, held this office for six hundred years until recently. Two marks are put on the beaks of the Dyers and Vintners' swans and five marks on the royal swans and this is quite painless.

1. MIDDENHYTHE
2. RAY THE MILLER
3. SWAN UPPING
4. GAIETY ROW
5. THE FLOODS OF 1947
6. A STEAMER RIDE
7. FULL CIRCLE ON RAY MILL ISLAND

ERRATA. The Turk family have been river people since 1760. Frederick, and later his son John, were Queen's Swan Masters from 1922-1992

1. MIDDENHYTHE

The barge horse pulls it's load of freight along the well-worn path
Timber cut from Bisham Woods en route for Middle Wharf.
    And still the tranquil river scythes it's chosen path through
    Middenhythe.

Long gone the barge weighed down with freight, a different craft's afloat
The punt, the skiff, the motor launch, the twenties pleasure boat.
    And still the tranquil river scythes it's chosen path through
    Middenhythe.

Long gone the punt, the skiff, the launch, a different craft's afloat
The awesome river cruiser, the nineties pleasure boat.
    And still the tranquil river scythes it's chosen path through
    Middenhythe.

The River Thames flows West to East from the Cotswold Hills to the North Sea. Up to 1950 it had become so polluted that it was almost devoid of fish but since then great efforts have been made to clean it up, and by 1972, 63 specifies of fish had returned to the river.

2. RAY THE MILLER

The visitor to Maidenhead thought he'd lost his way
Each turn he took down by the lock the road began with Ray
Ray Lea, Ray Drive and then Ray Street
Ray Mill Road both West and East
Ray Park Road, Ray Park Avenue
Ray Mead Road and Ray Lane too
The stranger stopped to ask because
He was intrigued to know who was
Ray the Miller.

Ray the Miller ground the corn to make the finest bread
To feed the landed gentry in the town of Maidenhead
With his profits he did speculate
Investing in local real estate
He bought the land ere which way you look
From Bath Road 'cross the Moor to Widbrook
The visitor was content because
He knew the secret of who was
Ray the Miller.

3. SWAN UPPING

All the swans may look the same as they glide so gracefully down the Thames.
But two parties on them have claims. Make way for the Queen's Swan Master!

Some swans belong to Her Majesty and others are the sole property
Of the Dyers and Vintners Company. Make way for the Queen's Swan Master!

Each year the swan uppers, with pageantry, mark the birds with the identity
Of the Queen or the Vintners Company. Make way for the Queen's Swan Master!

Some old swans take it in their stride but the younger ones they try to hide
And the cygnets are all petrified. Make way for the Queen's Swan Master!

The swans are herded into the Cut and a gentle mark on their beak is put
It's over in minutes and it doesn't hurt. Make way for the Queen's Swan Master!

The swans are released, a successful day, the marking's done, the uppers are away
Next port of call, the swans at Bray. Make way for the Queen's Swan Master!

4. GAIETY ROW

The naughty girls from London Town
Bedecked in silk and satin gowns
Came to kiss the soldiers of the crown
Heigh Ho for Gaiety Row.

The guardsmen chased the saucy girls
Who wiggled their hips and tossed their curls
And showed them the lace on their unmentionables.
Heigh Ho for Gaiety Row.

The lusty lads went in pursuit
Of the pretty girls of ill repute
Intent on pastimes rather rude
Heigh Ho for Gaiety Row.

In one short night, so it is said
One young blade slept in every bed
At break of day they found him dead
Heigh Ho for Gaiety Row.

The soldiers left, took up their guns
The war in Europe had begun
An end to the days of carefree fun
Heigh Ho for Gaiety Row.

5. THE FLOODS OF 1947

The heavy snow of '46 was heaven sent for play
Children clapped their hands as it continued day after day
Intricate patterns of hoar frost were woven across the grass
And icicles hung from the fences, bright as polished glass.

Cobwebs froze like delicate lace, adorning all the hedges
As adventurous boys slid down Boyne Hill on hastily improvised sledges
Cheeky snowmen, with coal for eyes, smiled as they sped by
Not comprehending that on the morrow a catastrophe was nigh.

In the spring of '47 the snowmen vanished overnight
The wet and dirty landscape was not a pretty sight
The sparkling, pure white snow had turned into a mushy grey
The pretty frost and icicles had instantly melted away.

Slush ran down the gutters and by the second morning
The River Board was forced to issue 'A DANGEROUS FLOOD' warning
The river burst its banks and many roads had to be closed
Ray Mead, Ray Mill, Ray Park, Ray Lane, and all the other Ray roads.

Filthy turgid water , carrying verminous sewer rats
Seeped into the houses, ruining furniture and mats
People tried to keep it out with buckets and mops and brooms
But the relentless river overwhelmed them and they retreated to the upper rooms.

A bright young lad named Albert, who lived in the village of Bray
Commandeered a rowing boat and rowed up the Causeway
Taking people shopping, a novel way to ride
For the fare of just a shilling, all were satisfied.

In the cruel flood of '47, no riverside house was spared
And it was many years before the damage was repaired
New culverts have been dug since then, deeper, wider drains
But the proud and haughty River Thames will never be contained.

After the flood of 1947, when the river water came up as far as Maidenhead High Street and almost totally engulfed Bray Village, a relief ditch was dug from Blackamoor Lane across the town to upper Bray to divert flood water; to date this had been successful and there have only been minor pockets of flooding in the low-lying areas near the river, but constant vigilance is still necessary.

6. A STEAMER RIDE

All aboard the Bray Princess for an afternoon steamer ride
Plenty of room on the upper deck and room for more inside
Captain Mike is at the wheel, which way will be steer today
Up the river to Marlow or down the river to Bray
The open craft is heading for Bray as it noses through the arch
The arch which carries the ancient road from London through to Bath
Under the bridge which Brunel built to carry the railway train
Through Bray Lock to Windsor, turn, and back through Bray Lock again.

Year after year the lock-keeper at Bray
Wins LOCK OF THE YEAR for his floral display.

Oohs and Aahs of envy as the riverside mansions appear
Capt. Mike knows all the rich and famous people here
A film star, a pop singer, a television compere
An oil magnate, a comedian and an Australian artist live there
Capt. Mike keeps up the commentary, his passengers he regales
'That house was built for Lily Langtry by her beau the Prince of Wales
And Gaeity Row is respectable now, but it wasn't always so
I blush to tell you of the goings-on in those houses long ago'.

This stretch of river used to be
The playground of the aristocracy.

Oohs and Aahs of sentiment as the river creatures appear
Capt. Mike knows all the native water dwellers here
The swan, the grebe and the humble pigeon
The kingfisher, the gull and the chestnut-headed widgeon
The Canada goose, with it's honking cry
The majestic heron and the transparent dragonfly
The frog, the newt and the shy, timid otter
All make their homes alongside the water.

Back under the bridges, tie up at the bank
Let's give Capt. Mike a big vote of thanks.

Steamers can accommodate up to 150 passengers on two decks and steamer excursions along the river at Maidenhead were started by Salters Steamers at Boulters Lock in 1870. A steamer ride is not only a perfect way to see the beauty of the Thames, as the boats sail westerly past the Hanging Woods of Cliveden along to Marlow and easterly through Bray to Windsor, but an opportunity to learn the history and the ecology of the area from the commentaries given by the captains. The trade is now carried on by Bray Boats of Ray Mead Road and The Maidenhead Steam Navigation Company of Taplow.

7. FULL CYCLE ON RAY MILL ISLAND

SPRING

Whisperings, almost imperceptible, an air of anticipation
Is felt as life begins again, the miracle of creation
Buds upon the burgeoning trees blink at the pale spring sun
On Ray Mill Island in the Thames the cycle has begun.
Rustling noises in the reeds, stirrings in the bushes
A flurry of activity as nests are built in the rushes.

SUMMER

Parent swans watch proudly as cygnets try their wings
Perched high up in the rowan tree the tuneful blackbird sings
The graceful willow dips her branches deep to quench her thirst
The scorching summer sun has sered the grass and turned it into dust
In the cool of evening the dry, parched earth welcomes the warm showers
The seed pods burst and scatter abroad a kaleidoscope of flowers.

AUTUMN

With a 'Ker Hoink, Ker Hoink' the geese are gone, as the autumn mists swirl round
Trees shed their leaves to make a rustling carpet on the ground
Squirrels frantically rout for nuts to hoard inside their dreys
Then settle in to hibernate and dream of warmer days
No longer do the coquettish flowers flirt as visitors walk by
Their pretty gowns are torn and tattered, they wilt away and die.

WINTER

In full spate now, the ominous weir, leaps with a clamourous sound
Freezing water slowly rises, claiming the higher ground
Naked and defenceless now, the mighty chestnut tree
Stands stark against the sky-line like a carven effigy
Her feet now waterlogged and cold, the gentle willow is weeping
As Ray Mill Island in the Thames her winter watch is keeping.

Ray Mill Island is maintained by the council as a nature park, one of the most beautiful parks on the Thames, and is open to the public except when the water level is dangerously high. Across the river from the island can be seen the impressive Cliveden Woods. Until the second world war, Ascot Sunday was a great social occasion down by the Boulters Lock. When this event was re-enacted in 1951 as part of the Festival of Britain, a mild catastrophe occurred - a landing stage on Ray Mill Island collapsed and the actress Cecilie Courtnidge was plunged into the river; fortunately, she was not injured and carried off the incident with the dignity and aplomb of her profession. Another successful pageant was staged in 1995.

WORSHIP AND EDUCATION

England became a Christian country in 597 when Saint Augustine converted King Etherlred, a Saxon king, to the faith and in 635 St Birinus came over from Rome and baptised local people in a pond at Taplow by Middle Wharf.

The churches in the manors of Bray (St Michael's), Cookham (Holy Trinity) and White Waltham (St Mary the Virgin) date back to Saxon times and a chapel (SS Andrew and Mary Magdalene) was built in the centre of Maidenhead in 1280. The Quakers arrived in 1665, the Marlow Road Baptists in 1672 and the Congregationalists (now the United Reform) in 1785.

A church was built on the site of the chapel of SS Andrew and Mary Magdalene in 1452 and the town was adminsitered under the patronage of the church when the Guild of SS. Andrew and Mary Magdalene was formed. This Guild was dissolved by Henry VIII in 1547 and reinstated by the charter of Elizabeth I in 1582. The church was rebuilt in 1824 and demolished in 1961 when it became structurally unsound. The new church on the site, at the bottom of the High Street, is now the borough church of St Mary's.

The authority and influence of the established church on the administration of the town continued until Maidenhead was joined to Windsor to form the Royal Borough of Windsor and Maidenhead in 1974.

In Victorian Maidenhead many new churches were built:-
St Peter's, Knowl Hill (C of E) 1857, Methodist 1858, St Lukes (C of E) 1869, St Joseph's (RC) 1884, St Paul's (C of E, now demolished) 1889 and St Peter's (C of E), Furze Platt, 1898.

After the second world war, a Jewish synagogue was founded in Maidenhead and, more recently, a mosque has been built. Maidenhead also has branches of the Buddhists, Christadelphians, Christian Science, Salvation Army and Spiritualists.

When education became compulsory in 1870, schools were founded and run by the Christian churches to educate children in the three R's and the principles of the faith.

Today, most schools have been taken over by the state but a few have remained as church schools: All Saints, Altwoood (formerly Boyne Hill, Seniors), Bisham, Braywood, Burchetts Green, Holyport, Knowl Hill, St Edmund Campion (RC), St Lukes, primary, St Mary's (RC) and White Waltham. Alwyn Road, East Street, Ellington, Gordon Road, and North town school, all built in this century, were not connected to any particular church but their teaching was scripture- based. When secondary schooling became compulsory, girls had the choice of Boyne Hill (senior girls), or Gordon Road (mixed) and boys could choose St. Lukes (senior boys) or Gordon Road; unless they passed their eleven-plus exam and attended the County Boys (now Desborough) or County Girls (now Newlands). Since the Education Act of 1947, the three secondary schools have closed -Boyne Hill (senior), Gordon Road and St Lukes (senior) - and three new comprehensive schools have been built: Altwood, Cox Green and Furze Platt, all mixed. Grammar schools have been abolished in this area and any parents wishing to send their children to a single sex school can now opt for Desborough or Newlands. To meet the needs of the growing population of Maidenhead in the late 20th century, more infant and primary schools have been built: Courthouse, Furze Platt, Larchfield, Lowbrook, Oldfield and Wessex. Holyport Manor was opened to educate children with learning difficulties.

For parents who could afford to pay for their children's education, a number of private schools were opened: Elmslie (closed), Claires Court, The Convent of the Nativity (now Maidenhead College), Lynton House (closed), PNEU (Highfield), Ridgeway, Redroofs Theatre School, Silchester House, St Piran's and Winbury.

Evacuees (1939-1945) were housed in a house named Redriff in Boyne Hill Avenue; after the war the house was demolished and the East Berks College of Further Education now stands on the site. The Art College, which used to be in Marlow Road, where Social Services are now based, has moved to Raymond Road.

1. ST BIRINUS
2. PRAISE GOD IN HIS HOLY PLACE
3. THOMAS ELLWOOD
4. THE ROCK
5. TO BE SCHOOLED IN THE PRINCIPLES OF THE FAITH
6. IN GOD'S ARMS

1. ST BIRINUS AD 635

If good old Saint Birinus had never chanced to come
Up the river to Middle Wharf, on leave from his church in Rome
Would we still be heathens, worshipping Woden and Thor
And behaving just like savages, as we did before
Would we now know of Our Lord, or Mary his Blessed Mother
Would we not know that the babe in the manger was born to be our brother
Would the love of Jesus of Nazareth be a complete enigma to us
Would we not know of His compassion and deeds so miraculous
Would we look upon the star that shines so brightly in December
And not know it's significance, what it teaches us to remember
How could we know of the frankincense or myrrh or golden rings
Presented to the Holy Babe, the homage of three wise kings
The ten commandments, the beautitudes, would we know what all these meant
If Saint Birinus had not taught us from the Holy Testament
We could not possibly comprehend the blatant contradiction
Of the unconditional love of God and the heinous crucifixion
The ancient Gods of old taught us how to main and kill
But Jesus teaches us to treat each other with goodwill
To live in peace and serve our friends as we would have them serve us
Let's say a special prayer today for good old Saint Birinus.

2. PRAISE GOD IN HIS HOLY PLACE

The bells high in the steeple ring out loud and clear
Loud enough for every home within the parish to hear
In neighbouring synagogue the shofar, the ancient ram's horn, is heard
Inviting the faithful from all over town to come and hear the Word
Marching with fervour, along High Town Road, the blood and fire band
Tambourines tinkling and cymbals clashing, here come the Sally-Anns
From high up in the minaret a plaintiff chant goes out
And soon the mosque is overflowing with Moslems so devout
The bells of St Mary's were silent, the belfry hauntingly still
No sound marked the hour of prayer for the people of White Waltham Hill
Now the bells are recast and rehung in their place, the countryside rings with their chimes
'Come worship with us, come join us in praise,' they echo as in olden times
Beat the drum and sound the horn, ring the steeple bell
Let the sacred music flow from mosque and citadel
Let all the choirs in Maidenhead their songs of worship sing
With glory, praise and honour to God the Almighty King.

The bells of St Mary the Virgin, White Waltham, were re-cast at the original Whitechapel foundry in 1989; when they were re-hung, a service of blessing was held at the church at 3pm on Sunday 5 November 1989. My thanks to Simon and Lesley Graves, bellringer and chorister of St Mary the Virgin, White Waltham, for this information.

3. THOMAS ELLWOOD

As a Quaker gaily rode through town one bright and fine spring morning
The warden called Halt, Dismount, Sir! and seized him without warning
Thomas Ellwood was on his way to a meeting at Chalfont St Giles
His heart was light as he trotted in, his face was wreathed in smiles
Why do you stop my journey, please tell me, Sir, I pray?
Your are indicted, preacher man, for travelling on the Sabbath Day
In the year of 1660, 'twas against the law to ride
Or travel on a Sunday, but this the Quaker defied
On special application, a pass would be certified
From the nearby town of Reading, but Tom has not applied
The warden passed the bridle to the ostler at the inn
And took the Quaker before the court to answer for his sin
Tom Ellwood was a great preacher, his diction loud and clear
His voice rang out across the room for all his accusers to hear
I am going to the village of Chalfont to preach the Holy Word
My horse is but a relation of the ass which carried out Lord
If you hinder me on my mission you hinder The One sent before
And you will answer on the Day of Judgement for this ridiculous law
The warden hung his head in shame, he was a righteous man
He quashed the charge against the Quaker before the case began
Before you ride off, Preacher, while the ostler is grooming your horse
Please dine with me in the Greyhound Inn, at my expense of course
On a bright and fine spring evening the Quaker, wreathed in smiles
Continued on his journey to the chapel at Chalfont St Giles.

4. THE ROCK

The God-fearing people of Knowl Hill, beside the old Bath Road
Were downcast for they had no church in which to praise their Lord
They travelled to Hurley or Wargrave to make their intercessions
Until Queen Victoria came to the throne in eighteen thirty-seven.

With the help of neighbouring parishes, enough money was then found
To build the Knowl Hill parish church, well nigh two thousand pounds
The foundation stone was solemnly laid by Lady Clayton East
And in eighteen forty-one the Knowl Hill church was blessed.

Saint Peter is their patronal saint, Jesus' chief disciple
The Rock, whose venerable life is chronicled in the bible
Born in the village of Bathsaida, beside the Gallilean Sea
And martyred in Rome, by Nero, in sixty eight A.D.

The God-fearing people of Knowl Hill, beside the old Bath Road
Still congregate in St. Peter's church to pray and praise their Lord
They bring to God their sorrows, their hopes and joys, their fears
As faithful Christians have done for the last two thousand years.

My thanks to Neville and Jean Palmer for the information on St Peter's Church, Knowl Hill.

5. TO BE SCHOOLED IN THE PRINCIPLES OF THE FAITH

1819   When the NATIONAL SCHOOL was founded, a charity called Merry and Spoor
Paid nine pounds per annum towards the education of the poor.

1848   The Congregationalists opened the BRITISH SCHOOL to teach their children well.

1857   Then the children of ALL SAINTS SCHOOL first heard the dreaded school bell.

1863   The WESLEYAN'S taught their children alongside the Methodist Hall

1871   The Roman Catholics sent their children to the newly-built CATHOLIC SCHOOL.

The education in the schools had need to be very thorough
For it was subsidised by a tax upon the borough.

Attendance was compulsory and a truant officer states
That every child who missed a day cost tuppence on the rates.

The non-conformists were incensed, they did not think it fair
That religion should be taught on the rates, and they withheld their share.

1894   DESBOROUGH (The COMMON SCHOOL), for older boys was begun

1901   Young ladies attended the COUNTY SCHOOL not to be outdone.

The multi-cultural composition of the present population
Sees synagogue, mosque and temple teaching religious education.

Every parent is now guaranteed the right to make the important decision
To have their children educated in the genre of their chosen religion.

The County Girls, now Newlands in Farm Road, was originally sited at the bottom of Castle Hill where there is now a youth centre; Queen Anne House was for some time the junior department. Desborough School still stands in Shoppenhangers Road.

Alongside the compulsory schools, during the 1940's ad 50's, there were two schools in Maidenhead which taught dancing, the Cybil Bennet School of Dancing and the La Roche School of Dancing. Those who could not afford the fees of these private dancing schools could attend the League of Health and Beauty; the League hired local halls and taught physical exercises for a small fee and, for another small fee, the enthusiast could stay on for lessons in tap dancing. The uniform of the League was a white satin blouse and black satin shorts but those who could not afford the uniform were allowed to wear any white blouse and navy blue knickers.

6. IN GOD'S ARMS

The churchyard at All Saints church is a peaceful place to stroll
And offer up a silent prayer for the long departed souls.

Those who died in adulthood had served their earthly purpose
But why are children, some only infants, tragically taken from us?

'There's a home for little children above the bright blue sky'
Is written on the grave of a little girl who died.
      Rose Ethel Keeley 1885-1892

A boy and his little sister died trapped in a tragic fire
They stayed such a short while here on earth before their time expired.
      Arthur Farington 1850-1857 and Frances Farington
      1852-1857

This young boy is 'In God's Arms', flowers cover his stone
A tragic accident claimed his life so very far from home.
      Andy Watts 1973-1988

Another teenage boy lies here within this hallowed ground
While playing, as all lads will do, the adventurous boy was drowned.
      Frederick Ambrose 1858-1873

A newborn babe lies in this plot, no time to choose a name
Just a fleeting visit here, then God called it back again.
      Baby Headlong-Moore - October 1993

Merciful God, hold these children in Your arms, let them in heaven remain
Until the Day of Glory, when they return to their loved ones again.
Amen.

'Then there were brought to Him little children, that He should put His hands on them and pray, and the disciples rebuked them. But Jesus said: Suffer little children and forbid them not to come unto Me, for of such is the Kingdom of Heaven; and He laid His hands on them and departed thence'. St Matthew, Chapter 19, Verses 13-15.

ALL SAINTS CHURCH, Boyne Hill, was built in 1857 and a vicarage, school and almshouses were soon added. It was paid for by two spinster sisters, the Misses Hulme, and the land was given by the Grenfell family of Taplow Court, who owned most of the land in the area. Two more spinster sisters, the Misses Lamotte, also became benefactresses of the church complex. In 1910 a new nave was added. The first vicar was the Rev. William Gresley and the second the renowned Canon Arthur Hislop Drummond. The church continues to serve the parish as a spiritual and pastoral centre under the ministry of the present incumbent, Fr. Norman Brown, MA.

74. THE TWENTIETH CENTURY

In the 20th century, Maidenhead has expanded into a sprawling, industrial and commercial metropolis; the population has risen from a few people in the year 1, 1,000 in 1801, 13,000 in 1901, 27,000 in 1948, 4.000 in 1965 49,000 in 1983 to an estimated 70,000 in the year 2000. In 1974, Maidenhead was amalgamated with Windsor to form the Royal Borough of Windsor and Maidenhead; at that time the link between the church and the corporation was ended with the reorganisation of local government.

Maidenhead played her part in the two world wars. White Waltham aerodrome was an important base for the Air Force through 1939-1945 and there was a munitions factory, the Anti-Attrition, which was staffed mainly by women. Those men who were fit enough went to war and the others did duty at home with the Civil Defence, Home Guard and firewatching as well as the regular services of police, ambulance and fire brigade. Women who were not working on munitions or in the Land Army joined the Womens Voluntary Service (now thee WRVS). Many families, escaping from the London blitz, made Maidenhead their home for the duration of the 39-45 war and some made it their permanent home. Some child evacuees were never reclaimed by their families and stayed on in the town.

A memorial outside the town hall pays tribute to the men of Maidenhead who died on active service.

With the coming of the film industry, three cinemas were built in Maidenhead, from the silent pictures to the talkies; The Colonnade 1905 (renamed The Ritz), The Picture Theatre 1910 (renamed the Rialto) and The Plaza 1913. A society - THE MAIDENHEAD AND DISTRICT PREVENTION AND RESCUE ASSOCIATION (the mad paras) - was set up, under Canon Drummond, vicar of All Saints, Boyne Hill, to have them closed down as it was considered that they would be a corrupting influence on the people of Maidenhead. After the last war, The Rialto cinema (the ABC), started Saturday morning cinema for children, the ABC Minors. Children in the 1940's were very well-behaved (or so we are led to believe) but the astute cinema manager anticipated trouble from some local lads who, having just been released from the constraints of wartime, were beginning to feel their feet. He had the brilliant idea of giving them the responsibility of being monitors and this ploy worked, the Saturday morning flicks at Maidenhead were probably the most smoothly run of all the ABC chain, under the administration of Monty Collins, Alby Hole, Slasher Page, Bernie Rawlings and Sniffy Smith. Slasher Page, about twelve at the time, drove to the cinema, at the bottom of the High Street, on his father's farm tractor - traffic wardens had not been invented at that time. By the 1990's, with the coming of television and bingo, all the cinemas were closed.

Some of the post-war developments and buildings have enhanced Maidenhead and some have not. The new library, with it's scaffolding effect architecture, still infuriates many people and the 'Jolly Green Giant', a large office block painted green, was considered to be an eyesore at the entrance to Maidenhead by the railway station.

The railway, road and motorway which traverse the town have all been the causes of contention between the rate-payers and the councillors, from felling trees to widen the motorway and keep leaves off the railway lines to putting traffic lights on the middle of three roundabouts on the A4; the lights were turned off after the first outcry from the ratepayers but then turned back on again, only finally being dismantled after a concerted campaign by irate motorists, in Feb 1995.

St Luke's Cottage Hospital was demolished in 1977 and not replaced. The modernised Workhouse Union buildings and St Marks Infirmary are now used for geriatric care and clinics.

Much industry has come to Maidenhead in the second half of the 20th century; Corwallis Estate, Reform Road, Maidenehad Business Campus, Norreys Drive, Priors Way, Woodlands Park Business Centre, and Vanwall Business Park. There was industry at Cordwallis prior to that, more than 1,000 cars were produced there from 1914-1936 including the 2-seater 10.8hp GWK and the Mandaraz Special, and during the war St Martin's jam factory and the Koola Fruita ice lolly factory were in Cordwallis. Vandervells came to Cox Green soon after the war to make car bearings and they built their own racing car, the Vanwall Special, which was raced successfully by Stirling Moss. Stirling Moss's parents had been rally drivers and his sister, Pat, was a showjumper and rally driver; the Moss family lived in Bray.

Commerce is also well served in Maidenehead by the plethora of office blocks which have sprung up at the end of the century.

Some of the old coaching inns are still in Maidenhead, but the Sun at the bottom of Castle Hill, the coaching inn for the first Royal Mail, disappeared under the road-widening scheme of the 1970's at the same time as Queen Anne House. The Cross Keys, a back street tavern in West Street, was pulled down after the last war but two more 'common lodging houses' remain - the Crown (now a restaurant) and the Model Lodging House (now the British Legion) in the High Street. Because the Crown was so disreputable at the turn of the century the Model Lodging House was built by J D M Pearce, of the Temperance Society, to steer the dusty-footed traveller away from the demon drink, but it failed. Skindles Hotel, on the river bridge, is now empty awaiting development but the Boulters Inn, the Riviera and the Thames Hotel have recently been refurbished . The Brigade of Guards is no longer stationed at Maidenhead but Guards' Club Island is maintained as a park.

To house the post-war rising population of Maidenhead, the council built new housing estates across the town at Cookham, Cox Green, Furze Platt, Holmanleaze, Holyport, Larchfield, Pinkneys Green and Woodlands Park; many private housing estates were also built. Building had now slowed down as the town is in danger of encroaching on the Green Belt.

Most of the family-based shops have gone from the town, including Budgens (John Budgen, opened 1876), Butlers, Carters (saddlers, opened 19th century), the Co-op, Home and Colonial, the International, Liptons, McIlroys, Neves (Julius Neve, opened 1847), Nicholsons Brewery (started 1840), Stuchberries (Opened 19th century) and Webbers (James Webber, opened 1864) together with countless small traders.

These shopkeepers have been replaced by supermarkets, such as Sainsburies, Tesco and Waitrose, and fast food outlets, Budgens still have stores on the outskirts of town. The shopkeepers used to live above their shops in High Street, King Street, Market Street and Queen Street until the town was redeveloped; now the town centre is a ghost town at night and prey to vandals.

Bray has been linked with Maidenhead through history, being on the Thames between Maidenhead and Windsor. Once rural, it is now mostly a commuter village; the M4 motorway makes it possible for people to live in the pleasant village and commute daily to London. The two village shops that had served the village for so long, through all the vagaries of war rationing, are now shut: Bowlers, by the village hall, was started by Mr Bowler sen. and carried on, until his retirement, by his son Stan. The other general store was run by the Jones family. The famous Hotel de Paris in Old Mill Lane has disappeared together with the Tan House in Ferry Road. The Monkey Island Hotel, and the Hinds Head still remain and Chauntry House has become an hotel; the George Hotel by the river in Ferry Road is now called the Waterside and is run by the world-renowned chefs, the Roux Brothers. The Albion, The Crown, The Stag and Hounds at Braywick (now the Pig in Hiding) and the Ringers (now the Fat Duck) are still open but the Ferry Inn (formerly the Waterside) and the Hare and Hounds at Braywick are gone. Pubs now have a swift turnover of managers but until recently they were the family home as well as the business - the Marks family at the Albion, the Woolmingtons at the Crown, George and Cinders Cox at the Ferry, and Jean and Fred Johnson at the Ringers.

St Michaels church (1293) and Jesus Hospital almshouses (1609) still stand proudly at either end of Bray village.

Bray Studios opened in 1950 and many famous film stars came to Bray in that era, staying at the local hotels; later the studio became famous for the Quatermass films and the Hammer House of Horrow films. Today the studio makes advertising and promotional films. Oakley Court was the home of the Free French during the German occupation of France during the last war and General de Gaulle visited there; it is now the Oakley Court Hotel.

The riverside houses at Bray are a favourite domicile for show business people and business tycoons and in the 1950's Diana Dors and Mr Teasy-Weasy Raymond, the hairdresser, lived in Monkey Island Lane.

The Brick and Tile Company at Pinkneys Green, started in 1820 by Charles Cooper and which provided the materials for much of Maidenhead's beautiful architecture, is no longer there, it has been replaced by modern industry. Furze Platt Laundry, started by Mr. Edwin Rogers in 1880, is still there (now called Clean Linen Services). Exlers Garage, started at the beginning of the century as a bicycle repair shop, has only recently been sold by the family.

The Primitive Methodist chapel, built in Cox Green in 1874, was purchased by All Saints church, Boyne Hill, in 1911. Named The Good Shepherd, it became a branch of the main church, together with St. Paul's in High Town Road.

Opposite to The Good Shepherd, a village hall was built after the 1914-1918 war to celebrate the victory. The Church of The Good Shepherd and the Victory Hall have been demolished and are now incorporated in the new Cox Green Community Centre in Highfield Lane; St Paul's was demolished to make way for the new road development and not replaced.

Maidenhead High Street is now pedestrianised and traffic by-passes the town on the M4 motorway on one side and the A4 on the other. In the last half of this century, Maidenhead has had a new ambulance station, fire station, leisure centre, library, police station and town hall and plans are afoot to build a heritage centre next to the library; all the cinemas have closed, the bus station has closed and the hospital (1879-1977) has not been replaced.

My thanks to Tony Clifton, FRICS, for his information on modern Maidenhead.

1. THE MAIDENHEAD AND DISTRICT PREVENTION AND RESCUE ASSOCIATION
2. THE LIBRARY
3. THE EVACUEE
4. THE VICTORY TEA
5. THE BOMBER ESTATE
6. THE CADILLAC
7. SAINSBURIES' LIGHTS
8. SPARE OUR TREES
9. and finally THE WATER LILY

1. THE MAIDENHEAD AND DISTRICT PREVENTION AND RESCUE ASSOCIATION

The animated picture show which was staged at the Colonnade
In 1905 was greeted with righteous rage
The MAD PREVENTION AND RESCUE ASSOCIATION
Viewed the entertainment with moral indignation
Canon Drummond, vicar of All Saints, Boyne Hill
Denounced it from his pulpit as one of society's ills.
The Picture Theatre in Bridge Road was built in 1910
And the fervent, pious Canon called down the wrath of God again
Banners were waved around the town at protest demonstrations
But the killjoys could not spoil the excitement of the occasion
The Canon, busy preparing for the dedication of his new nave
Predicted that such entertainment could only corrupt and deprave
In 1913 the Plaza showed novel moving films
The MAD PARAS paraded outside, praying and singing hymns
The good Canon was getting old by then, but others took up the crusade
Which had started when a picture show was staged at the Colonnade
In 1927 the Rialto showed talking pictures
The MAD PARA'S gathered outside and read passages from the scriptures
The pious Canon Drummond can lie easy in his grave
The moving, talking pictures will no longer corrupt and deprave
No latter-day moral rescue crusading association
Need fear for the downfall of the local population
The Colonnade, the Plaza and the Rialto have all gone
The M.A.D. PREVENTION AND RESCUE ASSOCIATION has finally won.

2. THE LIBRARY

A philanthropist, Mr Carnegie, donated five hundred pounds
To build a public library for the benefit of Maidenhead town
Mr Nicholson, the brewer, gave land in St Ives Road
And other local benefactors other money bestowed
King Teddy sent his apologies, he was sorry he could not be there
So the library was declared open by our own illustrious mayor
It was the smell that struck you first as you entered through the door
Of the Maidenhead Public Library, built in 1904
In the entrance hall were cabinets with weird and wonderful displays
Of artefacts which had been dug up and preserved from bygone days
And stuffed animals, stoats and foxes, which really frightened me
My sister said they came alive when the library closed for tea
SILENCE said the notices all around the walls
We children were so quiet, we hardly breathed at all
As we gazed in awe and wonder at the magic world of books
The steely eyed librarian watched which ones we took
My sister said the librarian, in her twin-set and pearls
Was really a wicked witch who ate noisy little girls
We were sad and quite nostalgic when the old library came down
It had served it's literary purpose for seventy years in the town
But a new library has been built, a striking, modern one
We must have progress and move with the times when all is said and done
My sister said it will be very nice when the scaffold is there no more
But they will never reproduce that special smell of the library of 1904.

3. THE EVACUEE

I know that I am lucky to get my school dinners free
But I wish that all the others were not served in front of me
By the time it is my turn the meat is nothing but fat
And I get the lumpy custard from the bottom of the vat
As soon as I find a seat to eat my dinner at last
The bell rings to leave the hall and go back to our class.

My friend Bernice asked her mother if she could take me home to tea
Her mother said 'No, certainly not, she's an evacuee'
I don't know why she said that, I have never understood
I have been taught my manners and I'm always very good
When I come home from school I am not allowed out anyway
I have to do the ironing and put it all away.

I have to get up early and the worst job that I hate
Is cleaning out the ashes and blackleading the fire grate
My mother came to see me once, she came here on the train
But I haven't seen her since that day, she didn't come again
My dad said he would write to me but I haven't had a letter
He had a hangover when I left home, I hope that he is better.

Lil, the lady I live with, drinks quite a lot of stout
Sometimes when I come home from school she's on the floor spark out
Lil did not want to take me in, for two days she resisted
But I was the last child left in the hall and the billeting officer insisted
I had long ringlets when I came and I was very distraught
When Lil put a basin on my head and cut my hair very short.

It was kind of Bernice's mother to send me her outgrown shoes
But Bernice takes a size four, and my feet are only size two
Lil put screwed up paper in the toes, it doesn't hurt a lot
I have to wear them anyway they're the only shoes I've got
My teacher says I should be grateful that Lil looks after me
But I hope that the war finishes next year in nineteen forty-three.

The Mayo came to our school today, it was Empire Day
I wanted so to see him but they pushed me out of his way
I am really so unhappy, I miss my Mum and Dad
I wish the war would finish, then I would be so glad
To go back home to London, I expect my Dad will fetch me
Then I'll be his little girl again and not an evacuee.

In 1939 alone, over 6000 children and pregnant women were evacuated from London to Maidenhead and many more followed; the reception and billeting of the evacuees was the responsibility of the WVS (WRVS). Many of the children were desperately unhappy, being separated from their parents.

4. THE VICTORY TEA

August 1945, the ending of the war
Blackout curtains were taken down, the light came in once more
The evacuees packed their bags and went to catch the train
To take them back to London, to live in peace again
We held a party in Desborough Park
With races and ices and other good larks
The women saved up from their few clothing rations
To deck themselves out in the latest of fashions
The mothers stayed up all night to make
Jellies and tarts and scrumptious fruit cakes
The dads put the stalls up and then promptly went
To sample the contents of the beer tent
The sun was so hot, 90 degrees in the shade
We sat on the grass with our fizzy lemonade.
A pirate, a gypsy, a sweet milking maid
'Step up, everyone, for the fancy dress parade'
The tressles were covered with white cotton sheets
And groaning with sandwiches, buns and sweetmeats
With everything rationed through six years of war
We young ones had not seen ice-cream before
Before tea was served we said a short prayer
For the husbands and fathers who could not be there
They had paid with their lives to keep us all free
To enjoy the delights of the victory tea.
They came from all over and ate of their fill
From neighbouring Cox Green, across to Boyn Hill
Altwood Road and Boyn Valley, the Gullet, Lock Lane
All joined in to celebrate peacetime again
Mr Climo played music, patriotic melodies
From speakers strung out all through the trees
The children stayed up 'til well after dark
When we celebrated peace in Desborough Park.

On 20th August 1945, the Mayor, Alderman Oldershaw, stood on the Town Hall steps and declared that the war was over. Street parties were held all over town and bonfires were lit on the Moor. Later in the year, the town centre was packed as crowds jostled to get a glimpse of Field Marshal Montgomery of Alemein who led a triumphant parade through town; he posed for photographs with the Mayor and civic dignitaries on the forecourt of the Rialto cinema. Rationing was gradually phased out and the street lights were switched on again.

5. THE BOMBER ESTATE

As they taxied down the runway of White Waltham aerodrome
So many brave young pilots would never again see home
Into the darkness they flew out, not knowing what lay before
Precious lives, so willingly given to bring an end to war.

To honour their memory and acknowledge their brave deeds
Houses fit for heroes were built at Pinkneys Green
Each road now marks the name of a wartime bomber plane
In hope that such a sacrifice will never be called for again.

Sunderland, Blenheim, such dependable kites
Which had flown into danger, night after night
The Lancaster, give credit where it is due
Was the greatest single factor in winning World War Two.

Lincoln Road, Halifax Road, Halifax Close and Way
Remind us of the horror of war in those no-so-distant days
Remembering those brave fliers, it is a chastening thought
That the homes on the post-war bomber estate were very dearly bought.

During the 39-45 war, Maidenhead was the base of the Air Transport Auxiliary, a band of civilian flyers which ferried planes to their take-off points. The town suffered only minor damage through the war. White Waltham Aerodrome is now the West London Flying club.

6. THE CADILLAC

The car which was painted in turquoise green
Upholstered in leather and fit for a queen
In the dull post-war years was a sight to be seen
Where is the Cadillac now?

As it glided through Bray to go anywhere
The curious villagers all turned to stare
At the passenger with the platinum hair
Where is the Cadillac now?

Diana Dors was extremely amorous
She shocked the village and became quite famous
For her torrid affairs and looks so glamorous
Where is the Cadillac now?

Diana became a flamboyant film star
With her inestimable talent she was sure to go far
In her chromium- plated turquoise green car
Where is the Cadillac now?

She died from an illness she had to endure
But her films will live on for evermore
Farewell to the legend of Diana Dors
Where is the Cadillac now?

7 SAINSBURIES' LIGHTS

Drive we now with gay abandon
Tra-la-la-la-la-la-la-la-la
Unhindered on our route to London
Tra-la-la-la-la-la-la-la-la
The traffic lights on Sainsburies' junction
Tra-la-la-la-la-la-la-la-la
Have been switched off, they've ceased to function
Tra-la-la-la-la-la-la-la-la
No more the crash as glass is scattered
Tra-la-la-la-la-la-la-la-la
As car hits car and peace is shattered
Tra-la-la-la-la-la-la-la-la
The rate-payers' voice has now been heeded
Tra-la-la-la-la-la-la-la-la
Our campaign has at last succeeded
Tra-la-la-la-la-la-la-la-la
But the fight goes on while the iron is still hot
Tra-la-la-la-la-la-la-la-la
For greater safety on the Forlease blackspot
Tra-la-la-la-la-la-la-la-la
A safe New Year to you and yours
Tra-la-la-la-la-la-la-la-la
Including all our worthy councillors
Tra-la-la-la-la-la-la-la-la

8. SPARE OUR TREES

Sometime during the Pleistocene Age the surge of an ice-flow
Sculpted this fair valley, millions of years ago.

The trees became Windsor Forest in Mesolithic times
Flourishing in abundance in those drier, warmer climes.

Then Neolothic Man appeared, claimed this as his domain
And still the noble, life-giving tree was suffered to remain.

Now Commuter Man, in utter folly, fells oak and beech and pines
For ever wider motor ways and tidier railway lines.

Please spare our trees or we shall find one morning upon waking
A barren land, a vast dust bowl, a desert of our own making.

9. and finally, THE WATER LILY

Down the Thames, past reed and rush, the water lily glides
Smiling at the woodland folk who dwell by the riverside
On neighbouring banks the yeoman labour at their native crafts
Their only way to ford the Thames is by the ferry raft.

In the year of our Lord, twelve hundred and eighty, the ferrymen departs
A bridge is built, a handsome arch, and the coaching era starts
With a clatter of wheels and a snorting of horses, the sound of the post horn
Salutes the birth of a new town, Maidenhead is born.

The Royal Mail drives through the town in seventeen eighty four
Pursued by bandits and footpads, and highwaymen galore.
Another snorting beast roars in, in eighteen thirty-nine
When Brunel builds a bridge to carry the Great Western Railway line.

The town spreads wide, devouring farm and hamlet in it's quest
To be a town par excellence, the biggest and the best
What thinks the water lily of the woodland folk today
Is that a smile of plaudit, or a grimace of dismay?

WINDSOR CASTLE, in the ROYAL BOROUGH and MAIDENHEAD, was built in l070.

KINGS AND QUEENS FROM THEN TO THE PRESENT DAY;

1066-1087 WILLIAM I (THE CONQUEROR)
1087-1100 WILLIAM II (RUFUS)
1100-1135 HENRY I
1135-1154 STEPHEN
1154-1189 HENRY II
1189-1199 RICHARD I (LIONHEART)
1199-1216 JOHN
1216-1272 HENRY III
1272-1307 EDWARD I
1307-1327 EDWARD II
1327-1377 EDWARD III
1377-1399 RICHARD II
1399-1413 HENRY IV
1413-1422 HENRY V
1422-1461 HENRY VI
1461-1483 EDWARD IV
1483-1485 RICHARD III
1485-1509 HENRY VII
1509-1547 HENRY VIII
1547-1553 EDWARD VI
1553-1558 MARY I
1558-1603 ELIZABETH I
1603-1625 JAMES I
1625-1649 CHARLES I
1649-1660 PROTECTORATE*
1660-1685 CHARLES II
1685-1689 JAMES II
1689-1702 WILLIAM AND MARY
1702-1714 ANNE
1714-1727 GEORGE I
1727-1760 GEORGE II
1760-1820 GEORGE III

1820-1830 GEORGE IV
1830-1837 WILLIAM IV
1837-1901 VICTORIA
1901-1910 EDWARD VII
1910-1936 GEORGE V
1936   EDWARD VIII**
1936-1952 GEORGE VI
1952- Present ELIZABETH II

* Oliver Cromwell and his son Richard, presided over the Rump Parliament after Charles I was beheaded.

** Edward VIII married a divorced American woman, Wallis Simpson; he was not crowned and he abdicated because parliament would not agree to his wife being the queen.

POEMS

THE ROMANS: 1

VENI VELI VICI 2
CASTLE HILL VILLA 3
FATHERLY ADVICE 4
MORE FATHERLY ADVICE 5
A LONELY GRAVE 6

THE ANGLO-SAXONS: 7

CHIEFTAIN TAEPPA 9
THE LONGBOATS HAVE BEEN SIGHTED 10
THE WOOD CARVERS 11

THE MIDDLE AGES: 12

THE SERF 14
THE MANORS 15
SHALLOW PROMISES 16
THE SIEGE OF MAIDENHEAD BRIDGE 17
GOOD QUEEN BESS 18
THE GATECRASHER 19

THE REFORMATION 1534-1559: 20

CHARITY 22
THE FLANDERS MARE 23
WHICH HAT TODAY 24

THE SEVENTEENTH CENTURY: 26

THE COURT NOW STANDS AT MAIDENHEAD 27
THE SECRET MEETING 28
BRAYWICK CAMP 29

THE COACHING ERA:	**30**
THE HIGHWAYMAN	32
THE OSTLER	33
FIRE!	35
THE NEW BRIDGE	36
THE GOLDEN AGE OF COACHING	38
TRAVELLERS REST	39
A DAY AT THE RACES	40
THE VICTORIANS:	**41**
THE UNION WORKHOUSE	43
THE BRUNEL BRIDGE	44
THE COTTAGE HOSPITAL	46
QUEEN ANNE HOUSE	47
THE CLOCK TOWER	48
THE RIVER:	**51**
MIDDENHYTHE	53
RAY THE MILLER	54
SWAN UPPING	55
GAIETY ROW	56
THE FLOODS OF 1947	57
A STEAMER RIDE	59
FULL CYCLE ON RAY MILL ISLAND	61
WORSHIP AND EDUCATION:	**63**
St. BIRINUS	66
PRAISE GOD IN HIS HOLY PLACE	67
THOMAS ELLWOOD	68
THE ROCK	69
TO BE SCHOOLED IN THE PRINCIPLES OF THE FAITH	70
IN GOD'S ARMS	72

THE TWENTIETH CENTURY:	**74**
THE MAIDENHEAD AND DISTRICT PREVENTION AND RESCUE ASSOCIATION	81
THE LIBRARY	82
THE EVACUEE	83
THE VICTORY TEA	85
THE BOMBER ESTATE	87
THE CADILLAC	88
SAINSBURIES' LIGHTS	89
SPARE OUR TREES	90
THE WATER LILY	91